state of world population

UNFPA

SEEING THE UNSEEN

The case for action in the neglected crisis of unintended pregnancy

CONTENTS

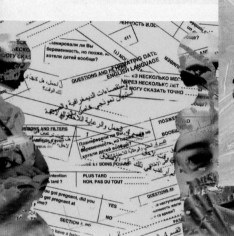

CHAPTER 1

The invisible crisis before our eyes

PAGE 9

CHAPTER 2

The evidence is in: Unintended pregnancy is linked to lack of development

PAGE 19

CHAPTER 3

Every woman is at risk: Erosion of agency leads to unintended pregnancy

PAGE 37

FOREWORD

A world where every pregnancy is wanted. This aim is a central pillar of our mission at UNFPA.

Every human being has the right to bodily autonomy, and perhaps nothing is more fundamental to the exercise of that right than the ability to choose whether, when and with whom to become pregnant.

The basic human right to determine freely and responsibly the number and the spacing of one's children has been recognized in numerous international human rights agreements over the past five decades. During this same period, the world has seen a vast expansion in the availability of effective, modern contraceptives — one of the greatest public health achievements in recent history. Why, then, are nearly half of all pregnancies unintended?

In 1994, the Programme of Action of the International Conference on Population and Development (ICPD) recognized that the empowerment, full equality and autonomy of women were essential to social and economic progress. Today, these aims are among the cornerstones for achieving the 2030 Agenda for Sustainable Development. It explicitly recognizes the role of sexual and reproductive health and gender equality in unlocking a more prosperous future, and contains specific indicators linked to women and adolescent girls' agency in making informed decisions regarding sexual relations, contraceptive use and reproductive health care.

That is why UNFPA's efforts focus on expanding access to the information and services women and girls need to exercise their reproductive rights and choices, which underpin gender equality and enable them to exercise greater power over their lives and realize their full potential.

We know the steep costs associated with unintended pregnancy — costs to an individual's health, education and future, costs to whole health systems, workforces and societies. The question is: why has this not inspired more action to secure bodily autonomy for all?

The topic of this report is a challenging one, in part because it is so common. Nearly everyone has an experience to draw upon, whether they have faced an unintended pregnancy themselves or know someone who has. For some, it is a personal crisis; for others, it is a blessing in disguise.

Beyond the personal context, unintended pregnancies have societal roots and global consequences. This, therefore, is not a report about unwanted babies or happy accidents. It is not a report about motherhood. And although abortion cannot be removed from the discussion — more than 60 per cent of unintended pregnancies end in abortion — this is not a report about abortion either. Instead, this report is about the circumstances that exist before an unintended pregnancy, when a person or a couple's agency to decide is critically undermined, and about the many impacts that follow, affecting individuals and societies over generations.

We see, through original research by the authors and in new data from partner organizations, that shame, stigma, fear, poverty, gender inequality and many other factors undermine women and girls' ability to exercise choice, to seek and obtain contraceptives, to negotiate condom use with a partner, to speak aloud and pursue their desires and ambitions. Most of all, this report raises provocative and unsettling questions about how much the world values women and girls beyond their reproductive capacities. Because recognizing the full worth of women and girls, and enabling them to contribute fully to their societies, means ensuring they have the tools, information and power to make this fundamental choice for themselves.

It is impossible to fully ascertain, let alone quantify, the overall toll of unintended pregnancies. Yet a growing body of evidence points to massive opportunity costs — from correlations tying unintended pregnancy rates to lower human development scores, to billions of dollars in related health-care costs, to persistently high rates of unsafe abortion and related maternal deaths. Unsafe abortion is one of the leading causes of the more than 800 maternal deaths occurring each day. This is a price tag the world simply cannot afford.

We are fast approaching 2030, the deadline for the Sustainable Development Goals and for UNFPA's own transformative goals — to end the unmet need for family planning, end preventable maternal deaths and end gender-based violence and harmful practices, including female genital mutilation and child marriage. Now is the time to accelerate, not retreat, to transform the lives of women and girls and reach those furthest behind. Preventing unintended pregnancies is a non-negotiable first step. When individuals are able to exercise real informed choice over their health, bodies and futures, they can contribute to more prosperous societies and a more sustainable, equitable and just world.

Dr. Natalia Kanem
Executive Director
United Nations Population Fund

DEFINITIONS

Definitions around unintended pregnancy and contraception are often fraught. Many of the terms commonly accepted in one community are incomprehensible in another. This report explores some of these terms and their uses, highlighting when these terms are confusing, misleading or used in multiple ways.

UNINTENDED PREGNANCY (N) — MAY BE WANTED OR UNWANTED.

A PREGNANCY THAT OCCURS TO A WOMAN WHO WAS NOT PLANNING TO HAVE ANY (MORE) CHILDREN, OR THAT WAS MISTIMED, IN THAT IT OCCURRED EARLIER THAN DESIRED. THIS DEFINITION IS APPLIED INDEPENDENT OF THE OUTCOME OF THE PREGNANCY (WHETHER ABORTION, MISCARRIAGE OR UNPLANNED BIRTH).

SYNONYM: UNPLANNED PREGNANCY.

FAMILY PLANNING (N) —

THE INFORMATION, MEANS AND METHODS THAT ALLOW INDIVIDUALS TO DECIDE IF AND WHEN TO HAVE CHILDREN. IT INCLUDES A WIDE RANGE OF CONTRACEPTIVES AS WELL AS NON-INVASIVE METHODS SUCH AS THE CALENDAR METHOD AND ABSTINENCE. IT ALSO INCLUDES INFORMATION ABOUT HOW TO BECOME PREGNANT WHEN IT IS DESIRABLE, AS WELL AS TREATMENT OF INFERTILITY.

USAGE NOTE: THE TERM "FAMILY PLANNING" DOES NOT RESONATE WITH CERTAIN POPULATIONS. (PAUL AND OTHERS, 2019).

SYNONYMS: CONTRACEPTION, BIRTH CONTROL.

UNWANTED PREGNANCY (N) —

1. A PREGNANCY THAT A WOMAN DOES NOT WANT TO HAVE.

2. (ACADEMIC) WHEN MEASURED IN SURVEYS, A PREGNANCY THAT OCCURRED WHEN A WOMAN DID NOT WANT TO HAVE ANY CHILDREN AT ALL, OR ANY MORE CHILDREN. THE ACADEMIC DEFINITION DOES NOT RECOGNIZE THAT A WOMAN MIGHT DECIDE SHE WANTS THE PREGNANCY AFTER IT OCCURS, EVEN IF SHE WAS NOT PLANNING TO HAVE ANY (MORE) CHILDREN.

USAGE NOTE: UNWANTED PREGNANCY SHOULD NOT BE USED AS A SYNONYM FOR UNINTENDED PREGNANCY.

COMPREHENSIVE SEXUALITY EDUCATION

A CURRICULUM-BASED PROCESS OF TEACHING AND LEARNING ABOUT THE COGNITIVE, EMOTIONAL, PHYSICAL AND SOCIAL ASPECTS OF SEXUALITY, AIMING TO EQUIP CHILDREN AND YOUNG PEOPLE WITH KNOWLEDGE, SKILLS, ATTITUDES AND VALUES THAT WILL EMPOWER THEM TO REALIZE THEIR HEALTH, WELL-BEING AND DIGNITY; DEVELOP RESPECTFUL SOCIAL AND SEXUAL RELATIONSHIPS; CONSIDER HOW THEIR CHOICES AFFECT THEIR OWN WELL-BEING AND THAT OF OTHERS; AND UNDERSTAND AND ENSURE THE PROTECTION OF THEIR RIGHTS THROUGHOUT THEIR LIVES (UNESCO AND OTHERS, 2018).

SYNONYMS: LIFE SKILLS EDUCATION, FAMILY LIFE EDUCATION, SEXUALITY EDUCATION, SEX ED.

MISTIMED PREGNANCY (N) —

1. A PREGNANCY THAT OCCURRED AT A TIME IN A WOMAN'S LIFE WHEN SHE DID NOT INTEND TO BECOME PREGNANT, EVEN THOUGH SHE DESIRED HAVING A CHILD AT A FUTURE POINT.

2. (ACADEMIC) WHEN MEASURED IN SURVEYS, THIS IS TYPICALLY DEFINED AS A PREGNANCY THAT OCCURRED TWO OR MORE YEARS BEFORE A WOMAN WANTED TO HAVE A CHILD.

USAGE NOTE: THESE PREGNANCIES ARE GENERALLY CONSIDERED UNINTENDED.

CONTRACEPTION (N) —

THE ACT OF INTENTIONALLY PREVENTING PREGNANCY, SUCH AS THROUGH THE USE OF DEVICES, PRACTICES, MEDICATIONS OR SURGICAL PROCEDURES (BANSODE AND OTHERS, 2021; JAIN AND MURALIDHAR, 2011). MODERN CONTRACEPTIVES ARE THOSE "HAVING A SOUND BASIS IN REPRODUCTIVE BIOLOGY, A PRECISE PROTOCOL FOR CORRECT USE AND EVIDENCE OF EFFICACY" (FESTIN AND OTHERS, 2016); TRADITIONAL CONTRACEPTIVES REFERRING TO OTHER METHODS.

SYNONYMS: FAMILY PLANNING, BIRTH CONTROL.

ABORTION (N) —

1. (COLLOQUIAL) THE DELIBERATE TERMINATION OF A PREGNANCY THROUGH A PROCEDURE OR USE OF MEDICATION. SYNONYMS: INDUCED ABORTION, ELECTIVE ABORTION, THERAPEUTIC ABORTION.

2. (CHIEFLY MEDICAL) ANY PREMATURE EXIT OF THE PRODUCTS OF CONCEPTION RESULTING IN THE END OF A PREGNANCY, INCLUDING BOTH INDUCED ABORTION AND MISCARRIAGE, ALSO KNOWN AS A SPONTANEOUS ABORTION.

USAGE NOTE: WHEN THIS REPORT USES THE TERM "ABORTION", IT IS REFERRING TO INDUCED ABORTION.

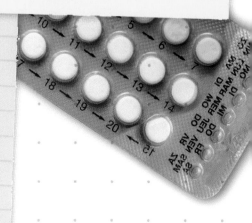

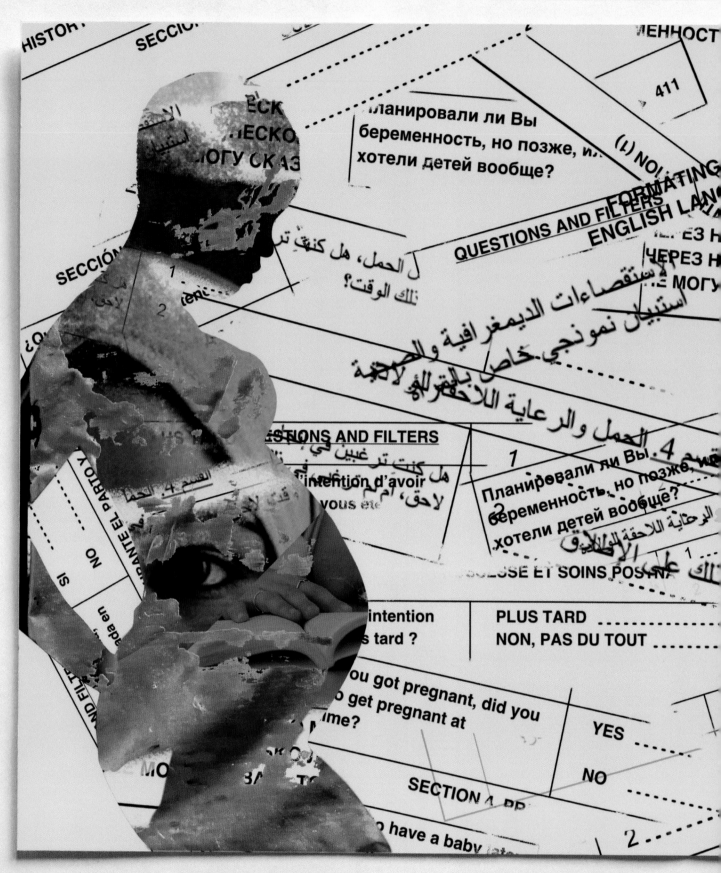

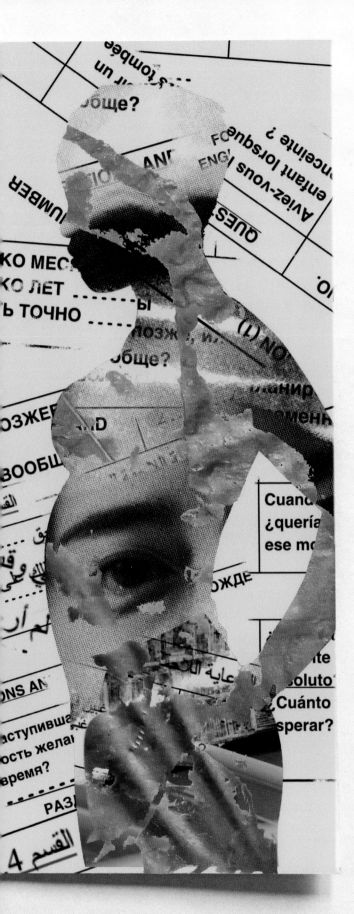

CHAPTER 1

The invisible crisis before our eyes

Half.

That's the share of pregnancies that women and girls do not deliberately choose (Bearak and others, 2020).

This share is startlingly high. Nothing is more fundamental to bodily autonomy than the ability to decide whether or not to become pregnant. And yet for far too many people, this most life-altering reproductive choice is no choice at all.

The basic human right to choose whether to have children, and to decide on their number and spacing, is contained in many global agreements (UNFPA, 1994; UN General Assembly, 1989; UN General Assembly, 1979).

Modern, effective contraception is widely — though not universally — available. Why, then, are half of all pregnancies unplanned, and many of them unwanted?

This is a reminder of how many people, especially women and girls, are limited in exercising their basic rights. It is a sign that gender discrimination continues to wind through the lives of women and girls, as well as transgender, non-binary and gender-expansive people. It points to deep gaps in rights and justice, gender equality, human dignity and broader social well-being.

So many unplanned and unwanted pregnancies raise questions about how much the rights and potential of more than half of humanity are prioritized and valued. They signal that the world could fail to reach its development goals for health, education and gender equality, derailing the shared ambitions of the international community.

> **So many unplanned and unwanted pregnancies raise questions about how much the rights and potential of more than half of humanity are prioritized and valued.**

A neglected crisis — and opportunity

The number of unintended pregnancies that occur every year — 121 million, or 331,000 per day on average — represents a global failure to uphold a basic human right. And that failure is expected to grow. While recent data also show that, worldwide, the unintended pregnancy rate fell between 1990 and 2019 (Bearak and others, 2020), continued global population growth means that the absolute number of unintended pregnancies will keep rising without decisive action.

Delivering the sexual and reproductive health services individuals and communities need will only become more difficult in the face of tectonic shifts like climate change, conflicts, public health emergencies and mass migration. These megatrends will test the capacity of health systems even as demand grows, especially in the world's least-developed countries, where crises will be felt most acutely and where services and resources are already in critically short supply (Starrs and others, 2018).

The international community has committed to a rights-based roadmap to guide humanity through these monumental changes: the 2030 Agenda for Sustainable Development. It is a framework for sustainable and inclusive development that expressly recognizes, in targets 3.7 and 5.6, the role of sexual and reproductive health and gender equality in unlocking a more prosperous future. These targets are linked to the right of every individual and couple to choose whether to have children and their number and spacing — where every birth is wanted and every child is valued.

Based on original analysis (in Chapter 2), this report finds that social and economic development and higher levels of gender equality strongly correlate with lower rates of unintended pregnancy. Coupled with what is known about the consequences of unintended pregnancy (explored in Chapter 5) to individuals and societies, the report confirms the powerful development case for intensifying efforts to uphold reproductive rights as fundamental to reducing unintended pregnancies.

Many factors linked to reducing unintended pregnancy are themselves core development goals, from poverty reduction to improved maternal health. One clear illustration of these intersecting forces is the extraordinary cost — to individuals, health systems and whole societies — of unsafe abortion, an issue that undercuts both rights and development. Over 60 per cent of unintended pregnancies end in abortion, safe or unsafe, legal or illegal (Bearak and others, 2020). Given that an estimated 45 per cent of all abortions remain unsafe (WHO, 2020), this is a public health emergency. Unsafe abortion hospitalizes about 7 million women a year in developing countries (Singh and Maddow-Zimet, 2016), costing an estimated $553 million per year in post-abortion treatment costs alone (Vlassoff and others, 2008), and resulting in an estimated 193,000 maternal deaths per year (Say and others, 2014). By contrast, reducing unintended pregnancies, and therefore recourse to unsafe abortion, can enable health systems to allocate resources towards comprehensive sexual and reproductive health services, including maternal and newborn health, investments that yield positive impacts across the board.

© UNFPA/Fidel Évora

Contraception is key — but not enough

Contraception is one of the most obvious areas for investment in reproductive health and rights. Globally, an estimated 257 million women who want to avoid pregnancy are not using safe, modern methods of contraception, and of them, 172 million women are using no method at all (UN DESA, 2021). In response, UNFPA has emphasized contraception access, providing 724 million male condoms, 80 million cycles of oral contraceptives and tens of millions of other forms of contraceptives in 2020 alone (UNFPA, 2020). Many other governments, donor agencies and non-governmental organizations have also provided large quantities of contraceptives.

But while such commodities are critically important, they are insufficient by themselves. Research (detailed in Chapter 4) shows that lack of awareness about, and lack of access to, contraception are no longer leading causes for non-use. Instead, these barriers are now overshadowed by concerns over side effects, myths, stigma and opposition from others. Addressing these reasons for unmet need will require a much broader range of responses.

Common assumptions must also be erased. In too many circles, the term "unintended pregnancy" evokes the image of an unmarried teenager, a girl met with pity or derision or both. In fact, since no contraceptive method is 100 per cent reliable and the intention to practise abstinence commonly fails — or is undermined by pressure, coercion or violence — effectively any fertile woman or girl of reproductive age can become pregnant unexpectedly. Overcoming the popular narratives around unintended pregnancy will require determined efforts to change discriminatory social norms, to address laws that codify these stigmas, and to expand interventions that must continue to reach adolescents but extend beyond them as well.

The sensitivity of this issue poses yet more challenges. Decision-making, or its absence, often plays out in the most intimate spheres of an individual's life, touching on fundamental elements of bodily autonomy and reproductive rights. In these spaces, women and girls too often see their choices narrow, or disappear, at every turn. A woman may be unable to negotiate condom use with her partner. She may not be able to say no to sex, as is the case for 23 per cent of all women where data are available (United Nations, 2022). She may be a victim of rape at home or by a stranger.

If comprehensive sexuality education is not offered in her school, she may lack accurate information. Pregnancy may be her default option because she has few opportunities and choices in her life. Without a chance to finish her education, for instance, she may not see a reason to postpone childbearing.

She may not want children at all, a desire that may be unacceptable in her family or community. To reflect the fact that "family planning" does not resonate with some groups, such as adolescents or individuals who do not want to have children, this report typically refers to "contraception" instead.

Unintended is not always unwanted. Some unintended pregnancies will be celebrated. Others will end in abortion or miscarriage. A share will remain unwanted but carried to term. And many will be met with ambivalence. These pregnancies may be not quite unintended but not fully deliberate either, taking place when an individual lacks the possibility to fully articulate what they want in their lives — or even to imagine a life in which pregnancy is a choice.

Questions of power and choice are too often matters of life or death: once an unintended pregnancy happens, its consequences can last a lifetime and extend through whole communities. Maternal mortality rates will soar, for example, for young girls who have not developed enough to carry a pregnancy safely to term or for women with underlying medical conditions (Singh and Maddow-Zimet, 2016). Pregnant girls may be forced to get married and/or leave school with no other options to continue their education, at which point they typically face a lifelong deficit in earnings. Women may experience an unexpected loss of income if they are forced to interrupt or even leave their jobs because they are pregnant. Poverty may be more likely if they have the child and must stretch already scarce household resources.

All these issues can be worse for people who face multiple forms of discrimination and vulnerability that erode agency and bodily autonomy even further. The quality of services, information and support is generally poorer for women in rural areas and informal settlements, in both developed and developing countries. In some contexts, service providers may legally refuse care to adolescents and to transgender people. Disabled people are more vulnerable to violence, including sexual violence (UNFPA, 2018). Among people caught in conflict and other forms of crisis, with limited access to health care and high rates of violence, vulnerability to unintended pregnancy escalates.

Unintended pregnancy from a human rights angle

Not every unintended pregnancy is necessarily the result of, nor results in, a human rights violation. Human rights come into play whenever bodily and reproductive autonomy is an issue (UNFPA, 2021). In important international agreements, such as the Convention on the Elimination of All Forms of Discrimination against Women (also known as CEDAW or the Women's Convention), States have asserted that all individuals and couples have the right to the information and means to choose whether or not to have children, when to have them, and how many to have (UN General Assembly, 1979). When those obligations are unmet, human rights are undermined or violated. This is the case when individuals are unable to exercise informed choice because they lack access to quality reproductive health information or the agency to act on that information, when an individual experiences sexual violence or coercion, and when discrimination and inequality circumscribe a full range of opportunities, leaving individuals with an incomplete set of choices.

The ICPD Programme of Action, a foundational document endorsed by 179 countries that has guided the work of UNFPA since 1994, calls on all States and the international community to "use the full means at their disposal to support the principle of voluntary choice in family planning". It should be noted that the Programme of Action stresses "abortion... in no case should be promoted as a method of family planning" (UNFPA, 1994). (See more on page 21 about abortion.)

179 countries

And yet these challenges — the jumble of social and legal concerns, the taboos and blame and discriminatory norms — are not insurmountable. Far from it. A virtuous cycle of progress can and must begin.

Unintended pregnancies reflect society's priorities

Can any society, whatever its stated intentions, claim to fully value women and girls when their ambitions, desires and human potential are curtailed? When they are not able to exercise their agency to avoid an unintended pregnancy? Can society truly claim to value motherhood if it results from abridged agency, coercion, stigma or violence?

The agency of women and girls is devalued when sexual and reproductive information and services are not fully supported and prioritized. This was evident during the onset of the COVID-19 pandemic, when contraceptive services were among the most extensively disrupted health-care services (WHO, 2020a). In the first 12 months of the crisis, the disruption of supplies and services lasted on average 3.6 months, leading to as many as 1.4 million unintended pregnancies (Luchsinger, 2021). By 2021, as disruptions continued, albeit with some degree of adjustment and catch-up, services to provide contraception were still among those most affected (Luchsinger, 2021).

When health-care systems fail to offer universal coverage, when sexual and reproductive care is not person-centred or comprehensive or is of low quality, the commitment of governments to ensure the universally agreed right to health remains unfulfilled. This is particularly true when health-care systems fall short in providing accessible, appropriate, tailored care to adolescents. The consequences of unintended pregnancy may be most severe for this age group — after all, complications in pregnancy and childbirth are the leading cause of death among girls aged 15 to 19 years (WHO, 2020b).

The right to health is also undermined when health-care practices are unresponsive to patient rights and concerns, as is evident in widely reported concerns over side effects (Bellizzi and others, 2020; Sedgh and others, 2016), difficulty with consistent use, and the fact that many unintended pregnancies happen among contraceptive users (Frost and Darroch, 2008). The bodily autonomy of individuals and their dignity, confidence and well-being are all eroded when health services do not meet their needs. The What Women Want campaign on reproductive and maternal health care surveyed 1.2 million women and girls in 114 countries in 2018–2019 and found the leading request was for more respectful and dignified care (White Ribbon Alliance, 2019).

Despite some progress, too many legal systems and policies continue to reflect the low value assigned to the rights of women and girls. Some still require third-party consent for using contraception or allow involuntary sterilization as a "solution" for unintended pregnancy among persons with disabilities (UNFPA, 2021). Far-reaching legal constraints continue to limit access to safe abortion (UNFPA, 2020a), even though these do little to limit the practice and instead increase the proportion of unsafe abortions and deaths caused by them (Ganatra and others, 2017). Policymakers can restrict or eliminate funding even in settings where contraception is socially acceptable and where health-care systems have the capacity to provide services (Gold and Hasstedt, 2017).

Much effort has gone into finding a magic bullet to "solve" unintended pregnancy, such as new forms of contraception, more accessible and reliable supplies, and more choice in methods — but many dimensions of the issue remain under-addressed. This is especially true when it comes to one core solution, a key to unlocking full agency and bodily autonomy for all: gender equality.

© UNFPA/Fidel Évora

Gender equality has been an elusive development goal for decades. It has yet to be fully achieved in any country. But we know that it works: empowered women and girls, who experience equality, are better able to address an unintended pregnancy or avoid it in the first place (explored in Chapter 2). Their ability to exercise autonomy improves their lives and leads to benefits for everyone else.

Human rights conventions and agreements have long called for gender equality. In 1994, the Programme of Action of the International Conference on Population and Development (ICPD) helped make clear that the full equality of women and girls requires that they have a command of their bodies, lives and futures equal to that enjoyed by men and boys. Achieving the Sustainable Development Goals (SDGs) (including not only SDG 5 on gender equality but many other goals and targets related to poverty reduction and economic growth, for example) requires reducing gender disparities.

Comprehensive efforts are required. It is time to strengthen health systems, and also go beyond them. It is time for high-quality, empowering education to reach all boys and girls, and for changes in the expectation that a girl's destiny unfolds mainly in the form of reproduction and motherhood. It is time for women to have opportunities for education and decent work, and to gain a greater sense of power and autonomy. Social protection must secure the rights of the most vulnerable. Leaders should model more progressive gender norms and set new directions in laws and public policies.

It is difficult to foresee a world where *every* pregnancy is intended. But we can work towards one where the vast majority of pregnancies are planned, welcomed and wanted, and where all women and girls live from a position of strength and empowerment, claiming choices and intentions that are their own. The body of evidence, discussed in the following chapters, shows what needs to be addressed to support individual agency in making reproductive choices. These are starting points for researchers, policymakers and advocates, backed not only by data but also by a long line of international agreements, human rights documents and the collective global ambitions of the 2030 Agenda for Sustainable Development.

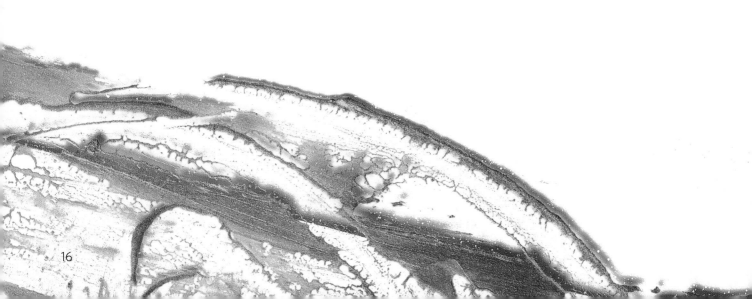

A framework of factors contributing to unintended pregnancy and outcomes

Sociodemographic studies suggest some of the pathways leading to an unintended pregnancy. This framework identifies key opportunities for intervention, with the caveat that the factors included are complex and not necessarily linear. For example, lack of reproductive autonomy, low educational attainment and poverty are associated with unintended pregnancy, but the causal pathways are not always clear.

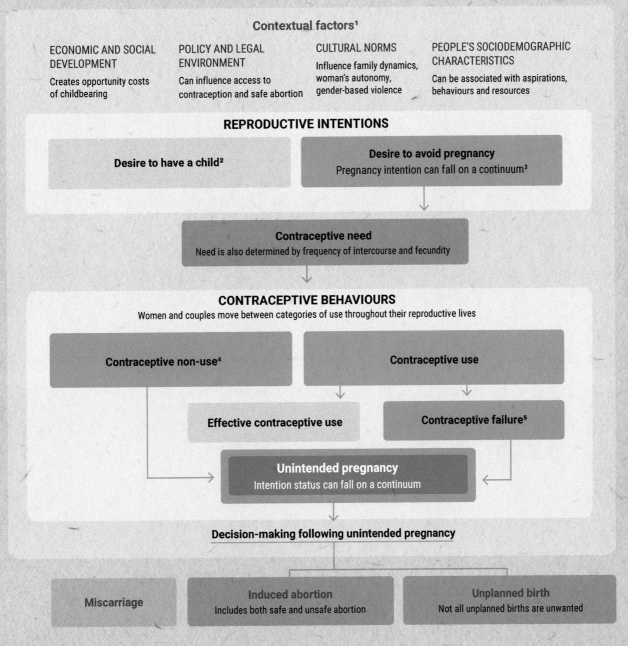

Contextual factors[1]

ECONOMIC AND SOCIAL DEVELOPMENT
Creates opportunity costs of childbearing

POLICY AND LEGAL ENVIRONMENT
Can influence access to contraception and safe abortion

CULTURAL NORMS
Influence family dynamics, woman's autonomy, gender-based violence

PEOPLE'S SOCIODEMOGRAPHIC CHARACTERISTICS
Can be associated with aspirations, behaviours and resources

REPRODUCTIVE INTENTIONS

Desire to have a child[2]

Desire to avoid pregnancy
Pregnancy intention can fall on a continuum[3]

Contraceptive need
Need is also determined by frequency of intercourse and fecundity

CONTRACEPTIVE BEHAVIOURS
Women and couples move between categories of use throughout their reproductive lives

Contraceptive non-use[4]

Contraceptive use

Effective contraceptive use

Contraceptive failure[5]

Unintended pregnancy
Intention status can fall on a continuum

Decision-making following unintended pregnancy

Miscarriage

Induced abortion
Includes both safe and unsafe abortion

Unplanned birth
Not all unplanned births are unwanted

Source: The authors.

Grey boxes: not at risk of unintended pregnancy. **Blue boxes:** outcomes of unintended pregnancy

Notes: (1) Economic, social, policy and cultural environments can influence each other, as well as the unintended pregnancy pathway. The prevalence of unintended pregnancy can also influence some contextual factors. (2) Even a desired pregnancy can be followed by circumstances that would make it difficult to have a child. (3) The pregnancy intention continuum includes ambivalence about having a child, as well as absence of conscious decision-making about childbearing (see Chapter 2). Pregnancy intentions include the desire to delay childbearing or to avoid having a child altogether. (4) Reasons for contraceptive non-use include concerns about methods, uncertainty about risk of pregnancy, limited access to quality services and the contextual factors noted in the framework (see Chapter 4). (5) Contraceptive failure is explored on page 52.

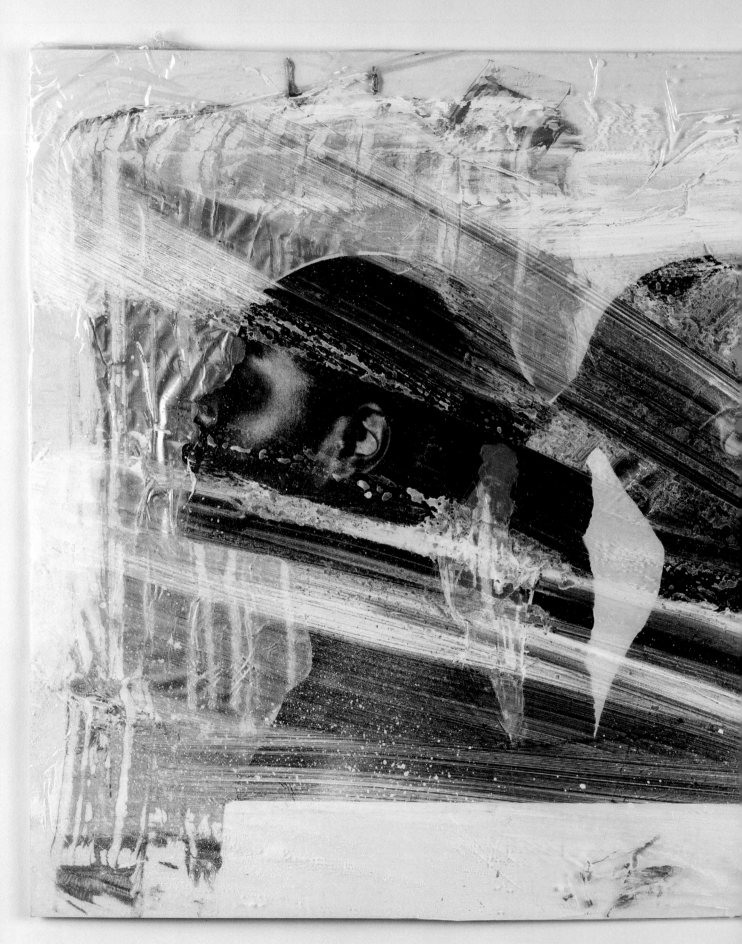

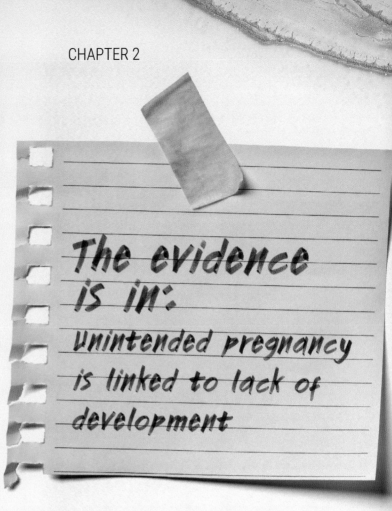

CHAPTER 2

The evidence is in: unintended pregnancy is linked to lack of development

In 2015, every United Nations Member State agreed to the 2030 Agenda for Sustainable Development, which sought as one key goal the achievement of gender equality — recognized as a pillar of human development. One of the indicators of that agenda is "the proportion of women aged 15 to 49 years who make their own informed decisions regarding sexual relations, contraceptive use and reproductive health care".

> **Only 57 per cent of women are able to make their own decisions over their sexual and reproductive health and rights.**

This indicator, SDG 5.6.1, emphasizes that rates of unintended pregnancy are a reflection of overall social development, and that higher levels of informed choice in reproductive decision-making are part of a positive cycle fuelling other development gains. The most recent data on SDG 5.6.1, looking at partnered women of reproductive age in 64 countries, show that 23 per cent are unable to say no to sex, 24 per cent are unable to make decisions about their own health care and 8 per cent are unable to make decisions specifically about contraception. Together, this means that only 57 per cent of women *are* able to make their own decisions over their sexual and reproductive health and rights (United Nations, 2022). This is the context in which we must understand the incidence of unintended pregnancy.

Globally, the latest data show that in 2015–2019, there were roughly 121 million unintended pregnancies each year, with some 48 per cent of *all* pregnancies being unintended (Bearak and others, 2020). Sixty-one per cent of these unintended pregnancies ended in an induced abortion.

The current rate of unintended pregnancies represents a decline from previous years — likely reflecting development gains made during that period. Between 1990 and 2019, the annual unintended pregnancy rate fell from 79 to 64 unintended pregnancies for every 1,000 women aged 15 to 49 years. While the falling rate of unintended pregnancy offers some comfort, the absolute number of women who experience an unintended pregnancy has actually *increased* by about 13 per cent, because of population growth over this 30-year period. The current rate of 64 unintended pregnancies per 1,000 women means that roughly 6 per cent of the world's women experience an unintended pregnancy each year.

New, model-based estimates reinforce the fact that rates and incidence of unintended pregnancy vary widely between countries (Bearak and others, 2022). Why would national and regional boundaries seem to demarcate the frequency of unintended pregnancies? After all, pregnancy is typically described in terms of personal behaviour and responsibility. Yet these trends show that national and regional conditions can play a critical role in supporting or suppressing bodily autonomy, and that, conversely, the loss or exercise of bodily autonomy can materially affect societal well-being. Both of these notions shift some measure of accountability for these issues away from individuals and onto States.

Which national conditions exert influence on, or are influenced by, the exercise of choice? Evidence to date has not provided definitive answers, but there are compelling possibilities, particularly when it comes to development conditions.

Trends in abortion

Though the rate of unintended pregnancy has declined, the global abortion rate is virtually unchanged, and is estimated at 39 per 1,000 women of reproductive age in 2015–2019 (Bearak and others, 2020) (see technical note on page 141). Globally, 29 per cent of all pregnancies — both intended and unintended combined — end in abortion. This amounts to an estimated 73 million abortions per year, on average, in 2015–2019. Where these abortions are unsafe, women risk short- and long-term morbidity and even death.

The steady abortion rate alongside the declining incidence of unintended pregnancy means that the proportion of unintended pregnancies ending in abortion has increased since 1990–1994, from 51 to 61 per cent (Bearak and others, 2020). Taken together, these findings suggest that women may be exercising moderately more autonomy over their reproductive outcomes, in the form of both pregnancy prevention and termination of unintended pregnancies, compared to women 30 years ago.

This broad trajectory can be mapped alongside increasing availability of contraceptive options, gains in gender equity and improving indicators of development, generally speaking; both development progress and decreasing unintended pregnancy rates are found in the great majority of countries for which data are available.

On a country or regional level, however, the proportion of unintended pregnancies ending in abortion varies widely. There is no discernible association between the national incidence of unintended pregnancy and the proportion of those pregnancies ending in abortion; in many places women tend to exercise reproductive choice in one way but not the other.

This chapter presents an original ecological analysis to explore some of the correlations between development metrics and newly available country-level data on unintended pregnancy. While this analysis does not demonstrate causality, it does raise critical questions about how development progress and, relatedly, policy choices can influence the incidence of unintended pregnancy. Conversely, this analysis also suggests that women's empowerment and exercise of choice can affect development and national well-being.

New insights

The incidence of unintended pregnancy varies widely by region. There were about 35 unintended pregnancies annually per 1,000 women aged 15 to 49 years in Europe and North America, compared to 64 in Central and Southern Asia and 91 in sub-Saharan Africa, in 2015–2019. But there are wide disparities within regions, too. For example, the estimated unintended pregnancy rate was 49 in Niger but 145 in Uganda (Bearak and others, 2022). Despite these intra-regional

> **More vigorous efforts to address unintended pregnancy could yield significant development benefits.**

variations, there are important overall trends that can be seen in the regional estimates.

Notably, in Europe and North America, by 2015–2019, the unintended pregnancy rate had dropped to about half what it had been in the early 1990s, while in Southern and Central Asia and Latin America it fell by about one quarter (28 per cent). The rate also fell in sub-Saharan Africa, but only by about 12 per cent.

What do these variations mean? To better understand, this analysis looked at correlations of key social, economic and policy indicators (UNDP, 2020) with unintended pregnancy rates, as well as the proportion of unintended pregnancies that end in abortion at the country level. It looked at 150 countries for which estimates are available, covering the period 1990–2019.

These analyses offer, in general, a strong indication that countries with higher levels of social and economic development, higher levels of gender equality and policies that include more legal access to safe abortion experience lower rates of unintended pregnancy. This highlights the interlinking and mutually reinforcing

relationship between unintended pregnancy and lack of development, suggesting that more vigorous efforts to address unintended pregnancy could yield significant development benefits.

Meanwhile, the proportion of unintended pregnancies ending in abortion varied widely, reflecting the wide diversity in cultural and legal environments around the world.

Socioeconomic development

The authors looked at the 2019 Human Development Index (HDI) data and two of its core components — namely, educational attainment and per capita gross national income (GNI) — against rates of unintended pregnancy. Globally, higher levels of social and economic development, as measured by these indicators, were strongly correlated with lower incidence of unintended pregnancy in 2015–2019. One explanation is that countries with higher development scores are likely to be those where contraceptive services are more widely accessible and where women face fewer cultural barriers to managing their fertility preferences. (Notably, the pattern was different in sub-Saharan Africa, a situation explored further in the technical note on page 141.)

Pregnancy *outcomes* tended to differ between high-income countries and low- and middle-income countries.

In low- and middle-income countries, higher levels of social and economic development were associated with a higher proportion of unintended pregnancies being aborted (even after controlling for differences in the legal status of abortion). This finding lends itself to the hypothesis that, as opportunity costs associated with childbearing increase, women who experience an unintended pregnancy are more strongly motivated to avoid having a child. The same pattern was true with respect to trends over the 30-year period between 1990 and 2019 in these countries: improvements in development scores at the country level were associated with increases in the proportion of unintended pregnancies that were terminated.

In high-income countries, higher HDI scores were associated with a *lower* likelihood that pregnancies would be terminated, although high-income countries with lower development scores were linked to a greater likelihood of abortion. One hypothesis is that, in high-income countries with higher levels of development, women who are motivated to avoid having a child are better able to avoid pregnancy, including through the use of contraception. It is also possible that social and economic safety nets make it easier for women to carry an unintended pregnancy to term in more developed countries.

One might assume that income and education levels among women and girls are more closely linked to lower rates of unintended pregnancy than are the levels of income and education among men and boys, but that was not the case. Per capita GNI scores and levels of educational attainment among females were *not* more strongly correlated with the incidence of unintended pregnancy or the proportion aborted than were male scores for per capita GNI and educational attainment. This indicates that *overall* country GNI and education level is linked to lower unintended pregnancy, rather than exclusively per capita GNI and education among women and girls. In other

words, and importantly, *overall* development is a likely factor in lowering rates of unintended pregnancy.

Gender equality
The authors also assessed the relationship between gender equality and unintended pregnancy, with the gender inequality index (GII) used as a measure of women's and girls' status. The GII measures three aspects of gender equity — reproductive health, empowerment and economic status — with higher GII scores indicating higher levels of gender inequality. Countries (and territories) with higher levels of gender inequality, as measured by the GII, had higher rates of unintended pregnancy in 2015–2019, in both low- and middle-income countries and in high-income countries. This correlation persisted even after controlling for the role of the HDI,

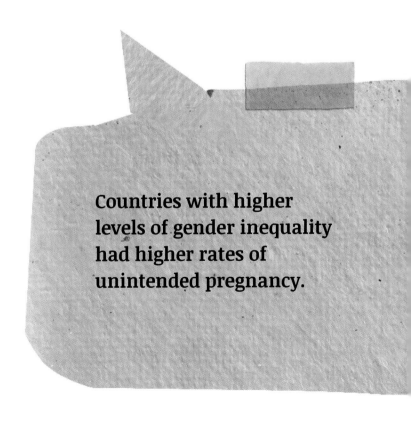

Countries with higher levels of gender inequality had higher rates of unintended pregnancy.

FIGURE 1

Correlation between unintended pregnancy rate 2015–2019 and gender inequality index, 2019

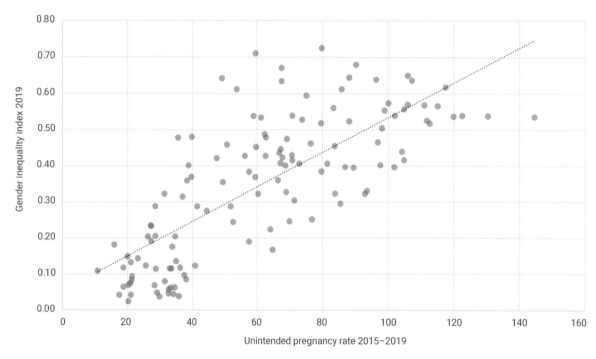

R-squared=0.5744
P-val for slope of fitted line: 0.0000

Source: The authors, using data from Bearak and others, 2022.

and stood out as the strongest of all predictors examined in these analyses (see Figure 1).

In terms of pregnancy outcomes, the patterns that emerged were similar to those observed with respect to the HDI: in low- and middle-income countries, *lower* levels of gender equality were associated with *smaller* proportions of unintended pregnancies that were aborted. This correlation held after accounting for wide variations in abortion laws across those countries. By contrast, in high-income countries, higher scores in gender equality were slightly but non-

significantly associated with lower proportions of unintended pregnancies aborted.

Taken together, these findings suggest that initial gains in gender equality, as seen in low- and middle-income countries, result in women with an unintended pregnancy being more likely to take advantage of the option to have an abortion. However, in higher-income settings more gender equality had no noticeable impact on recourse to abortion (Figure 2), perhaps because in these settings women are better able to avoid unintended pregnancies in the first place.

FIGURE 2

Unplanned birth and abortion rates, and proportion of unintended pregnancies that end in unplanned births, abortions or miscarriages, 2015–2019, by gender inequality index (GII)

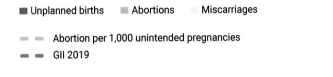

■ Unplanned births   ▨ Abortions   ░ Miscarriages

▬ ▬ Abortion per 1,000 unintended pregnancies
▬ ▬ GII 2019

A. Countries and territories with GII less than 0.35

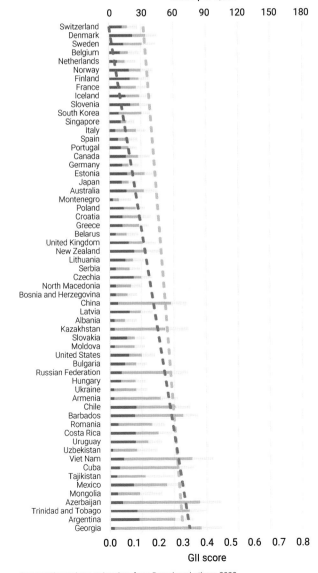

B. Countries and territories with GII greater than 0.35

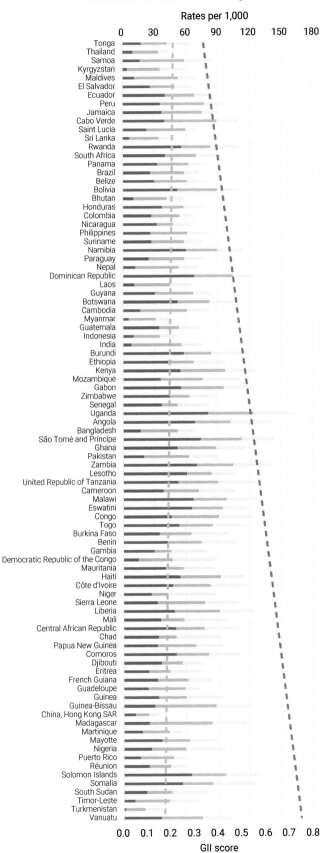

Source: The authors, using data from Bearak and others, 2022.

Maternal mortality ratio

The relationship between maternal mortality ratio (MMR) (a component of the GII) and unsafe abortion is well known. Unsafe abortion is one of the leading contributors to maternal deaths around the world: Between 4.7 per cent and 13.2 per cent of maternal deaths can be attributed to unsafe abortion annually (WHO, 2020). But the relationship between unintended pregnancy and maternal mortality has been less clear.

In the authors' analyses, using only available data on MMR (WHO and others, 2019) (a very important measure of development, especially of the health sector) and the unintended pregnancy rates from 2015 to 2019, it was found that higher maternal mortality was indeed correlated with higher rates of unintended pregnancy. This association held for countries in all income categories (with the exception of sub-Saharan Africa, discussed in the technical note on page 141).

Why would unintended pregnancies be associated with a higher risk of maternal mortality than intended pregnancies? There are many possible explanations. Central among these is that unintended pregnancies are more likely than intended pregnancies to lead to abortion, including unsafe abortions. Women with unintended pregnancies are also less likely to use health services (explored further in Chapter 5 on page 94). Still, evidence on the impact of unintended pregnancy on maternal health outcomes is limited, and the pathways for this association are yet to be fully unpacked in the scientific literature (Gipson and others, 2008).

Abortion laws

Rates of unintended pregnancy tend to be *lower* in countries with more liberal abortion laws (i.e., countries in which abortion is allowed on socioeconomic grounds or on request) than in those with more restrictive laws (where abortion is prohibited altogether; where it is only allowed to save a woman's life; where it allowed to preserve a woman's physical health; and where it is also allowed to preserve a woman's mental health).

This is a notable correlation, though not a matter of causation: liberal abortion laws themselves likely have no impact on the incidence of unintended pregnancy. Instead, it is possible that liberal abortion laws are a reflection of broader sexual and reproductive health services that are more user-friendly and accommodating to the needs of sexually active people.

In terms of unintended pregnancy *outcomes*, low- and middle-income countries saw no significant association between abortion laws and the proportion of unintended pregnancies that ended in abortion. In other words, restrictive abortion laws in these countries were *not* shown to reduce recourse to abortion. But in high-income countries that had more liberal abortion laws a significantly *smaller* proportion of unintended pregnancies resulted in abortions, compared to high-income countries with more restrictive laws. These findings support those of other researchers (Bearak and others, 2022).

Abortion from a human rights angle

Not all unintended pregnancies are unwanted. But the majority of unintended pregnancies end in abortion, making the human rights perspective on abortion highly relevant to States and policymakers. Reproductive rights are human rights; everyone has the right to make informed decisions about their body and health and to decide whether, when and how many children to have (UN General Assembly, 1979). These rights, and the rights to health and life, are inclusive of safe abortion access, which is protected "where the life and health of the pregnant woman or girl is at risk, or where carrying a pregnancy to term would cause the pregnant woman or girl substantial pain or suffering, most notably where the pregnancy is the result of rape or incest or is not viable" (UN CCPR, 2019). Safe abortion access is not a standalone right. It depends upon the protection and enjoyment of other human rights: to information, to health, to equality, to privacy and to live free from violence, gender-based stereotypes and discrimination (OHCHR, 2018).

While abortion access is principally governed through national law (UNFPA, 1994), human rights norms increasingly affect the scope of national legislation. In 2019, for instance, the United Nations Committee on Civil and Political Rights indicated that all States should decriminalize abortion and ensure that legal abortion be available to preserve a woman's life and health; furthermore, States may not place administrative or other barriers in the way of women seeking a legal abortion (UN CCPR, 2019). Many other international human rights treaties and bodies and regional human rights treaties consider abortion a human right when pregnancy is the result of

force and coercion. (Fine and others, 2017). In all cases, whether or not the abortion or attempted abortion is legal, post-abortion care as a lifesaving medical intervention must be available to all those who require it (UNFPA, 1994).

Abortion is, in fact, legal in the majority of countries, although often with restrictions. In 96 per cent of the 147 United Nations Member States that reported data, abortion is legal on some or all grounds, including to save a woman's life, to preserve a woman's health, in cases of rape and in cases of fetal impairment. However, a husband's consent is required for married women to access the service in 28 per cent of these countries, and judicial consent is required for minors in 36 per cent. Furthermore, women can be criminally charged for an illegal abortion in 63 per cent of the countries (United Nations, 2022).

In situations where abortion is illegal or otherwise inaccessible, unwanted pregnancies have been described as "compulsory childbearing" (UN ESCWA, 2004). This idea, that an individual should be compelled to continue with an undesired pregnancy, is rooted in gendered stereotypes and reflects the discriminatory notion that the worth of girls and women lies solely in their reproductive capacities. States are obliged by human rights conventions to transform such harmful stereotypes and end the practices through which they are reinforced. Laws and policies must, at the very least, enable individuals to avoid unintended pregnancies to the greatest extent possible (UNFPA, 2020b).

Supporting or suppressing choice

These analyses are just a first step in examining these new estimates. More extensive research is needed. Still, at present, this glimpse into the data offers important insights, many of which affirm existing assumptions and findings, such as the clear correlation between many measures of development, especially those related to gender inequality, and unintended pregnancy. Other findings help uncover nuanced differences across parts of the world in how women experience and deal with unintended pregnancies, as reflected in the relationships between gender equality and pregnancy outcome.

Taken together, these data show that overall country and community circumstances could create environments that enable or hinder the exercise of affirmative choice over whether and when to become pregnant, and that bodily autonomy and agency can play a reciprocal role in improving community and national development.

Unintended, unwanted or uncertain? The limits of current measures

This chapter presents some of the most comprehensive and recent data on the topic of unintended pregnancy. Yet it is also important to note that this topic — though critically important socially and economically, and while ubiquitous as an experience — is often poorly or inconsistently described, and often poorly understood, leading to limitations in how it has been measured.

First of all, the large proportion of unintended pregnancies that end in abortion — more than three in five (Bearak and others, 2020) — highlights the likelihood that most of these pregnancies are not only unintended but unwanted as well. Given the legal restrictions on abortion in many countries, as well as the social, economic and geographical barriers to abortion in many communities, the actual proportion of unintended pregnancies that are undesired could be much higher.

But it would be a mistake to assume that all unintended pregnancies are unwanted. In some cases, women do not actively plan to get pregnant, but they might react positively to the pregnancy and decide they want to continue it. This is underscored by a large survey in France, in which respondents were more likely to say a pregnancy was unplanned than they were to report it was unwanted (Moreau and others, 2014).

Researchers have long noted, and struggled to precisely capture, how women's attitudes toward getting pregnant can fall on a spectrum (Hall and others, 2017; Aiken and others, 2016). Many women, for instance, are ambivalent about having, or expanding, a family. Some want to have a baby but are uncertain about their life circumstances, partner or future. A woman's desire for pregnancy may ebb and flow before, and even during, a pregnancy. And in many settings, the very notion of intentionality is fraught. Women and girls in these scenarios may be unable to exercise personal volition or they may have a fatalistic approach to pregnancy and childbearing. They may think their intentions do not matter, and — tragically — in the eyes of their families or communities, many of them are right.

This uncertainty has an impact on the data. Many metrics assume that women make conscious and binary decisions about whether or not they want to have a child. Most current estimates of the incidence of unintended pregnancy are derived from questions used in population-based surveys, such as Demographic and Health Surveys (DHS) in low-income countries. The DHS asks women a single question about each pregnancy that occurred, up to five years in the past. It is usually a version of: "At the time you became pregnant, did you want to become pregnant then, did you want to wait until later, or did you not want to have any (more) children at all?" Women who respond that they did not want to become pregnant or that they wanted to wait are considered by these estimates to have had an unintended pregnancy. This approach is imperfect (Population Council, 2015): for instance, some women who have a child from an unintended pregnancy may later go on to reframe their experience of a pregnancy after they have adapted to their new reality (Ralph and others, 2020). After giving birth and bonding with a baby, or after enduring the stigma attached to unintended pregnancy, a woman may recast a prior aversion to pregnancy as simply ambivalence, or ambivalence may be recast as openness to pregnancy. Measures based on retrospective reporting of pregnancy intentions may thus underestimate the prevalence of unintended pregnancy.

Women may, for religious or other reasons, make a deliberate choice to not choose — leaving their fate to faith or destiny, for example. These women evade easy classification; they could be described as having an open-ended intention to become pregnant but, equally, their pregnancies could be described as unplanned. Finally, DHS and other surveys usually collect information on unintended pregnancy from women only. Therefore, little is known about male partners' attitudes towards pregnancy, or the degree to which they are able to exercise reproductive choice in their own lives.

There are efforts underway to improve measures of unintended pregnancy to better reflect women's nuanced experiences. One approach, the London Measure of Unplanned Pregnancy, measures the extent to which a pregnancy was planned on a scale of 0–12 (Hall and others, 2017). Model-based estimates of the incidence of unplanned births and abortion were published in 2016 (Sedgh and others, 2016a), and these have been followed by the first-ever model-based country estimates for nearly all countries in the world (Bearak and others, 2022). Still, these are estimates; a deep and reliable evidence base will emerge only when these experiences can be reported without shame, and sufficient resources are dedicated to measuring abortion incidence.

Adolescent pregnancy and choice

Unintended pregnancy is often conflated with the issue of teen pregnancy, but the relationship between these two concerns is actually more complex. Not all adolescent births result from unintended pregnancies. A majority of births among girls under the age of 18 take place within a marriage or union, a finding reaffirmed by new research from the United Nations Population Division (UN DESA, 2022). Many of those pregnancies may well be classified as "intended" by existing surveys, self-reports and other measurements even though young girls' ability to decide when and with whom to have children is severely constrained, if they have any choice at all. A closer look at adolescent fertility, particularly among the youngest adolescents, shows the limitations of looking only at current measures of pregnancy intention when examining autonomy and choices.

Motherhood in childhood

New UNFPA research (UNFPA, 2022) looking at 96 per cent of the world's adolescent population, excluding China and high-income countries, finds that, across the developing world, *nearly one in three* young women aged 20 to 24 years gave birth in adolescence, defined as ages 10 to 19. Nearly half of these adolescent mothers were children (aged 17 years and younger) and they commonly went on to experience additional births while still in childhood.

In other words, 13 per cent of all young women in developing countries begin childbearing while still children, and these adolescents go on to account for a strikingly large portion of all adolescent births. Three-quarters of girls with a first birth at age 14 and younger had a second birth before turning 20, and 40 per cent of those with two births went on to have a third birth before turning 20. Half of girls with a first birth between ages 15 and 17 had a second birth before turning 20.

Furthermore, more than half of the additional births (after the first birth) to adolescent mothers were rapid repeat births; that is, they occur within 24 months of a previous birth and come with elevated risk of infant mortality and morbidity (Molitoris and others, 2019; Rutstein, 2008).

These new findings show:
- **45 per cent** of first-time adolescent mothers are children themselves — that is, 17 years and younger.
- **50 per cent** of all adolescent births occur to girls who start childbearing in childhood.
- **54 per cent** of all non-first births to adolescent mothers are rapid repeat births.

Progress has been made in increasing the age at first birth, but not enough. In the data spanning nearly six decades, the proportion of first-time adolescent births occurring to girls aged 17 years and younger fell from 60 to 45 per cent. The proportion of all adolescent births that occurred to these girls fell from 68 to 50 per cent. In both cases, this corresponds to a decline of only about 3 percentage points every 10 years, with an acceleration in the decline over the past two decades. At this rate, it will take 160 years to end motherhood in childhood. For rapid repeat births, the decline is even more limited — only 1 percentage point decrease every 10 years over the last six decades.

In all regions of the world, a significant proportion of women start their reproductive lives in adolescence (Figure 3).

FIGURE 3 Proportion of women who began childbearing in adolescence, by SDG region, excluding China and high-income countries

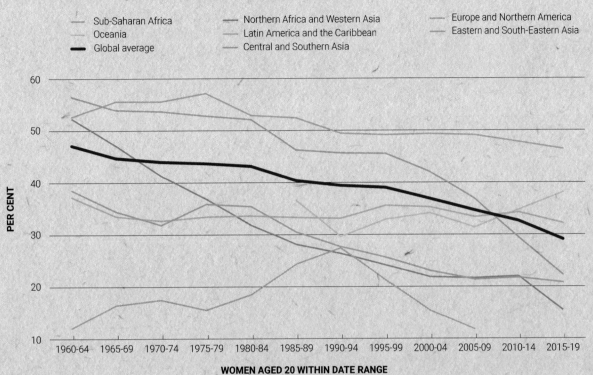

Source: UNFPA, 2022.

FIGURE 4 Completed fertility by motherhood entry age, global average, excluding China and high-income countries

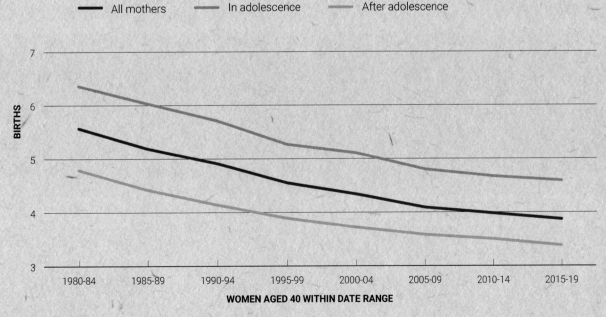

Source: UNFPA, 2022.

Women who have their first birth in adolescence end up having nearly two births more over their lifetimes than women who start at age 20 or later (Figure 4).

The role of child marriage

In 54 developing countries with data, the majority of first births to girls under the age of 18 occur within a marriage or union, according to a new, previously unpublished, analysis from the United Nations Population Division (UN DESA, 2022). Countries in Central and Southern Asia and in Northern Africa and Western Asia most consistently show high proportions of marital births.

What is the relationship between adolescent childbearing and marriage? Many young brides are expected to bear children or demonstrate their fertility early in their marriage, in which case pregnancy occurs soon after marriage.

But we also know pregnancy can be a driver of child marriage, owing to cultural beliefs or gender-stereotyped attitudes about childbearing and wedlock, premarital sex, family honour and lack of access to sexual and reproductive health services including safe abortion (Petroni and others, 2017). The survey data show that many first births among girls under the age of 18 occur less

than seven months after marriage or the start of cohabitation suggesting that premarital conception often precedes the marriage of girls (Figure 5). In some countries — Bangladesh, Benin, Chad, Comoros, Indonesia, Lesotho, Niger, Papua New Guinea and the Philippines — more than a fifth of first births to girls under the age of 18 fall into this category. Still, there is significant variation across regions and countries (see technical note on page 142 for more information).

Some adolescents get formally married or enter informal unions as part of an emancipatory strategy (Horii, 2021); rather than seeing their own marriages as "forced", they view them as a solution to the prohibition against premarital sex and romantic relationships, and even a way to escape violent conditions in the home. Yet these self-described voluntary marriages have many of the same harmful consequences of forced marriage, including accelerated and unsafe transitions to adult roles and responsibilities, including adolescent childbearing.

Women and girls married as adolescents tend to have less education, less household and economic power and less mobility than unmarried adolescents and older women. They tend to be isolated and lack the knowledge

and skills to negotiate situations that are detrimental to their health and well-being — including how many children to have and when. The age gap between spouses tends to be larger among women who marry at younger ages compared to women who marry at older ages (UN DESA, 2022; Haberland and others, 2004). Early sexual activity with an older partner has been linked to poor gender relations and poor reproductive health outcomes (Ryan and others, 2008).

Addressing these underlying conditions means addressing gender inequality by giving adolescents and young people education, employment and participation opportunities as alternatives to early marriage and pregnancy; providing comprehensive sexuality education; ensuring adolescent-friendly sexual and reproductive health services and contraceptive supplies; enabling parents and families to provide information, support and care to shape adolescents' healthy approach to sexuality and relationships (UNESCO and others, 2018); establishing the minimum legal age of marriage for girls and boys, with or without parental consent, at 18 years; and avoiding "criminalizing adolescents of similar ages for factually consensual and non-exploitative sexual activity" (UN CRC, 2016).

FIGURE 5   First births by age 18, by SDG region

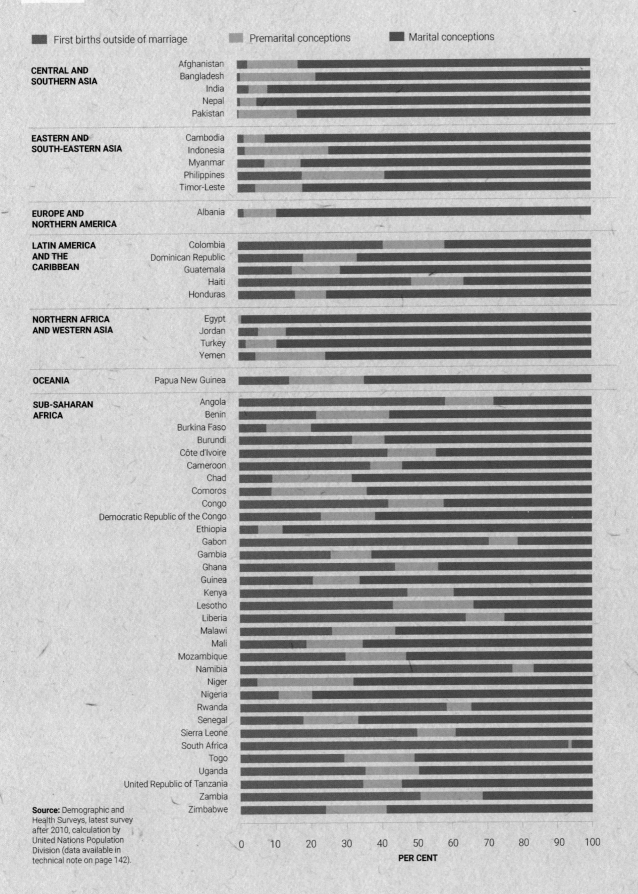

■ First births outside of marriage   ■ Premarital conceptions   ■ Marital conceptions

Source: Demographic and Health Surveys, latest survey after 2010, calculation by United Nations Population Division (data available in technical note on page 142).

THE ILLUSION OF CHOICE: ADOLESCENT PREGNANCY

For Yajaira and for so many young women – especially those marginalized by poverty and a lack of employment or educational opportunities – there is a certain inevitability to early pregnancy and marriage. © UNFPA/Wilton Castillo

EL SALVADOR/PHILIPPINES — When she was just 16, Yajaira was impregnated by her 18-year-old boyfriend the first time they slept together. They married soon after. "That was the start of a new stage in my life," recalls Yajaira. "It was an abrupt change because I had to take responsibility for my pregnancy. I had only finished the ninth grade."

Her situation is all too common. In El Salvador, where she lives, adolescents make up one quarter of all pregnancies (UNFPA El Salvador, 2021). This is a sign of overall disempowerment: teen pregnancies and early marriages are linked to cycles of domestic and sexual violence (UNFPA El Salvador, 2021), a scourge that was already common before it soared by 70 per cent in the COVID-19 pandemic (IRC, 2020). Sexuality education has only recently been added to the national curriculum, and abortion is strictly banned under all circumstances – with no exceptions for rape, incest

or if the lives of the mother and baby are at risk.

One might assume, then, that most teen pregnancies are unintended. But in fact, over half of adolescent pregnancies in El Salvador, 58 per cent, were reported as intended by women, while 75 per cent of the men involved considered them intentional (Carter and Speizer, 2005).

When asked if she had made the choice to have a baby at 16, Yajaira does not answer directly. She says that she didn't have any sexuality education, and that sex and pregnancy just seemed to happen. For her, and for so many young women – especially those marginalized by poverty and a lack of employment or educational opportunities – there is a certain inevitability to early pregnancy and marriage. More than one quarter of Salvadorian girls are married or in informal unions by age 18 (ECLAC, 2020).

While Yajaira did not make an affirmative choice to become pregnant, marriage was a different matter. "My mother didn't want me to," she says, "but I didn't want to repeat my situation for my child, of being raised without a father, so I decided to get married and I went to live with my boyfriend's parents. It was the most difficult stage of my life. As I was on my way to the city hall to get married, my classmates were at an event to mark the start of high school... It was a reality check. I thought, 'What am I doing?'"

Her husband had promised she could continue her education, but the reality was different. In addition to caring for her infant son and helping with expenses by making and selling cheese, she attended school in the departmental capital every Saturday. Afterwards, she rushed home to prepare meals for her husband, a situation that irked her mother-in-law. "That nonsense about studying is over," Yajaira recalls her saying.

On the other side of the world, in Maguindanao in the Philippines, Rahmadina was a typical school girl – until she finished sixth grade. At 14 years old, she fell in love with and married 16-year-old Morsid, giving birth to their first child soon after. These were her own decisions, she says. But she did not expect what followed.

"When we got married, I still managed to finish the first year of high school," Rahmadinah says, cradling her second child, a newborn. Then her desire to continue school crashed into a harsh reality. After her husband travelled to Manila for work, "he told me to quit because he had stopped studying".

Despite their financial hardships and the difficulties she sometimes faces raising two children so young, Rahmadinah loves being a mother. Still, she says she thinks about the life she would have had if she had made different choices.

Today, she wants to find work overseas "so that my children could have the things they need," she says. "But my husband isn't going to let me. He tells me I can't. He'll abandon me if I ever work abroad. So I just stay quiet; I don't plan on going anywhere anymore."

Yajaira, too, felt stuck. Though she had made the choice to get married, other life choices were beyond her control. Her husband was unfaithful and emotionally abusive. When Yajaira wanted to leave, he and his parents used her son as leverage: "They asked me to go and to leave my son, not to take him." Finally, five years into the marriage, she reached a breaking point. She moved back to her mother's home, taking her son with her. "I wasn't going to leave my son there. Nobody was going to take my son away from me."

Determined to chart a different course for herself, she finished her studies and joined the police force, supporting survivors of gender-based violence. She experienced another unintended pregnancy – this time she was using contraception, but it failed. When she told her partner she was pregnant, he left town.

These days, at 34, Yajaira exudes an air of confidence. She is happy with

Rahmadina Talusan Malang, 18, mother of two. © UNFPA/Rosa May DeGuzman

her career, proud of her 6- and 17-year-old boys, and excited about the degree in social work she is soon to complete. And she is raising her sons to be responsible men who reject gender-unequal norms and speak openly about issues like contraception: "It is very common for mothers not to open up and talk to their children about these issues. But it is good to talk to them so that they gain some confidence."

As for Rahmadina, she too is making decisions to secure her future. She has learned about available contraceptive options and is about to receive her first contraceptive injection. She wants her daughter to have more choices, too. "I want her to finish school, not end up like me, and to achieve her goals before she marries," she says.

CHAPTER 3

Every woman is at risk: Erosion of agency leads to unintended pregnancy

Unintended pregnancy affects women and girls (as well as transgender men and non-binary people) from all cultures, economic strata, religions and marital statuses. In many cultures and countries, stigma is attached to the pregnancy of an unmarried woman or girl. On the other hand, married women are often assumed to be open to, or accepting of, the prospect of pregnancy at any time — an erasure of their desires and choices. In that worldview, the concept of unintended pregnancy among married women does not exist.

The truth is that any fertile woman of reproductive age can experience an unintended pregnancy.

Contraceptives have failure rates and access barriers (explored further in Chapter 4), sexual violence and reproductive coercion remain ubiquitous, and some 23 per cent of women, in countries with available data, report they are unable to say no to sex (SDG data). Together, these facts mean that nearly all fertile women and girls of reproductive age have a non-zero chance of becoming pregnant without planning, desiring or assenting to do so.

Still, there are many factors associated with greater vulnerability. These are not moral qualities but sociodemographic circumstances, as the previous chapter highlights. And rather than *driving* unintended pregnancy, which suggests they propulsively direct women and girls in the inexorable direction of pregnancy, these factors may be better described as conditions that *erode* human agency. This chapter examines how these sociodemographic circumstances can, and often do, affect the decision-making power of women and girls who experience unintended pregnancy.

The truth is that any fertile woman of reproductive age can experience an unintended pregnancy.

Factors that support or undermine choice

Poverty and income inequality take a toll on women's agency

The relationship between poverty and unintended pregnancy is often assumed, but it is far from straightforward. The degree of intentionality with which a woman regards her pregnancies is often coloured by contextual circumstances. Poor women with fewer opportunities may see pregnancy as an inevitability or live under economic conditions that favour large families.

Studies looking at developing countries have found that women in the poorest income categories have higher rates of unintended pregnancies than women with higher family income levels (Sarder and others, 2021; Bain and others, 2020; Ameyaw and others, 2019). In a broad overview of DHS data from 29 countries in sub-Saharan Africa, spanning 2010–2016 (Ameyaw and others, 2019), researchers found that the proportion of pregnancies considered unintended was *highest* among the poorest women. Similar findings have been reflected in studies from the United States (Finer and Zolna, 2016).

One explanation for this correlation is that poorer women are often less able to afford modern contraception (Garraza and others, 2020). Lower-income women are also disproportionately less educated than their peers, and therefore may lack knowledge about contraception. They are additionally more likely to be rural or living in the underserved parts of urban areas, and therefore may lack access to services.

Couples' concordance

DHS data from 18 sub-Saharan African countries, collected between the mid-1990s to the mid-2000s, show that men overwhelmingly expressed a desire for more children than women did (Westhoff, 2010). More recent research from 2019, looking at four sub-Saharan African countries, similarly found husbands' desired number of children generally exceeded their wives' ideal number (Atake and Ali, 2019). A key issue, therefore, is the ability of couples to articulate and negotiate their fertility preferences — in a way that realizes the autonomy and agency of both. Distressingly, evidence shows that many women are unable to participate in this critical area of decision-making: the most recent data show that, in 64 countries, more than 8 per cent of women lack the power to decide on contraception, and nearly a quarter of women lack the power to say no to sex (United Nations, 2022). Many women resort to covert methods of contraceptive use in order to reassert autonomy when their reproductive choices are being undermined.

Researchers at Avenir Health have created a couples' concordance index (CCI), measuring not only agreement over family size but also power imbalances within the relationship known to affect fertility choices (using factors such as education levels and age difference between partners, as well as gender norms), with greater CCI values representing a larger degree of both agreement and shared decision-making. The analysis finds that a higher CCI correlates strongly with a higher prevalence of modern contraceptive use. Tellingly, no country in the review exceeded a prevalence of 55 per cent for modern contraceptive use if it did not have a relatively high CCI score (Bietsch and Emmart, 2022). This suggests that when couples are able to jointly plan their reproductive futures, under gender-equal conditions, women are more likely to be empowered to use modern methods of contraception.

Here it should be noted, as well, that men themselves have only one traditional method of contraception (withdrawal) and two modern methods (condoms and male sterilization) available to them. Only one of these modern methods, male sterilization, meets the World Health Organization (WHO) definition of being "very effective" based on common use. The other modern option for which men are considered the primary user, the male condom, is considered "moderately effective" based on common use (though, it should be emphasized, condoms have other advantages, such as protecting users from sexually transmitted infections, including HIV) (WHO, 2020c). (See more in the male contraceptive feature on page 70.) The paucity of contraception options available to men leaves women to bear most of the contraceptive burden, which can include costs, time seeking health-care services, and side effects, even as gender-unequal social norms leave many women with little decision-making power over contraception and sex. See the list of methods available to women on page 58.

© UNFPA/Fidel Évora

Still, not all studies find a direct or linear correlation between wealth and unintended pregnancies (Habib and others, 2017), indicating that the correlation is contextual, depending on the country, and that other factors tied to poverty, like lack of education, have an important role to play.

Age and agency

Teenagers with unintended pregnancies are often deployed as cautionary tales to illustrate the dangers of premarital sex. This stereotype has led many people, and even policymakers, to assume that unintended pregnancies largely or even primarily affect younger women and girls. But the data paint a much more complex picture.

In a recent study of pregnant women who were or had been married in six South Asian nations — Afghanistan, Bangladesh, India, Maldives, Nepal and Pakistan — fully 90 per cent of women and girls aged 15 to 19 years classified their pregnancies as intended, more than any other age group, seemingly refuting the assumption that this age group would have a large number of unintended pregnancies. However, after controlling for potential confounding factors (such as poverty status and education), it did appear that adolescents faced the greatest odds that their pregnancies were unintended (Sarder and others, 2021). Another study, covering 29 sub-Saharan African countries, in which never-married women were *included*, it was true that unmarried adolescents were more likely than older unmarried women to report their pregnancies as unintended. However, among all women and girls, including those who were married or cohabiting (or divorced or widowed), those aged 15 to 19 years had rates of unintended pregnancy lower than other age groups. Taking into account all age groups and every marital status, in the African countries it was the *older* women who were more likely to experience unintended pregnancies than women aged 15 to 19 years (Ameyaw and others, 2019).

Easy conclusions are elusive in part because study methodologies and quality of data can be so variable. Unintended pregnancy rates among women can vary widely depending on whether the studies look at all women in a cohort or just those who are sexually active (Finer and Zolna, 2016; Finer, 2010). Additionally, many young women, especially if they are married, are culturally expected to have children to prove their fertility, and because many young women do desire children, they may provide what they think is the "correct" answer when asked by the DHS if they intended their first pregnancy. If intention status were measured differently — for instance, if girls were asked whether, at the time they became pregnant, they would have preferred to be pregnant or to continue their education — the incidence of unintended pregnancy among adolescents might look different.

Another explanation for inconsistent findings across study settings is that different age groups face differing vulnerabilities. Many adolescents

Many adolescents in low- and middle-income countries face particularly acute risk factors.

in low- and middle-income countries face particularly acute risk factors (Neal and others, 2020). They are known, for instance, to face challenges in accessing contraceptive information and services (Smith, 2020; UN CRC, 2003), and have their modern contraceptive demands satisfied at lower levels than any other age group (Kantorová and others, 2021). Furthermore, studies show that individual, familial and community factors make some girls and adolescents even more vulnerable to an unintended pregnancy, including low educational attainment, substance use/abuse and intimate partner violence (Chung and others, 2018).

Recognizing these added vulnerabilities, human rights norms direct States to ensure quality health-care services for adolescents that respect their rights to privacy and confidentiality on the basis of non-discrimination (UN CRC, 2016). These services should be available and accessible without necessarily requiring parental or guardian authorization by law, policy or practice. But these rights are not realized in many parts of the world, meaning that adolescent girls and young women require special attention in reducing unintended pregnancies. It is also worth noting adolescents bear disproportionate costs as a result of unintended pregnancy (explored further in Chapter 5).

Meanwhile, women at the other end of their reproductive lives also experience unintended pregnancies. Their risks are often markedly different, resulting not necessarily from barriers to contraceptive services or insufficient knowledge about sex and contraception, but from widespread misconceptions about their waning reproductive capacity. Information about mid- and later-life fertility and menopause is often scarce (Ilankoon and others, 2021; Im and others, 2010), and while fecundity does indeed decline as women age, many women remain fertile through perimenopause. Yet the perception that they have aged beyond fertility, or beyond sexual activity, may discourage the use of effective contraception (Bakour and others, 2017; Wellings and others, 2013). Women may confuse perimenopausal menstrual irregularity with infertility, and health providers may be unfamiliar with mid-life sexual health needs (Taylor and James, 2012). In fact, pregnancy among older or mid-life women can occur at ratios similar to younger women (Chae and others, 2017; Baldwin and Jensen, 2013).

The consequences of unintended pregnancies in this age group are different, as well. Older pregnant women face a higher risk of complications and miscarriage (Frederiksen and others, 2018). While they are less likely to see their own education interrupted by a pregnancy, they face opportunity costs in the form of workforce participation, investments in children they may already have, caretaking for other family members or grandchildren, and savings for their own retirement or old-age care.

Abstinence from sexual activity is considered by many to be a "fail-safe" method of controlling fertility. This is, of course, not true in the case of rape or coercive sex, which can be widespread in some places and circumstances, such as humanitarian crises (see page 54). But even among those who do not experience coercion or violence, abstinence can be ineffective if it is not reliably practised. DHS respondents frequently report using periodic abstinence as a method of contraception, for example, but about 40 per cent of those individuals discontinue the method within 12 months (Ali and others, 2012).

More generally, "abstinence-only" education is often promoted as a way of preventing sexual contact among unmarried young people. Yet programmes promoting abstinence-only are found to be ineffective in delaying sexual initiation, reducing the frequency of sex or reducing the number of sexual partners. By contrast, programmes that combine a focus on delaying sexual activity with content about condom or contraceptive use are effective (UNESCO and others, 2018).

Education as an enabler of choice and equality

Within the 2030 Agenda, education and gender equality are recognized as pillars of development. We know that the more formal education girls and women receive, the more agency they have over their life course. They are better equipped to make choices about whether and when to marry, and if, when and how many children to have. They are also better supported when they make those choices. But these two things should not be confused: while education does empower girls with knowledge about their bodies and rights, it should not burden them with the entire responsibility for preventing an unintended pregnancy. Communities bear responsibility as well, because when societies value formal education for girls, there is an implied acceptance that girls and women have more to offer than exclusively reproduction and motherhood. Thus, female educational attainment can be seen as both a reflection of, and vector for, overcoming gender inequality and stereotypes.

Numerous studies have found that women with more education have less risk of having unintended pregnancies compared to women with fewer years of education. This is true in studies across sub-Saharan Africa, where women with primary and secondary education were respectively 26 and 29 per cent less likely to have an unintended pregnancy than women with no education (Ameyaw and others, 2019). And it is true in higher-income countries such as the United Kingdom (Wellings and others, 2013) and the United States (Finer and Zolna, 2016).

Higher educational attainment among male partners has also been linked to lower unintended pregnancy rates (Seifu and others, 2020). That is, women are less likely to experience an unintended pregnancy when their husbands are more educated. In part, this could reflect that the women married to educated men are more likely to be educated themselves, but it also indicates that, with education, men become increasingly aware of the advantages of planning births for the well-being of the family unit.

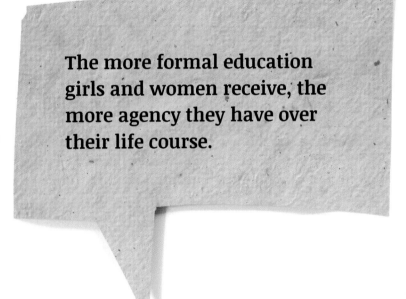

The more formal education girls and women receive, the more agency they have over their life course.

Marital status offers no clear protection from unintended pregnancy

Historically, concerns about unintended pregnancy have been attached to marital status. Pregnancy outside of marriage has long been considered scandalous or dishonourable, a norm that persists across cultures and religions. While marital status offers no direct protection against unintended pregnancy, one might assume that the stigma and negative repercussions of unmarried, unintended pregnancy produce a deterrent effect. Yet a look at the data shows no

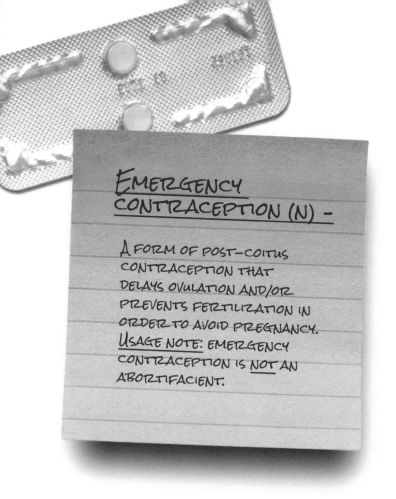

EMERGENCY CONTRACEPTION (N) –

A form of post-coitus contraception that delays ovulation and/or prevents fertilization in order to avoid pregnancy. Usage note: Emergency contraception is NOT AN ABORTIFACIENT.

clear association between marital status and risk of unintended pregnancy (Hall and others, 2016; Ikamari and others, 2013; Melian, 2013), with some studies finding unmarried women to be at higher risk, while others indicate married women are (Ameyaw and others, 2019; Nyarko, 2019). For example, in the study of 29 sub-Saharan African countries, unmarried women had a higher *prevalence* of unintended pregnancy than married women overall, but after researchers controlled for other factors (such as age), married women ended up having a much higher *likelihood* of unintended pregnancy (Ameyaw and others, 2019).

It might also be assumed that married women, whose unintended pregnancies tend to be more socially acceptable, are less likely to obtain an abortion. Again, the available data paint a more nuanced picture: According to one study from 2016 (Sedgh and others, 2016a), the abortion

rate globally was higher among *married* women, although this varied considerably among regions.

Family size and intention

In many studies, women with more children appear to be more vulnerable to unintended pregnancies. A study of women with HIV in Uganda found that "a higher number of pregnancies increased the likelihood of experiencing unintended pregnancies" (Napyo and others, 2020). Across six South Asian countries, an average of 22.7 per cent of women with three or more children had experienced an unintended pregnancy, compared to only 5.5 per cent of the women who had no children (Sarder and others, 2021).

There are many possible explanations for this association. Researchers have posited that the women with more children may have more inconsistent use of contraception, under-use of emergency contraception, more experience of contraceptive side effects like excessive bleeding, or they may have more experience of partner refusal or stock-outs at accessible health facilities. Other explanations centre around women's fertility preferences: because women's fertility preferences tend to be lower among more empowered women — those who are more educated, who have greater decision-making power, who exercise greater control over household resources (Atake and Ali, 2019) — it may be the case that women with lower levels of empowerment tend to both prefer larger families and *also* exercise less agency over their fertility, therefore resulting in higher levels of unintended pregnancy.

Still, the connection between family size and pregnancy intention is far from definitive, with a

Risks across the gender spectrum: not just a heterosexual concern

Marginalization of every kind can take a toll on the agency of people who are able to become pregnant. While prevailing wisdom suggests that only women in heterosexual relationships are at risk of an unintended pregnancy, studies indicate that this vulnerability extends to — and may be even greater among — sexual minorities.

Researchers have found that the presumption that sexual minority women, such as lesbian and bisexual women, are not at risk can actually contribute to their increased vulnerability (Everett and others, 2017). These women are less likely to use contraception, and have lower levels of access to reproductive health care than heterosexual women, and they face additional social stress and stigma.

A meta-analysis of studies from several countries found that lesbian and bisexual adolescents were at greater risk of pregnancy than their heterosexual peers (Hodson and others, 2016). In another study, lesbian women reported having had male sexual partners, and bisexual women reported more male sexual partners, on average, than heterosexual women (Xu and others, 2010), a counterintuitive finding that can be explained, in part, by social pressures, coercion and the significantly higher rates of sexual violence experienced by sexual minorities (Rothman and others, 2011). Researchers have reported that, among pregnancies experienced by a sample of self-identified transgender, non-binary and gender-expansive people, some 54 per cent were unintended, compared to 48 per cent overall (Moseson and others, 2021). Sexual minorities can also experience specific consequences linked to these unintended pregnancies, including additional stigma, discrimination and dysphoria, and challenges finding non-judgmental and knowledgeable health-care providers (Everett and others, 2019; Müller and others, 2018).

number of studies showing a correlation, others finding none (Napyo and others, 2020), and some finding that unintended pregnancy actually *decreases* as women have more children (Ameyaw and others, 2019; Nyarko, 2019).

Spacing between births can also shine a light on a woman's exercise of agency. Unintended pregnancy (Ahrens and others, 2018; Hall and others, 2016; White and others, 2015) and intimate partner violence (Maxwell and others, 2018) have both been linked to shorter

intervals between births. Births so close together are associated with adverse maternal, perinatal and infant outcomes (WHO, 2007), illustrating the vulnerabilities that accrue to women with less agency over their bodies and choices.

Labour force participation supports choice
Numerous studies have found that absence from the paid labour force is correlated with higher experience of unintended pregnancy. In Ethiopia, unemployed women were 6.8 times more likely to experience an unintended

pregnancy compared to women working as civil servants, for example (Moges and others, 2020). And in sub-Saharan Africa generally, women who were not working experienced much higher levels of unintended pregnancy than women in four different categories of employment (managerial, clerical, sales, agricultural) (Ameyaw and others, 2019).

A key takeaway is that participation in the paid labour force has an empowering effect on women's exercise of agency and bodily autonomy. Women with financial resources are better able to access and afford contraceptives, and have more decision-making power in the household (Acharya and others, 2010). The opportunity costs of an unintended pregnancy therefore become much higher for women with access to income, indicating that labour remuneration creates strong incentives to avoid unintended pregnancy (Ameyaw and others, 2019). Additionally, greater labour force participation by educated women is understood to be a key driver of development, one which reciprocally supports their exercise of choice (as seen in Chapter 2).

Reproductive coercion (n)

Behaviour that actively interferes with a woman's reproductive autonomy, including contraceptive sabotage, stealthing, forced abortion or preventing a desired abortion; this is recognized as a form of intimate partner violence, but can also be committed by family members or others.

The rural/urban divide

Many studies have shown that rural women are more likely than urban women to have unintended pregnancies, in some cases more than twice as likely (Ameyaw and others, 2019). The simplest explanation for this difference would be that rural women have less access to modern contraception, and this is true in many circumstances (an issue explored further in Chapter 4), but it is far from the complete story. By many measures, women living in rural communities may have greater barriers to empowerment and autonomy overall. For instance, rural women in countries in Asia (Acharya and others, 2010), Latin America (Chant, 2013) and Africa (Darteh and others, 2019) experience lower levels of autonomy when looking at health-care decision-making, household decision-making and contraceptive use. Social and gender norms in rural areas may also tend to be more conservative and patriarchal. Interviews with rural women in the Democratic Republic of the Congo showed that sociocultural norms and poor communication between spouses discouraged use of contraception, for instance (Mbadu and others, 2017). Rural women in developing countries are also more likely to have lower education levels and higher poverty (Suttie, 2019; UN Women 2012), which, as we have seen, correlate with higher rates of unintended pregnancies.

When there are no choices

While the factors above play a critical role in supporting or eroding women's and girls' bodily autonomy, we also know that many women have little decision-making power, or none at all, when it comes to pregnancy or the sexual activity that precedes it. These women and girls — and gender non-conforming individuals — have their bodily autonomy critically compromised or denied, by violence, coercion or circumstances entirely beyond their control.

Violence and coercion

Violence, particularly sexual violence, is a clear and acknowledged human rights violation and is strongly associated with unintended pregnancy (Miller and others, 2010). A person who experiences violent, unwanted or otherwise non-consensual sexual intercourse may become pregnant as a result. But the various forms of violence also cast a pall on a survivor's decision-making capacity more broadly — affecting one's ability to exercise one's rights in myriad ways, such as the ability to speak up, to access health services (including safe abortion), or seek and use contraception.

Decades of research have shown that intimate partner violence and associated behaviours such as reproductive coercion have a strong bearing on survivors' sexual health, including use of contraception and prevalence of unintended pregnancy (Skracic and others, 2021; Silverman and others, 2019; Raj and others, 2015; Miller and others, 2010a; Coker, 2007). Survivors of violence are more likely to have partners who

Reproductive control

"Reproductive control" was first named as such in scientific literature in 2010 — although such practices are age-old (Miller and others, 2010a). Very different from the concept of "birth control", which is a synonym for family planning, reproductive control includes a wide variety of behaviours, such as emotional blackmail, verbal abuse, threats of violence and violence itself, that keep a woman from exercising control over her own body and fertility. Reproductive control can escalate to "reproductive coercion" (Paterno and others, 2021; Tarzia and Hegarty, 2021; Boyce and others, 2020; Grace and Anderson, 2018) in which a partner or family interfere with a woman's reproductive choices, such as preventing a woman from terminating her pregnancy if she wants to or, conversely, forcing her to have an abortion she does not want. Reproductive coercion also includes contraceptive sabotage, such as piercing a condom, throwing away oral pills, forcibly removing patches, vaginal rings or IUDs (Rowlands and Walker, 2019), and "stealthing", in which a male partner removes a condom during sex when consent was only given for intercourse with a condom (Brodsky, 2017). Not only are women who experience intimate partner violence twice as likely as other women to have a male partner who refuses to use contraception (Silverman and Raj, 2014), they could also risk an escalation of violence if they try to negotiate contraception use (Thiel de Bocanegra and others, 2010).

VIOLENCE, COERCION AND THE ERASURE OF AGENCY

FREETOWN, Sierra Leone — "I was not ready to get pregnant," Mamusu, now 18, tells UNFPA in Freetown, Sierra Leone. "But when I started dating this man, I didn't have anyone to take care of my education, someone who could assist me when I needed things for school... He was the one helping me."

Mamusu describes her baby's father as a "boyfriend", "husband", and "the man that impregnated me" – a sign that their relationship is many things, but it is not equal.

For one thing, Mamusu was a child, barely into her teenage years, when she met him. For another, she was desperate to stay in school, but poverty threatened that tenuous lifeline to a better future. "They were asking us to buy pens, books, to do everything, assignments, and I didn't have money... He said he wanted us to date, and so I explained to him my problems."

The help was short-lived: "When I realized that I was pregnant at age 14, I was not happy."

She is not alone. Girls in Sierra Leone often struggle to navigate a maze of impossible choices. The country has some of the highest rates of teen pregnancy (UNFPA, n.d.) and maternal mortality (UNFPA, n.d.a) in the world. Sexual violence is rampant (UNFPA Sierra Leone, n.d.), with much of it directed at children and leading to dire circumstances. The most vulnerable girls can be attacked or propositioned by older boys and men when they venture out to fetch water, sell goods or even attend school. If these girls do consent to enter into a sexual relationship – whether it is romantic, transactional or a blurring of the two – they often do so from a position of disadvantage, or as a survival strategy. But if they become pregnant, they too often find themselves cast out of their homes, left to fend for themselves.

"Girls do not become pregnant because that is what they want," says Mangenda Kamara, who co-founded and leads 2YoungLives,

Mamusu realized she was pregnant with her first child at age 14. © UNFPA/Michael Duff

a mentoring project for pregnant girls. "But extreme poverty, as well as violence and many levels of coercion, including transactional sex, limit their options."

Girls have little autonomy, but face full responsibility for these situations, even if they result from rape. "When someone is raped and falls pregnant, the options are very limited," says Fatmata Sorie, a barrister in Freetown and chair of an organization of female lawyers, the Legal Access through Women Yearning for Equality, Rights and Social Justice. "The structures are not there to help rape victims," she continues. "Police stations do not even have rape testing kits, for instance."

Girls are often made to feel responsible for sexual activity, even when it results from pressure or coercion, and they receive little information about their rights or bodies. Until recently, sexuality education was largely unavailable and visibly pregnant girls were not allowed to return to school. (Ms. Sorie's group and UNFPA lobbied for a law changing these rules, but implementation of this policy has only just begun.) More than 86 per cent of girls aged 15 to 19 years have never used contraceptives, according to FP2030, and 21 per cent of them will have a baby by age 19 (FP2030, 2020; Stats SL and ICF, 2020). Meanwhile, abortion is a prosecuted criminal offence in Sierra Leone. When an abortion does take place, Ms. Sorie says, "it happens in the most unsafe and unprofessional circumstances."

These factors, together, are often fatal. "Before the quarantine, we did a survey and found that the maternal death rate for girls under age 18 [in East Freetown] was 1 in 10," says Lucy November, a midwife and researcher from King's College London (November and Sandall, 2018). Her research, conducted with Ms. Kamara, prompted the founding of the 2YoungLives.

Pregnant girls can be disowned and abandoned. That was the case for Dankay, also now 18. She, too, was propositioned by an older man who helped her get by: "When I accepted his proposals, it was him that was assisting me bit by bit. But when he impregnated me, he denied responsibility and started avoiding me. So my aunt sent me away, because she said it was disgraceful to become pregnant without a man claiming ownership." She stayed with a friend, but often went hungry and slept on a cold floor on the porch.

"They get this stigma from the community, schools and the hospitals – everybody," Ms. Kamara explains. Sometimes, "if there's nobody to help them out, like by mentoring them or advising them, they end up losing either the baby or even both lives."

But this is also a place where a little support goes a long way, she said. Mentoring, social support, child-care assistance, factual information, kindness – these are making a world of difference. Through 2YoungLives, Mamusu

Dankay, 18, says when she became pregnant she did everything possible to get the father to acknowledge his paternity; he refused.
© UNFPA/Michael Duff

started her own small business and proved to be an excellent student. She is committed to making the most of what she has, not only for herself and her child, but for her community. "After I have taken my exams and graduate from college, I want to become a nurse," says Mamusu. "Because when I visit the hospital I see the way nurses take good care of people."

Dankay, too, is getting help balancing school and motherhood. Their resilience and determination to create a better life for their children are examples decision makers would be wise to follow. Theirs is a potential to be celebrated, not squandered – and they know it.

"To be a mother at this age is not really easy," Mamusu says, "but it will enable me to become stronger."

are non-monogamous and less likely to have their partner use a condom (Silverman and Raj, 2014). In some studies, women experiencing intimate partner violence are twice as likely to have a male partner refuse to use contraception and twice as likely to report an unintended pregnancy than women who do not experience violence in their relationships (Silverman and Raj, 2014). These studies have included such disparate countries as Bangladesh (Silverman and others, 2007 and New Zealand (Fanslow and others, 2008).

Those who experience violence are also more likely to resort to covert contraceptive use (Silverman and others, 2020; McCarraher and others, 2006), suggesting many abusive partners actively disapprove of, or seek to disrupt,

survivors' reproductive autonomy. One meta-analysis looked at seven studies encompassing almost 15,000 participants from five countries (Maxwell and others, 2015), finding that, overall, "the odds of women who had experienced [intimate partner violence] reporting contraceptive use were 53 per cent lower than the odds for women who had not experienced [intimate partner violence]". Another study, of married women in Nigeria, found that women who had suffered intimate partner violence were 1.28 times more likely to have discontinued contraception than those who had not been exposed to violence (Kupoluyi, 2020).

Forms of violence other than sexual violence also take a serious toll on women's and girls' reproductive agency. A study from the United

Laws and standards versus lived experience

There are numerous human rights laws and instruments that, together, represent near-universal agreement that sexual and intimate partner violence are violations of human rights. The right to be free from sexual and intimate partner violence has been clearly articulated for decades, notably by the UN Committee on the Elimination of Discrimination against Women (CEDAW) and the UN Committee on Economic, Social and Cultural Rights (CESCR) (UN CESCR, 2016; UN CEDAW, 2017). In part out of recognition that pregnancy often results from force and coercion, abortion is legal in a large majority of nations (Allotey and others, 2021) and is considered a human right by many international human rights treaty bodies and in regional human rights treaties (Fine and others, 2017).

The duty of governments to exercise due diligence in preventing, investigating, prosecuting and punishing acts of violence is also well settled in international human rights, regional human rights and national law (UN CEDAW, 2017). Furthermore, forced or "compulsory" pregnancy, under certain circumstances, is considered a crime against humanity and a war crime (UN General Assembly, 1998; ICRC, 1977). Yet despite overwhelming endorsement of these legal norms and instruments from around the world, sexual violence and coercion remain ubiquitous, and perpetrators continue to enjoy impunity.

States in 1999 found that unintended pregnancy was strongly correlated with having experienced psychological or physical violence in the household while growing up. This is a powerful demonstration of the long-lasting consequences of being disempowered, and indicates that the psychological impact of disempowerment can be a strong driver of unintended pregnancy (Dietz and others, 1999).

How often does sexual violence and coercive sex result in pregnancy? Too often, the data show. Surveys in Haiti, Malawi, Nigeria, Zambia and Uganda examined the incidence of pregnancy resulting from coercive sex among girls and young women aged 13 to 21 years. Of those surveyed, between 10.4 per cent and 18 per cent had been subject to sexual violence either from a current or former intimate partner or from a family member, acquaintance or stranger (Statmatakis and others, 2020). Among the adolescent girls who had experienced rape, the percentage who reported that they became pregnant as a result ranged from 13.2 per cent in Nigeria to 36.6 per cent in Malawi. The study concludes that, in some cases, more than one third of reported survivors experienced pregnancy related to their first or most recent experience of forced or pressured sex. Older studies look at the incidence of rape-related pregnancies and find that they occur at rates similar to, or exceeding (Gottschall and Gottschall, 2003; Wilcox and others, 2001), the incidence of pregnancy resulting from consensual sex.

Indeed, violence continues to be more widely socially accepted than might be thought. While such acceptance, by both women and men, declined significantly over the first decade of the

One review of sexual violence among refugees and internally displaced persons in 19 countries estimated the prevalence of sexual violence to be 21.4 per cent.

21st century (Pierotti, 2013), the rate of change in attitudes is uneven, and studies have shown that in some places a high percentage of women still believe violence is justified if a woman refuses sex (World Bank, 2021).

But violence is not the only way in which bodily autonomy and pregnancy decision-making are denied to those who experience an unintended pregnancy. Coercion — the use of force, threats, pressure and/or intimidation, as well as the absence of consent — can and does take place without violence, critically eroding one's capacity to exercise intention and choice. Women may yield decision-making over sex and pregnancy to their partner out of fear of violence or because violence is socially accepted or expected.

When pregnancy is the result of rape or sexual coercion, the harms and rights violations multiply. The sexual violence or coercion is itself a human rights violation, and in addition the act of forcing someone to become pregnant and the act of forcing someone to either stay pregnant or undergo an abortion against their

WHEN CONTRACEPTIVES FAIL

UNFPA — Contraceptives have changed history: for decades, modern methods have fortified women's agency over their reproductive lives and helped countries meet their development goals. But they don't always work.

After Mukul, in India, experienced life-threatening labour complications at age 24, she opted to use an IUD. Yet less than a year later, she was shocked to discover she was pregnant again – and five months along, too late to consider an abortion. She gave birth to a second daughter. "We welcomed our second child and continued rearing both," Mukul says. "It worked out well, and she was loved by all my family and friends."

Mukul had no reason to expect she would become pregnant. The IUD, a long-acting method, is considered one of the most reliable forms of contraception. Yet no contraceptive is infallible – not oral contraceptives, implants, injectables or even vasectomies. When used consistently and correctly, these methods all have failure rates lower than a single percentage point, and

sometimes far lower, but they do fail. In the United Kingdom, for example, one in four abortions is attributed to failure of hormonal contraception (BBC, 2017), a figure that nearly doubles when other methods, including condoms, diaphragms and withdrawal, are added to the mix.

> ## *"I realized the contraceptive hadn't worked when I got the result at six months. I was in shock and thought, 'What happened?'"*

Several years later, while still using contraception, Mukul found herself pregnant again. She was certain she did not want another child, even though her father had been pressuring her to try for a boy. (Despite Mukul's own successes – she is an accomplished academic – her family continued to harbour a strong preference for boys.) "I chose to have an abortion so I could meet my responsibilities to my two daughters, which would have been divided with the birth

of a third child," she says. "I have no regrets about that."

Dalila*, in rural El Salvador, had a very similar experience. Soon after her wedding, a family planning counsellor paid her and her new husband a visit. But she held off on using contraception. "I wanted to have a child," Dalila explains. "Then my daughter came along and I was happy."

Like Mukul, she started using contraception after her first child was born. And also like Mukul, she learned she was pregnant well into her second pregnancy. "I realized the contraceptive hadn't worked when I got the result at six months. I was in shock and thought, 'What happened?'"

These stories are no surprise to Dr. Ayse Akin, a medical doctor in Turkey whose career in reproductive and public health spans half a century. She has witnessed many breakthrough pregnancies, both in individuals with IUDs and in those using other methods. "Sometimes people don't recognize their

No contraceptive is infallible.
© Shutterstock

Dalila and Mukul continued to rely on contraception, even after experiencing contraceptive failure. Mukul's husband underwent a vasectomy to keep their family at their desired size. Dalila – who says her surprise second pregnancy left her "filled with joy" – also decided her family was complete with two children.

These days, Dalila's daughters are teens, and she advises them to find partners who are supportive of them and their ambitions – and to consider family planning. She is firm that each of her girls will be in command of their own future: "Nobody is going to demand that she brings a baby into the world if she doesn't feel ready to be a mother."

Name changed for privacy and protection

pregnancy until much farther along, because they're not expecting it," she explains.

But contraceptive failure does not affect all women the same way – or even at the same rates. A 2019 study found that, for certain methods, the youngest contraceptives users had failure rates up to 10 times higher than older women (Bradley and others, 2019). There are many possible explanations: younger women may be more fecund, more sexually active, have less experience using contraceptives, or face worse access to quality contraceptive counselling. The poorest women also experienced significantly higher contraceptive failure rates. These findings indicate that those least able to cope with an unintended pregnancy – the youngest and

the poorest – are more likely to experience one, even when they are doing their best to prevent it.

The consequences can be dire, Dr. Akin explains. She helped many patients who arrived after undergoing a clandestine and unsafe abortion. They would arrive bleeding, anaemic or septic; many had lasting complications, or didn't survive. "It was terrible," she says. One month, out of four women admitted after unsafe abortions, "three of them died. Only one was saved." The situation improved after 1983, when abortion was legalized in Turkey, but even now safe abortions are not available in many hospitals, she said, and many doctors do not have the time or inclination to provide contraceptive counselling.

© UNFPA/Fidel Évora

often lose access to sexual and reproductive health services, including contraceptives, even as they face increased exposure to sexual violence (Heidari and others, 2019). The risk of rape is widely acknowledged to increase in emergency settings as protection mechanisms break down. Actual numbers are difficult to surmise due to underreporting; however, one review of sexual violence among refugees and internally displaced persons estimated the prevalence of sexual violence to be 21.4 per cent based on the 19 selected studies (Vu and others, 2014).

Sexual violence is also used as a weapon of war. Studies show this is not the case in all conflicts, but it is all too frequent (with examples including the Bosnian war in the 1990s, the targeting of Yazidi women by the Islamic State of Iraq and the Levant in the last decade, and violence committed by the Boko Haram in northern Nigeria [Oladeji and others, 2021]). The most recent report of the United Nations Secretary-General on conflict-related sexual violence highlights ongoing patterns of rape in situations of armed conflict in Afghanistan, Central African Republic, Colombia, Democratic Republic of the Congo, Iraq, Libya, Mali, Myanmar, Somalia, South Sudan, Sudan, Syrian Arab Republic and Yemen (United Nations, 2020).

will (forms of reproductive coercion), are recognized forms of violence and are human rights violations (Grace and Anderson, 2018; Miller and Silverman, 2010).

Humanitarian crises deny agency at all levels

Humanitarian crises, including natural disasters as well as human-induced calamities such as armed conflict, also deny women and girls the right to proactively exercise bodily autonomy. People in such emergencies

Humanitarian programmes must both protect people at risk (including boys and men) and meet the sexual and reproductive health needs of survivors, including clinical management of rape and emergency contraception (Austin and others, 2008). The revised Inter-agency Field Manual on Reproductive Health in

Humanitarian Settings underscores this by including prevention and treatment of unintended pregnancy — and explicitly incorporating safe abortion care — into the Minimum Initial Service Package for reproductive health and gender-based violence (Heidari and others, 2019; Foster and others, 2017).

Method failure and inconsistent/incorrect use

Contraceptive access is not itself a silver bullet that can prevent all unintended pregnancies. Even when used correctly and consistently, every modern method of contraception has a failure rate. (Traditional methods are even less reliable.) This means that unintended pregnancy cannot and will not be eliminated with currently available methods.

In addition, as data from the Centers for Disease Control and Prevention and WHO show, there is an even greater incidence of method failure when looking at contraceptives as used in real-world conditions — up to a 21 per cent failure rate in the case of female condoms (see page 58 for more information on contraceptive effectiveness rates).

Method failure and use under real-world conditions are cited by women throughout the world as one of the chief reasons for experiencing unintended pregnancy. In the United Kingdom, for example, the British Pregnancy Advisory Service, an abortion provider, reported that of the approximately 60,000 women who had

UNFPA and unintended pregnancy

To prevent unintended pregnancy and recourse to unsafe abortion, UNFPA works in more than 150 countries to support access to and demand for comprehensive sexual and reproductive health care and services from a life-course approach, recognizing that people have different and changing needs throughout their lives and at different stages of their sexual and reproductive lives.

UNFPA's Strategic Plan 2022–2025 sets out the organization's commitment to scaling up the provision of high-quality comprehensive sexual and reproductive health information and services, as part of universal health coverage plans.

Upon request from respective governments, to the full extent of the law of each country, in line with WHO guidance and consistent with paragraph 8.25 of the ICPD Programme of Action, UNFPA supports governments, other implementing partners and stakeholders in their efforts to ensure access to, inter alia: comprehensive sexuality education for young people in and out of school; quality contraceptive services and commodities, including for adolescents; and post-abortion care for all; as well as services that prevent and respond to gender-based violence and harmful practices such as child marriage.

an abortion at one of their centres in 2016, more than half had been using at least one form of contraception. The chief executive officer of the service told the BBC, "Our data shows that women cannot control their fertility through contraception alone, even when they are using some of the most effective methods" (BBC, 2017).

One study shows that pregnancies among contraceptive users accounted for nearly half of all unintended pregnancies, with 9 in 10 of those pregnancies being attributable to inconsistent or incorrect use, and 1 in 10 to method failure occurring under optimal use (Frost and Darroch, 2008).

Other forms of marginalization

Additional and overlapping forms of marginalization further erode human agency and increase vulnerabilities related to unintended pregnancy. Sex workers, for example, face legal and social barriers to contraceptive use, leading to high numbers of unintended pregnancies (Faini and others, 2020; Ampt and others, 2018). Persons with disabilities face an extreme risk of sexual violence — women with disabilities are up to 10 times more likely to experience sexual violence than those without disabilities — and can also be subject to forced abortion if they become pregnant (UNFPA, 2018). Racial and ethnic inequalities and other disparities compound an individual's vulnerability to unintended pregnancy. All of these factors warrant deeper exploration than is possible here.

Turning toward data means turning away from blame

Despite how it is often wrongly portrayed or understood (as, for example, the result of a fleeting moment of passion or incaution), unintended pregnancy is a complex issue eluding simple explanations. As the evidence in Chapter 2 and here highlights, it reflects a broader set of political, economic, sociocultural and technological forces affecting girls, women and other persons who can get pregnant, at all levels. There is a strong case for taking on a holistic approach to reducing unintended pregnancy, one that moves away from moralizing attitudes that censure those affected. Stigmas against unintended pregnancy among adolescents and unmarried women mean that they often encounter barriers to accessing contraception. Among married women, the widespread expectation that they should bear children means that their experience of unintended pregnancy is often under-acknowledged and under-examined. Stigma can also affect women who would otherwise feel happy about their pregnancy or who need space to work through their ambivalence.

The story of unintended pregnancy reflects the way that societies do and do not value women and girls.

Ultimately, the story of unintended pregnancy reflects the way that societies do and do not value women and girls. By failing to sufficiently empower women and girls to choose whether to become pregnant, society implies motherhood is an inevitability rather than an aspiration. By contrast, when societies empower women and girls to make reproduction a deliberate choice, they recognize women's inherent human value — beyond and inclusive of motherhood.

Contraceptive effectiveness, side effects and benefits

Modern methods of contraception can be extremely effective in preventing unintended pregnancy, but users may find a method unsuitable for medical, socioeconomic or supply-related reasons. The information below is excerpted from the latest WHO guidelines (WHO, 2020c; WHO, 2018). It should not be used for medical counselling or treatment purposes; health providers should instead refer to the original sources.

Type of contraception	Duration or time of use	Pregnancies per 100 women per year with consistent and correct use	Pregnancies per 100 women per year as commonly used	Potential side effects (an incomplete list)	Potential health benefits (an incomplete list)
INTRAUTERINE METHODS					
Levonorgestrel intrauterine device (LNG IUD)	3–7 years (depending on type)	0.2–0.8	0.2–0.8	Changes in bleeding, acne, headaches, breast tenderness or pain, nausea, weight gain, dizziness, mood changes, ovarian cysts	Can protect against anaemia, endometrial and cervical cancers, may reduce cramps, bleeding and symptoms of endometriosis
Copper-based intrauterine device (IUD)	Up to 10–12 years (follow national guidelines)	0.6	0.8	Changes in bleeding, as well as cramps during monthly bleeding especially in the first 3-6 months	Can protect against endometrial cancer
HORMONAL METHODS					
Implant	3–5 years (depending on type)	0.1	0.1	Changes in bleeding, headaches, abdominal pain, acne (can worsen or improve), weight gain, breast tenderness, dizziness, mood change, nausea, rare complications	Can protect against symptomatic pelvic inflammatory disease, anaemia
Progestin-only injectable (can be DMPA, DMPA-SC or NET-EN)	Every 2 or 3 months (depending on type)	0.2	4	Changes in bleeding, weight gain, headaches, dizziness, abdominal discomfort, mood changes, lowered sex drive, loss of bone density	Can protect against endometrial cancer, fibroids, symptoms of pelvic inflammatory disease and others (DMPA), and protects against anaemia (DMPA and NET-EN)
Monthly injectables or combined injectable contraceptives	Monthly	0.05	3	Changes in bleeding, weight gain, headaches, dizziness, breast tenderness	Data limited, benefits could be similar to combined oral contraceptives
Combined oral contraceptives ("the pill")	Daily	0.3	7	Changes in bleeding, headaches, dizziness, nausea, weight gain, mood change, breast tenderness and other rare and extremely rare health risks	Can protect against endometrial and ovarian cancer and symptoms of pelvic inflammatory disease
Progestin-only pills ("the minipill")	Daily	0.3	1–7 (depending on whether user is breastfeeding)	Changes in bleeding, headaches, dizziness, mood changes, breast tenderness, abdominal pain, nausea	Protects against risks of pregnancy, safe for breastfeeding women and their babies because does not affect milk production
Patch	Once a week for 3 weeks	0.3	7	Skin irritation, changes in bleeding, headaches, nausea, vomiting, breast tenderness and pain, abdominal pain, flu symptoms, vaginitis	Data limited, benefits could be similar to combined oral contraceptives
Contraceptive vaginal ring – combined –hormone releasing	Wear the ring for 3 weeks	0.3	7	Changes in bleeding, headaches, vaginitis, discharge	Data limited, expected to be similar to combined oral contraceptives
Contraceptive vaginal ring – progestin releasing	90 days	1–2	1–2	Changes in bleeding, abdominal pain, breast pain	No changes to milk production for breastfeeding women

Type of contraception	Duration or time of use	Pregnancies per 100 women per year with consistent and correct use	Pregnancies per 100 women per year as commonly used	Potential side effects (an incomplete list)	Potential health benefits (an incomplete list)
BARRIER METHODS					
Cervical cap	Before intercourse	9–26 (depending on whether user has given birth)	16–32 (depending on whether user has given birth)	Some users report irritation, possible vaginal lesions	May protect against certain STIs, as well as cervical precancer and cancer
Diaphragm	Before intercourse	16	17	Some users report irritation, possible vaginal lesions	May protect against certain STIs, as well as cervical precancer and cancer
Male condom	Single use	2	13	Extremely rare allergic reaction to latex can occur	Provides dual protection against pregnancy and STIs (including HIV)
Female condom	Single use	5	21	None	Provides dual protection against pregnancy and STIs (including HIV)
Spermicides	Before intercourse	16	21	Some users report irritation, possible vaginal lesions	Helps protect against risk of pregnancy
FERTILITY AWARENESS-BASED METHODS					
Calendar-based method (Standard Days method)	Monthly; avoidance of intercourse on fertile days – or use of barrier method on those days	5	12	None	Helps protect against risk of pregnancy
Symptoms-based methods (TwoDay method, Ovulation method, Symptothermal method)	Monthly; avoidance of intercourse on fertile days – or use of barrier method on those days	<1–4	2–23	None	Helps protect against risk of pregnancy
Lactational amenorrhoea method (LAM)	Up to 6 months after birth during amenorrhoea while fully breastfeeding	0.9 (in 6 months)	2 (in 6 months)	None	Encourages breastfeeding patterns, healthy for mother and baby
WITHDRAWAL					
Withdrawal (coitus interruptus)	During intercourse	4	20	None	
EMERGENCY CONTRACEPTION					
Copper IUD	Inserted within 5 days of unprotected sex	No data	No data	Changes in bleeding, as well as uncommon and rare risks and complications	Can protect against endometrial and cervical cancer
Emergency contraception pills	Up to 5 days after unprotected sex	<1–2	N/A	Changes in bleeding, nausea, abdominal pain, fatigue, headaches, breast tenderness, dizziness, vomiting	Helps protect against risk of pregnancy, does NOT disrupt an existing pregnancy
PERMANENT METHODS OF BIRTH CONTROL					
Female sterilization (tubal ligation)	Permanent – effective immediately	0.5	0.5	Uncommon to extremely rare complications may occur	Can protect against pelvic inflammatory disease, may protect against ovarian cancer
Male sterilization (vasectomy)	Permanent – but another method should be used for the first 3 months	0.1	0.15	Uncommon to rare complications may occur	Can protect partner against risk of pregnancy

DMPA, Depot-medroxyprogesterone acetate • **DMPA-SC,** Subcutaneous depot-medroxyprogesterone acetate
NET-EN, Norethisterone oenanthate • **STIs,** Sexually transmitted infections

Testimonials

An informal questionnaire elicited about 60 responses from nearly 30 countries at the end of 2021. Responses here have been excerpted and edited for clarity.

Where did you learn about reproduction and contraceptives?

Response	Respondent
Medical school.	India, male, 59
I learned in medical school.	Brazil, female, 46
A youth-led organization.	United Republic of Tanzania, male, 53
I learned about reproduction during my undergraduate education.	Nigeria, female, 37
Health provider.	Mali, male, 43
From a project in my community.	Burkina Faso, female, 23
Thanks to my mother, and from the media.	Algeria, female, 44
From the organization where I work.	Morocco, female, 24
From official training and social media.	Jordan, female, 40
After the birth of my first child, from a gynaecologist.	Ukraine, female, 39
School, college, television, internet.	Nepal, female, 23

Is it ever difficult to get accurate sexual health information?

Response	Respondent
Adolescents and youth struggle a lot. They are given inaccurate and fear-triggering information.	United Republic of Tanzania, male, 53
My girlfriend in high school took a bus for 30 miles to get to a library that had a book on reproduction.	USA, female, 70
Many people believe in old wives' tales.	Jordan, female, 44
Almost every young person I know has difficulties, as well as unmarried people of all ages.	Sudan, female, 31
Most of this information is accessible only in urban areas.	Uganda, male, 35
People do not talk about sex openly.	Tajikistan, female, 30
I met a lady with six children. She did not want any more but did not know what to do.	Lao People's Democratic Republic, female, 58
People around me are given false information full of stereotypes. The people responsible for informing them are not well trained.	Benin, male, 24
Yes. My parents didn't talk about those things.	Peru, female, 53
Yes, there was little information about this. The topic was stigmatized.	Ukraine, female, 39

Have you ever been told myths about contraception?

Response	Respondent
I've been told birth control pills cause infertility.	USA, female, 39
Some people incorrectly believe urinating after sex can prevent pregnancy.	India, male, 59
Even doctors believe things like IUDs cannot be used by nulliparous women.	Brazil, female, 46
I've heard that contraceptives make people grow fat.	Ghana, female, age not stated
I've heard contraceptives do not work, they can move all around the body.	Nigeria, female, 37
A pharmacist told my friend she could not use emergency contraception because she was breastfeeding. That's why she had her fourth baby.	Spain, female, 40
People believe it causes infertility, cancer, that it's a foreign idea.	Sudan, female, 31
No. I am not married and not looking for information about this. For me, discussing these topics is taboo.	Morocco, female, 24
We were told contraception makes you sterile.	Burkina Faso, female, 43
Yes. Condoms should only be used for sex outside marriage, the Pill makes you sterile, the IUD causes haemorrhages, etc.	Algeria, female, 44
There is a lot of misinformation that doctors pass on to women.	Brazil, male, 75
An aunt told me that talking about contraceptives was an invitation to have sex.	Mexico, female, 35
Excessive use of emergency contraception can cause infertility.	Nepal, female, 23

Have you or your friends ever used a method of contraception that was NOT modern?

Response	Respondent
No, but many patients use withdrawal.	Brazil, female, 46
One woman said she washed herself after sex.	Uganda, female, 46
Yes, a special type of melon.	Nigeria, female, 60
No, but I have heard of traditional methods such as herbs.	Nigeria, female, 37
The natural method.	Burkina Faso, female, 50

Is it ever difficult to get contraceptives?

Response	Respondent
I had a health insurance plan that made it impossible to access oral contraceptives.	USA, female, 39
Women in slums had difficulty during COVID-19 lockdowns. This led to many unintended pregnancies and many abortions.	India, male, 59
Yes, as a doctor, it is difficult to get implants and IUD placement kits.	Brazil, female, 46
Yes, mostly young people. They are insulted and called names.	Nigeria, female, 60
Yes. There is fear and a lack of privacy.	Trinidad and Tobago, female, 65
There are regular stock-outs.	Uganda, male, 35
Unmarried girls are scared… because of a lack of privacy. Doctors might not keep it secret.	Tajikistan, female, 30
Not at all.	Benin, female, 27
No.	Jordan, male, 42
Minors are not allowed to go to the doctor's office without an adult.	Panama, female, 56
Yes! When I was 21, the doctor scolded me... then I went to another doctor, who put an IUD in me very badly.	Mexico, female, 38
Yes, shame.	Peru, male, 26

Have you ever pressured a partner not to use contraceptives?

Response	Respondent
No!	USA, female, 39
No, I have never put such pressure on my partner.	Benin, male, 24
No.	India, male, 59
Yes, I want to have children, but my husband does not want to.	Sudan, female, 37
No.	United Republic of Tanzania, male, 53
No.	Brazil, female, 46
I was the one that pushed for contraceptives.	Nicaragua, female, 50
No.	Trinidad and Tobago, female, 65
No.	Tajikistan, female, 30
Yes.	India, female, 35
No, the agreement is always mutual.	Peru, male, 26
No.	Ukraine, female, 39

Have you ever experienced unwanted side effects from using a contraceptive?

Response	Respondent
Weight gain, acne, nausea, moodiness, headaches, diarrhoea, stomach cramps.	USA, female, 39
I had blurry vision and mood swings. No one told me about the side effects beforehand.	Jordan, female, 44
Yes, heavy bleeding and abdominal pain in the first few months.	Nigeria, female, 37
No.	India, female, 62
Yes, mood swings.	Sudan, female, 31
Not applicable.	Uganda, male, 35
My wife had cramps from using an IUD.	Brazil, male, 75
Yes, with the implant. Fatigue and decreased libido.	Mexico, female, 38
No.	Panama, female, 56
Gained weight.	Ukraine, female, 39
No.	Jordan, male, 42

Have you ever had sex without using contraception even while not intending to have a child?

Response	Respondent
Yes, but my partner and I used the withdrawal method.	Jordan, female, 29
Yes.	India, female, 62
Yes. I personally don't like using condoms, especially when I am not familiar with the brand or type, so I have engaged in unprotected sex.	Country unlisted, female, 24
Yes.	United Republic of Tanzania, male, 53
Yes. Because of a lack of access to contraception, plus in some cases because of my partner's pressure.	Sudan, female, 31
Rarely.	USA, female, 30
Yes, due to lack of access to contraception.	Trinidad and Tobago, female, 65
Yes.	Tajikistan, female, 30
No, I always used a condom together with another method, even when married.	Brazil, female, 65

In your community, who makes decisions about contraception? Do men and women have the same power to decide?

Response	Respondent
It's usually seen as the woman's responsibility to get on oral or long-acting contraceptives. But when it comes to condoms, it's often a man's responsibility.	USA, female, 39
Men and women have the same power, but families and communities have a say, too.	Lao People's Democratic Republic, female, 50
Men have greater decision-making power. Women may have to act secretly/discreetly to get contraception services.	India, male, 59
Generally men are not in favour of using condoms, and many discourage women from taking contraceptives.	Brazil, female, 46
Men have more power.	United Republic Tanzania, male, 53
Women were not allowed to decide.	Nigeria, female, 60
Men can easily access condoms but females receive judgemental looks when purchasing them. When getting a family planning method in a clinic, most females still need to consent from their partners. And since most women get the funds from partners, men get to influence women's decisions.	Nigeria, female, 37
It is a patriarchy. Males have dominance over decision making.	Jordan, female, 44
Most men don't want their wives to use contraception. Same for families and communities.	United Republic of Tanzania, female, 51
Men hold the ultimate decision-making power. It is common practice for providers to ask for the husband's consent.	Sudan, female, 31
In most cases, contraceptive options are determined by availability, instead of choice.	Uganda, male, 35
My husband and mother-in-law interfere a lot in my choices.	Jordan, female, 29
Even when women go to the hospital to get contraception, they have to be accompanied by their husbands.	Benin, male, 24
Many men believe that contraception is not allowed.	Morocco, female, 24
In my congregation, women don't use birth control... and men don't even try to use it. I was pressured to get pregnant 30 years ago, by the father of my children.	Nicaragua, female, 50
In some couples, men force women not to use contraceptives; they claim it causes discomfort or does not give them pleasure. Women concede out of fear or submission.	Peru, female, 20
There is pressure to have children even if it is not my wish. I am the abnormal one for not wanting to have children.	Mexico, female, 38

Have you or someone you know ever experienced an unintended pregnancy? If it happened to you now, how would you react?

Response	Respondent
I am currently pregnant from an unintended pregnancy. I was consistently and correctly using a condom with my long-term partner, but it slipped off. We did not plan to have children, but I've decided to keep the baby. Unfortunately it ended our relationship and I'll be a single mother.	*USA, female, 39*
Yes, my sister. She was 19.	*Brazil, female, 46*
Not that they have told me…. I would get a medical abortion as soon as possible.	*USA, female, 30*
I was 18 when it happened to me. My friend was around 35 years old when it happened to her.	*Nigeria, female, 37*
Yes, at 23 a friend got a surgical abortion. If it was me, I would seek a safe abortion even if it meant I had to travel.	*Country unlisted, female, 24*
No. For me, I would plan to take care of our child.	*Lao People's Democratic Republic, female, 58*
Yes, in my 20s and 30s, all my pregnancies were unplanned.	*Ukraine, female, 39*
My close friend used misoprostol to terminate her pregnancy. But abortion is not allowed in Tanzania except for preserving the mother's life, so if something like that happened again, I would advise her to cope with the situation and avoid unsafe abortion.	*United Republic of Tanzania, male, 53*
Yes. A relative was fairly young when she got married, and was pressured to get pregnant during her first year of marriage.	*Jordan, female, 44*
Yes, the person was 16 years old and had a stillbirth due to minimal care.	*Uganda, male, 35*

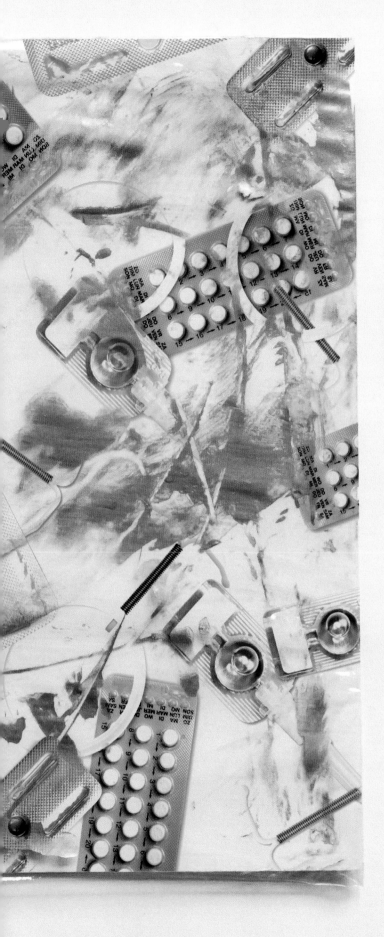

CHAPTER 4

Revealing the challenges to choice

The most obvious way to prevent an unintended pregnancy — aside from abstaining from sex, which, as explained (see page 42), is not "fail-safe" — is to use contraception, and a wide range of safe and effective methods of contraception have been developed. While all forms of contraception are subject to method failure, this accounts for a comparatively small proportion of all unintended pregnancies. Challenges with consistent and correct use also play an important role. But the biggest issue, by far, is the unmet need for contraception.

Globally, an estimated 257 million women who want to avoid pregnancy are not using safe, modern methods of contraception, and of these women, 172 million are using no method at all (UN DESA, 2021). SDG indicator 3.7.1 calls expressly for meeting this need, an acknowledgement of its importance in international development.

A reductive, yet all too common, reaction would be that pregnancy is an obvious consequence of unprotected intercourse, and that public policy can offer few remedies for couples or individuals who fail to account for this fact. Yet the latest SDG data show that, in 64 countries, more than 8 per cent of women are unable to make their own choices over contraception and 24 per cent are unable to decide about health care — clear rights violations requiring State rectification and norms changes. And millions more women face circumstances that have a less obvious, but no less real, impact on contraceptive use, non-use and disuse. A deeper exploration of these factors points to the responses that policymakers can undertake to support and protect the reproductive agency of individuals.

Family planning programmes work

It is first important to emphasize that family planning programmes have made a tremendous difference globally. Contraceptive use is increasing in every region in the world, and unmet needs are declining. In 2022, 1.1 billion of the 1.9 billion women of reproductive age (defined as ages 15 to 49) were considered to have a need for contraception, meaning they had a desire to limit or delay childbearing, and of them

858 million were using a modern method of contraception and 85 million were using a traditional method (United Nations, 2022).

Researchers have noted changes in the reasons women give for not using contraceptives, even when they want to avoid pregnancy (Sedgh and others, 2016). Lack of knowledge about contraceptives was the most common reason for non-use in the 1980s; it is now the least common reason cited, with larger proportions of women listing side effects and infrequent sex as their reasons for non-use. Access to contraceptives has also improved over time, and is less frequently mentioned as a reason for non-use. These studies show that progress can and has been made by effective family planning programmes — but they also point to gaps that must still be overcome. For example, lack of access and lack of knowledge persist in many places, particularly rural areas (Moreira and others, 2019).

To bridge these gaps, a closer look at the rates and reasons for non-use is needed. The starting point must be to ask what a woman wants. Only then is it possible to consider whether she is able to act on and realize this desire, and how that ability is affected by programmes, policies and norms. This chapter explores three overarching questions that researchers and policymakers should ask when considering unmet need for contraception. When looking at a woman who wishes to prevent or delay pregnancy: (a) does she want to use modern contraception; (b) can she get a method of her choice, particularly if and when her choices change; and (c) how does the environment facilitate or hinder her use of contraception?

While this chapter focuses on women in low- and middle-income countries — where unmet need is highest — many of the issues discussed are also relevant and common in countries at all income levels and in all regions.

Do women *want* to use modern contraception? Unpacking demand

Every individual has the right to make an informed, voluntary decision about whether to use a contraceptive method. This will, of course, relate to her or his desire to avoid a pregnancy, a desire that is not necessarily constant or clear. It is a desire that will likely change over time through different stages of an individual's life, informed by social norms, their family and their partner or partners, as well as their own experience and body.

Concerns about safety and side effects

Studies consistently show that non-use or discontinuation of contraception is most often a result of fear of, or experience of, side effects or health issues. Analyses of DHS data indicate that 38 per cent of women with an unmet need for modern contraception have used a modern method in the past but have chosen to discontinue it for a reason other than wanting to get pregnant (Castle and Askew, 2015). On average, over one third of women who start using a modern contraceptive method stop using it within the first year, and over half stop before two years. Studies show contraceptive failure and method-

What about men's needs?

It should be noted that men can and do have unmet contraceptive needs. Unfortunately, this fact is not well captured by existing metrics. Unmet need, like most reproductive health measures, is typically defined around women's behaviours. Women are considered primary users of contraception and available data tend to focus on women. Still, a more complete picture requires consideration of men's needs and knowledge, while ensuring that women's reproductive rights are not compromised. In fact, a more comprehensive approach to meeting contraceptive needs could actually advance women's rights and welfare by creating a more supportive environment for all people to express and realize their fertility preferences (see feature on male contraceptives on page 70; see couples' concordance text box in Chapter 2).

Additionally, most contraceptive methods focus on female biology: barrier methods such as diaphragms, cervical caps, sponges and female condoms, as well as hormonal methods such as injectables, some IUDs, oral contraception and emergency contraception. This is often justified by the disproportionate physical burden pregnancy presents to women, yet it raises the human rights and ethical issue of gender equality. Is it justifiable for women to disproportionately bear the responsibility for contraception? Why are men deprived of contraceptive choice, relative to women? Do governments have a duty to support the development of contraception for men and thereby equalize opportunities and responsibilities for individuals and couples in realizing their pregnancy intentions? Societies have largely left the answer to markets (Costantino and others, 2007). The obligation for States to address gender stereotypes (UN General Assembly, 1979) suggests that governments should do more, as marketability alone falls short.

THE NEXT MALE CONTRACEPTIVE: WHAT'S TAKING SO LONG?

UNFPA — "The hard part about reproduction should be deciding if and when to have children," says Logan Nickels, a researcher at the Male Contraceptive Initiative (MCI) in the United States. "Once that decision is made, the tools should be available to everyone to ensure that they're able to carry out their life plan easily and effectively."

Two male-driven methods – condoms and withdrawal – currently make up about 26 per cent of worldwide contraceptive use. But male condoms, as commonly used, have a failure rate of about 13 per cent, and withdrawal is one of the least effective forms of contraception (WHO, 2018). Vasectomy, on the other hand, is noted as being one of the most effective methods (WHO,

2018), but fewer than 3 per cent of couples rely on it for protection (Pile and Barone, 2009).

Promising possibilities for new male methods abound: pills, topical creams, microneedle patches, biodegradable injectables and a device that acts like a vasectomy but is designed to be reversible. More than 40 methods are listed in a database of contraceptive methods under exploration or development (Calliope, n.d.). So why aren't there better male contraceptive options out there yet? "I think the societal assignment of reproduction to women has played a big part in that – it's women who bear the burden of pregnancy," says Logan.

Cultural attitudes often assign women responsibility for

contraception. This can stand in the way of progress. "Men are often thought of as secondary in the equation because it's kind of a pervasive opinion that they have all the rights that they need," Logan says. "So I think that [contraceptive development] has been focused on providing rights to women and girls rather than bringing men into the equation in a way that's productive and helpful."

Research shows that men in many countries are interested in male-driven contraceptive methods. In a 2002 survey of 9,000 men in nine countries, more than 55 per cent of respondents said they'd be willing to use a new product (Heinemann and others, 2005). And in the United States, a 2019 study of some 1,500 men found that, of those who wanted to prevent a pregnancy, 60 per cent wanted to see a new male contraceptive method (Friedman and others, 2019). Yet the global pharmaceutical industry has not advanced in this arena. "They just don't have the incentive, because the products they have [for women] work and are safe," says Rebecca Callahan, who works in product development at the United States-based health and wellbeing non-profit FHI 360.

CONDOMS AND WITHDRAWAL

Comprise 26 per cent of worldwide contraceptive use

» Male condoms have a failure rate of about **13 per cent**

» Withdrawal is one of the **least effective forms of contraception**

VASECTOMY

Noted as being one of the most effective methods but fewer than

3 per cent of couples rely on it for protection

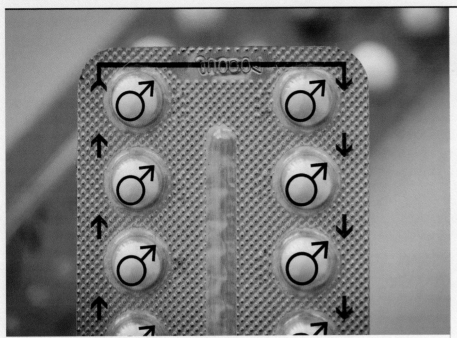
Research shows that men in many countries are interested in male-driven contraceptive methods.
Getty Images/Canopy

A new male contraceptive would have to be at least as effective as the best women's products on the market in order to compete. Meanwhile the safety thresholds for a novel contraceptive – male or female – are the highest of any pharmaceutical product, Rebecca says, "because you're giving it to young, healthy people to prevent a condition". And these standards are even higher for a new male method, as for women the risks of contraceptive side effects are weighed against the potential risks of a pregnancy – which can, after all, be deadly.

One study found that weekly hormonal injections in men were very successful at preventing pregnancy, with generally minimal side effects (Behre and others,

2016). There were some cases of acne, weight gain and mood swings – the kind of problems women often endure with hormonal contraception. But when one man developed severe depression and another attempted suicide, the study was cut short, even though depression is a known risk among female users of hormonal contraceptives (Skovlund and others, 2016).

Challenges extend beyond pharmaceutical research. New contraceptive methods require funding and extensive field-testing, marketing and distribution. Without support, even effective and desired methods can falter. Dr. Demet Güral saw this in the 1990s when she worked on a project to introduce non-scalpel vasectomies in Turkey.

"Our project demonstrated that men would accept the method in a heartbeat," she says. Of more than 2,000 vasectomies performed within a three-year period in four Turkish hospitals, over 60 per cent of the potential clients accepted the procedure after just one counselling session. But without long-term support from the donor, she says, the method never took off. Vasectomy has remained rare in the country (UN DESA, 2021a).

Yet any improved forms of male contraception will not, by themselves, be enough. For all people to be able to make responsible reproductive choices, they will also need accurate information about benefits and drawbacks of contraceptive methods, the ability to articulate their desires when it comes to reproduction, and a healthy respect for the needs and views of their partner.

In this area, too, there are signs of progress. Martha Brady, a global health expert in contraceptive development, says she has seen attitudes shifting: "[Younger men] see the world is changing dramatically. Norms have shifted for everyone from the US to Africa... I think there will definitely be young men who are willing to try things that maybe 50-year-old guys of a different era wouldn't," she says.

Reasons for non-use of contraceptives

An analysis in the Guttmacher Institute publication *Adding it Up* found that 77 per cent of unintended pregnancies in low- and middle-income countries are to women who, despite wanting to avoid a pregnancy, are using no method of contraception or are using a traditional method, meaning a method with lower efficacy such as periodic abstinence or withdrawal (Sully and others, 2020). A recent study in 36 low- and middle-income countries found that more than 65 per cent of women with an unintended pregnancy were either non-users of contraception or using traditional methods (Bellizzi and others, 2020). Researchers using DHS data from 52 countries between 2005 and 2014 found that the proportion of married women with an unmet need for a method of contraception (either modern or traditional) ranged from 8 per cent in Colombia to 38 per cent in São Tomé and Príncipe (Sedgh and others, 2016).

The most common reasons cited by women for not using contraception were: they were concerned about contraceptive side effects and health risks (26 per cent); they had sex infrequently or not at all (24 per cent); they or people close to them were opposed to contraception (23 per cent); or they were breastfeeding and/or hadn't resumed menstruation after a birth (20 per cent). Among sexually active never-married women wanting to avoid pregnancy, the most common reasons cited for not using contraception were also infrequent sex (49 per cent), the fact that they were unmarried (29 per cent) and concerns about contraceptive side effects (19 per cent) (Sedgh and others, 2016).

A 2019 study from 47 countries showed that, on average, 40.9 per cent of all sexually active women were not using any contraceptive methods to avoid pregnancy; in this study, too, the most prevalent reasons were health concerns and infrequent sex, but with significant variation across countries, populations and other socioeconomic factors (Moreira and others, 2019). For example: non-use due to "opposition from others" was higher among married than unmarried women; the prevalence of non-use due to "lack of access" or "lack of knowledge" was about two times higher in rural areas than in urban areas; and women with less schooling more often reported non-use due to "lack of access".

These reasons relate directly to issues of information accuracy, agency and health impacts (often framed as supply, enabling environment and demand, or the "SEED model"), areas where leaders, policymakers, health systems and others have considerable influence. For example, when women cite side effects as a concern, this can reflect both supply (limited method choices, poor counselling on side effects) and demand factors (negative experiences with contraception and/or myths and misperceptions). It is notable that women with unmet need for contraception rarely say that they are unaware of contraception, that they do not have access to a source of supply, or that it costs too much, indicating in part the success of family planning programmes. The countries where more than 10 per cent of women cited any of these reasons are in western and central Africa, regions where the prevalence of contraceptive use has remained low until recently (Sedgh and others, 2016).

related side effects or problems are among the most common reasons for discontinuation (Bradley and others, 2009). There were few discontinuations due to cost and access issues (Bradley and others, 2009), though this is unsurprising since women who have used a method did at some point succeed in accessing affordable contraception.

While rates and reasons for discontinuation vary by method, these reasons are fairly constant for each method over time (Castle and Askew, 2015; Bradley and others, 2009). Across surveys in 25 countries, the lowest 12-month discontinuation was for the IUD (13 per cent), and the highest was for the condom (50 per cent), while oral contraceptive pills and injectables, as well as the lower-efficacy methods of periodic abstinence and withdrawal, were discontinued by about 40 per cent of users within the first 12 months of use. Method-related reasons were the dominant cause of discontinuation for any method (Ali and others, 2012).

Women with moderate to severe side effects are more likely than those with mild side effects to discontinue contraceptive use (Jain and others, 2021). These findings validate, in many ways, the concerns of women who cite side effects as a major concern. Serious side effects, though rare, can be debilitating (see chart on page 58). In extremely rare circumstances, a side effect such as a blood clot can prove fatal. While it is well established that contraceptives, in general, are associated with many positive health outcomes for women, including lower risk of maternal mortality (Utomo and others, 2021) and reduced risk of certain cancers (Hannaford and others, 2010), this may not allay the

METHOD MIX (N) –

(1) The menu of contraceptive choices available to an individual, clientele or population.

(2) (Academic) The pattern, distribution or percentage of method use within a population.

concerns of women who have experienced, or witnessed in others, severe or intolerable side effects.

In fact, support for effective contraception methods and fear of their side effects often go hand-in-hand. Recent research in Ghana, focused on women and girls aged 15 to 49 years, found that women both valued hormonal methods for their effectiveness against pregnancy and also expressed concerns about side effects (particularly bleeding changes), future fertility impairment and long-term health issues that led some women to discontinue use of hormonal methods. Having experienced long-term health issues as a perceived result of hormonal method use more than halved the odds of current use (Keogh and others, 2021).

These issues are not unique to women in low- and middle-income countries. A systematic review of

Autonomy is at the heart of rights-based family planning

Family planning programmes typically use modern contraceptive method use as a primary marker of success. The focus on increasing contraceptive use can lead observers to regard non-use as a failure, but in fact it can be a legitimate choice for a woman. Researcher Leigh Senderowicz suggests the creation and use of a new indicator called "contraceptive autonomy", defining contraceptive autonomy as "the factors necessary for a person to decide for themselves what they want in relation to contraception and then to realize that decision" (Senderowicz, 2020). This type of perspective could better align programmes with a rights-based approach. Calculating this indicator would require adding questions to population-based surveys such as the DHS.

reasons for rejecting hormonal contraception by women and men in high-income countries found similar concerns, including: problems related to physical side effects; concerns about changes in mental health; negative impact on sexuality; concerns about future fertility; concerns about menstruation; fears and anxiety; and the experience of having concerns about side effects dismissed by health providers (Le Guen and others, 2021). A key takeaway is that health providers and systems must build, and sometimes restore, trust with women through emphasizing respectful, person-centred approaches, and understand that an individual's needs will likely change over time. Another takeaway is that the existing range of options is insufficient, pointing to a need for public investment into the development of new or improved contraceptives with fewer or milder side effects.

Side effects may also have adverse sociocultural consequences, contributing to a woman's decision to discontinue use (Castle and Askew, 2015). In communities with norms that prohibit women's participation in certain activities due to vaginal bleeding (usually

menstruation), discontinuation may occur if a contraceptive method causes abnormal bleeding or spotting. This can limit a woman's ability to pray, prepare food or have intercourse. Some women may experience amenorrhoea, or the absence of menstruation, as a side effect; these users may discontinue because amenorrhoea limits their ability to *avoid* intercourse or because they associate it with infertility (Polis and others, 2018; Chebet and others, 2015).

Side effects that could be detected by a partner, such as spotting, can be particularly troubling to covert users of contraceptives (women who conceal their contraceptive use from their partner) (Castle and others, 1999). Clandestine use of contraception can be common, particularly when women face a partner opposed to contraception, when there is trouble in the relationship or a desire to avoid conflict (Kibira and others, 2020; Castle and others, 1999). Covert contraceptive use can be dangerous for women — in some sub-Saharan African countries, such as Ethiopia, a woman using contraception without her husband's approval is considered a sign of being unfaithful (Alio and others, 2009) — further incentivizing discontinuation of methods that could be noticed by a partner.

While overall knowledge about modern contraception has improved around the world, many myths and misperceptions persist and contribute to non-use. Focus group discussions with women in Ghana, for instance, found that many women believed contraception can lead to infertility, particularly among young women. Hearsay about side effects and misinformation were also common reasons for non-use (Hindin and others, 2014). Young men and women in Kenya believed modern contraception jeopardizes future fertility, results in problems conceiving, causes birth defects, makes women promiscuous, is "un-African", and denies couples their sexual freedom (Mwaisaka and others, 2020). This highlights the importance of adequately involving and informing men about contraceptives, as they are often important decision-makers in this area.

Are contraceptive users satisfied?

In order to live up to their commitments to achieving universal sexual and reproductive health care, family planning and education by 2030, countries are monitoring data on the proportion of women of reproductive age (between ages 15 and 49) who have their need for contraception satisfied with modern methods, and those with unmet need. The most recent SDG data show, for instance, that in low- and middle-income countries the overall rate of unmet need for contraception is 9.2 per cent, and the overall rate of unmet need for modern contraception is 13.3 per cent.

These figures are important, but they are imperfect. Met and unmet need are broad measurements that divide women into the categories of users versus non-users of modern contraceptives, when the reality is more nuanced. While increasing numbers of women are using modern methods, the high levels of discontinuation clearly show a widespread lack of satisfaction with the methods currently available to them.

Researchers Rominski and Stephenson call for metrics that account for these complexities: "The current definition of unmet need for contraception assumes that all women who are using a method have a met need. We argue that without taking into account the level of satisfaction with a method, many women are classified as having a met need when in fact they have an unmet need. They are using a method that does not meet their preferences, either because it causes side effects they find untenable or has other characteristics they do not like. Given the large number of contraceptive episodes that end in discontinuation, reportedly often due to the experience of side effects, we argue that the current definition of unmet need undercounts the number of women with a true unmet need for contraception as it misses the many women who are using a method that does not meet their preferences" (Rominski and Stephenson, 2019).

One study of users of modern contraceptives in Kenya reclassified current users who were dissatisfied as having an unmet need. They found the prevalence of method dissatisfaction ranged from 6.6 per cent to 18.9 per cent. Applying this result nationally would greatly increase (by approximately 25 to 70 per cent) the country's estimate of unmet need for any form of contraception (Rothschild and others, 2021).

Lack of knowledge about sexuality, reproduction and pregnancy

Having demand or desire for contraception requires knowing about your body, sexuality, reproduction and contraception. While lack of knowledge is no longer one of the most significant reasons for unmet need, it remains strongly correlated with higher levels of unintended pregnancy (Huda and others, 2013). Many young people still lack access to comprehensive sexuality education, contributing to widespread myths and misperceptions about both contraception and human anatomy.

Essential information on sexual and reproductive health and rights should come from in-school and out-of-school programmes, including from health facilities. In fact, in many settings, knowledge about contraception comes largely via the health system. In a recent study in Ethiopia, for example, 68 per cent of women interviewed said their source of information on family

Human rights and comprehensive sexuality education

The absence of accurate sexual and reproductive health information not only has serious consequences, it is a human rights violation. Education on sexuality and reproduction is a basic component of the rights to health, education and non-discrimination, as articulated by the United Nations Committee on Economic, Social and Cultural Rights (UN CESCR, 2016). This means individuals, including children and adolescents, have the right to seek, receive and disseminate family planning information and ideas. To meet these human rights obligations, States and communities must ensure that sexual and reproductive health information is accessible, acceptable and medically accurate (UN CESCR, 2016), and "provided in a manner consistent with the needs of the individual and the community, taking into consideration, for example, age, gender, language ability, educational level, disability, sexual orientation, gender identity and intersex status" (UN CESCR, 2016). Access to comprehensive sexuality education is therefore a critical enabler of the human rights to health, well-being and autonomy, which are found in many human rights instruments, including the United Nations Convention on the Rights of the Child (UN General Assembly, 1989), the United Nations Convention on the Elimination of all Forms of Discrimination against Women (UN General Assembly, 1979), the International Covenant on Economic, Social and Cultural Rights (UN General Assembly, 1966), and the United Nations Convention on the Rights of Persons Living with Disabilities (UN General Assembly, 2007).

Comprehensive sexuality education also addresses many of the drivers of unintended pregnancy, such as gender-based violence, and offers tools for their prevention, including how to build equal relationships, respect for non-stereotyped gender roles, and how to discuss consent (Haberland and Rogow, 2015). Many studies have affirmed that quality comprehensive sexuality education is effective in reducing risky sexual behaviours and reducing the incidence of unintended pregnancy. This education is most effective when it is provided in diverse and linked ways, such as by linking school-based education with non-school-based, youth-friendly services (UNESCO and others, 2018).

planning came from a health worker. This study also found that those who had experienced at least one unintended pregnancy were less likely to have a subsequent one — in other words, they sought out information or used the information they were given at the time of delivering their first baby to plan the second (Moges and others, 2020).

It is important that all information and counselling be medically accurate, non-directive and supportive, to ensure autonomy in decision-making (UNFPA, 2021; UN CESCR, 2000). That means health-care providers and other professionals should provide evidence-based counselling and information about the function, benefits and risks of contraceptives, and deliver this information in a way that meets women (and, if appropriate, their partners) where they are. This information can and should dispel the misinformation, misperceptions, myths and fear that are often drivers of non-use. It should also disambiguate the manner in which emergency contraception works, distinguishing it from induced abortion; this is especially important among communities and individuals for whom abortion is culturally unacceptable.

Miscalculating pregnancy risk
One of the most common reasons for unmet need is infrequent sex or the perception of not being at risk. This highlights the importance of adequate knowledge about when one is at risk. It also highlights the need to ensure that a woman herself identifies when she has a need rather than others assuming that she does. The importance of infrequent sex as a reason for unmet need has led some in the reproductive health community to advocate for research to develop an effective pericoital method of contraception that a

woman can use only when she needs it. Ideally this would be a method that a woman could control and use without her partner's knowledge. Current methods that could be used in such a way tend to be less effective and require partner cooperation (e.g., condom, diaphragm or cervical cap). WHO convened a meeting in 2017 to discuss hormonal pericoital contraception; participants concluded that there was a need for such a method and that more research was needed (WHO, 2017). Such research is ongoing (Jackson and Dossou, 2021).

Are women *able* to get a modern contraceptive method of their choice?

Perhaps one of the most frequently asked questions when considering unmet need is: can individuals obtain contraceptives? But framing the question this way, while simple, is misleading. As discussed earlier, family planning programmes have been extremely successful in expanding the availability of modern contraceptives to communities where needs are greatest. And while continued investment is needed to reach those most marginalized, the fact is that most people can say some form or forms of contraception are available in their community. So the question should be more nuanced: can individuals reasonably obtain the contraceptive option of their choice, when and where they want it?

Individuals require a range of methods to

meet their diverse and evolving needs. These methods must be available, accessible and acceptable, and supplies and services must be of high quality. Within each of these areas, there remain significant barriers, as detailed below. Overall DHS data indicate that between 7 and 27 per cent of women stop using a contraceptive method for reasons related to the service environment, including service quality, availability of a sufficient choice of methods, commodity stock-outs and ineffective referral mechanisms (Castle and Askew, 2015).

Availability

Contraceptive availability means much more than simply having condoms on hand at the local store. It means that contraceptive services, including accurate and sensitive family planning counselling, are present, as are a wide range of contraceptive methods. It means there are an adequate number of health facilities, family planning programmes and trained health personnel to serve the population (UN CESCR, 2016). The United Nations Committee on Economic, Social and Cultural Rights has said that "unavailability of goods and services due to ideologically based policies or practices, such as the refusal to provide services based on conscience, must not be a barrier to accessing services" (UN CESCR, 2016).

Stock-outs also remain a significant issue for family planning programmes (see Figure 7). A multi-country analysis of DHS data found that up to 5 per cent of contraceptive discontinuations are due to stock-outs (Castle and Askew, 2015). A 2017 review of supply chain challenges in low- and middle-income countries found that supply chain issues contributed significantly to high stock-out rates for modern contraceptives (Mukasa and others, 2017). A 2020 systematic review explored the impact of contraceptive stock-outs and found

Not having access to effective contraception is a human rights violation

The obligation for governments to make quality family planning information and methods available to all — on a basis of non-discrimination and equality — is found explicitly in the Convention on the Elimination of All Forms of Discrimination against Women and the Convention on the Rights of the Child (UN General Assembly, 1989; UN General Assembly, 1979). It is also affirmed in many other human rights treaties, such as the International Covenant on Economic, Social and Cultural Rights, which guarantee access through the right to health (UN General Assembly, 1966). Sexual and reproductive health is a significant component of the right to a universal minimum standard of health to which all individuals are entitled. Therefore the human rights obligations undertaken by governments require that contraception and family planning methods and services are available, acceptable, accessible and of high quality (UN CESCR, 2000).

FIGURE 6

Distributions of contraceptive users by method, by region, 2019

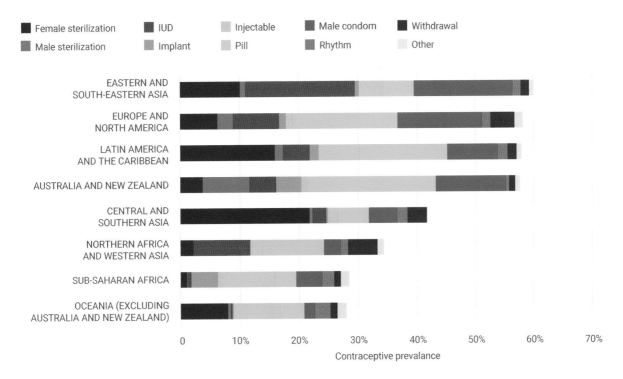

Data source: Calculations are based on the data compilation World Contraceptive Use 2019, additional tabulations derived from microdata sets and survey reports and estimates of contraceptive prevalence for 2019 from Estimates and Projections of Family Planning Indicators 2019. Population-weighted aggregates.

Source: United Nations, Department of Economic and Social Affairs, Population Division. (2020). *Contraceptive Use by Method* 2019.

Note: "Other" includes less-used modern methods, such as lactational amenorrhea method (LAM), vaginal barrier methods, emergency contraception, patches and vaginal rings as well as traditional methods, including douching, prolonged abstinence, gris-gris, incantation, medicinal plants, abdominal massage and other methods.

that they limited the ability to use a preferred method and influenced where methods were obtained and how much they cost. However, comparing the impacts was challenging due to varying definitions and measurements (Zuniga and others, 2020).

The stock-out situation has only been exacerbated by the COVID-19 pandemic, which seriously disrupted supply chains and limited access to health facilities. In Latin America, for instance, contraceptive stock-outs, alongside falling household incomes,

were estimated to result in discontinuation of use of modern contraceptives for between 9 and 20 million women (UNFPA, 2020c). To model the potential impact, an analysis by the Guttmacher Institute estimated that a 10 per cent decline in use of short- and long-acting reversible contraceptives due to reduced access would result in an additional 48 million individuals experiencing an unmet need for contraceptives and over 15 million experiencing an unintended pregnancy over the course of a year (Riley and others, 2020).

FIGURE 7

Percentage of facilities reporting stock-outs on the day of the survey, overall and by method, select countries*

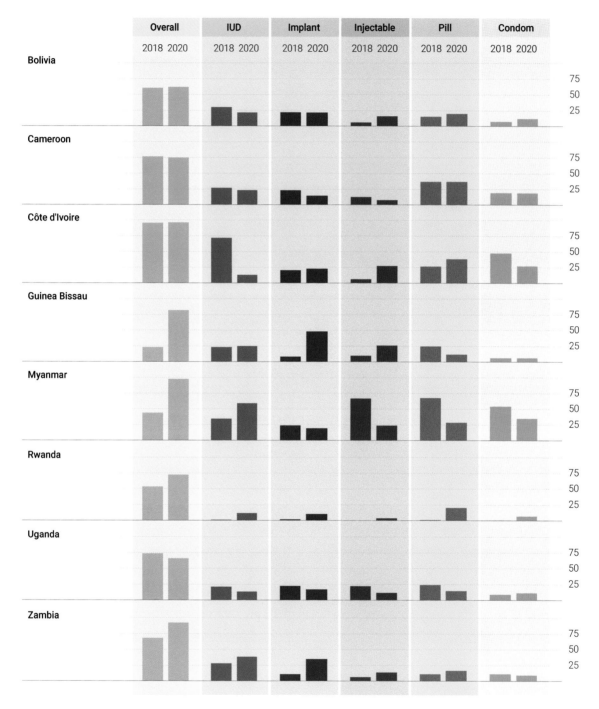

Source: UNFPA Supplies Facility Survey Reports, 2018 and 2020.

*Reporting provided in line with current national protocols, guidelines and/or laws.

The stock-out situation has only been exacerbated by the COVID-19 pandemic.

Accessibility

Even if methods are available, they might not be easily accessible. Accessibility means physically accessible, without discrimination, for all people, including persons with disabilities, those who live in remote locations, those displaced by armed conflict and natural disasters, and adolescents (UN CESCR, 2016). It also means family planning methods are affordable and provided with information in a manner that is accessible to the user, taking into consideration language ability, education level, disability status and other factors (UN CESCR, 2016). Barriers include economic and geographical considerations, costs (including the opportunity costs of travel and childcare), and age limits or marital requirements. The United Nations Committee on Economic, Social and Cultural Rights has determined that human rights standards require that these barriers be removed and addressed through budgetary measures, programmes, insurance schemes, public education and law reform (UN CESCR, 2000).

Stigma and discrimination have also been identified as barriers (Cook and Dickens, 2014). Closely related to harmful gender stereotyping, the idea that certain girls, women, non-binary individuals and persons with disabilities who are not "supposed" to be sexual can result in these people feeling inhibited, intimidated or stigmatized, interrupting their access to contraceptive services (Horner-Johnson and others, 2020; Cook and Dickens, 2014). Data from Peru, for example, show that the prevalence of modern contraceptive use among married women is more than double that among single women, and among adolescents it is seven times lower than among married women (ENDES, 2020). Women and men who defy social and cultural expectations and choose to be "child-free" face stigma as well (Ashburn-Nardo, 2017), and young and single people often face barriers in accessing voluntary sterilization (Kimport and others, 2017).

Acceptability

Contraceptive needs vary among women, and an individual woman's needs will change over time. But women are not always able to use a method that they find acceptable to them given their current circumstances and desires.

A key factor within acceptability is the relationship between the client and the health-care provider. This relationship is essential for establishing trust, ensuring satisfaction of both the client and health-care provider, and supporting retention of health-care personnel within the community (WHO, 2014). Health workers must provide family planning information and services in a manner that is respectful of individuals' culture and communities, and sensitive to their age, gender, disability and sexual diversity (UN CESCR, 2016). They must also be fully aware of, and able to communicate about, issues such as side effects, the potential need for covert methods, and social or community constraints. The WHO recommends health-care personnel receive gender-sensitive counselling and education tailored to meet the specific needs of individuals and communities. It also recommends health workers provide information and options for clients to switch contraceptive methods if they are, or become, dissatisfied, and follow-up services to help manage contraceptive side effects (WHO, 2014).

Quality

Quality of care and services means having choice among a wide range of contraceptive methods; being accurately informed about the effectiveness, risks and benefits of the methods; and being counselled and treated by technically competent, respectful providers who ensure the dignity, non-discrimination, privacy and confidentiality of users (UNDP, 2005). Ill-treatment within health-care facilities drives users away and is increasingly recognized as a human rights violation (Kholsa and others, 2016). Quality of care can also be compromised by failure or refusal to incorporate technological advances and innovations in the provision of sexual and reproductive health services (UN CESCR, 2016), such as emergency contraception (see page 82 for guide to policies).

One significant barrier to quality services is health-care provider bias. Service providers may believe they are better qualified to choose the most appropriate method for their client, and/or they may have a personal preference toward or against certain methods (Castle and Askew, 2015). Biases can be based on age, parity (number of births a person has had), marital status and other criteria, with many providers imposing barriers and restrictions beyond those included in normative guidelines or needed for any medical reasons (Solo and Festin, 2019). A bias against providing various contraceptive methods to adolescents is most common, often stemming from judgments about sexual activity among young people or concerns, not borne out by the evidence, about the impact of hormonal methods on future fertility. While it is challenging to measure the impact of provider bias, method mix skew (when 50 per cent or more of contraceptive users rely on a single method) has been identified as a potential macro-level indicator (Solo and Festin, 2019).

Bias can also extend to the level of policymakers, who can play a role in limiting method choice. For example, if decision-makers hold personal biases regarding a method like vasectomy or oral contraceptives, they can decide not to support programmes and policies that expand the provision of those methods to clients.

To address and improve quality of contraceptive services, WHO recommends that quality assurance processes (client feedback) be incorporated into contraceptive programmes, as well as ongoing competency-based training and supervision of health-care personnel (WHO, 2014).

Are women living in an *environment* that facilitates or hinders use of contraception?

Family planning experts call on policymakers and health systems to create an enabling environment for contraceptive use. Activities that increase uptake of contraceptives were, in the past, often referred to as "demand generation" or "demand creation", but these terms, which originate from marketing, incorrectly connote that women should be induced or persuaded to use contraception. In fact, human rights standards require that women, and all individuals who can become pregnant, are empowered with information, education and services, and supported by positive social norms to make this choice freely for themselves. No matter the language used, the environment remains, overall, poor for the exercise of free and informed choice.

Increased agency through advances in the self-care movement

In recent years, self-care — defined by the WHO as the ability of individuals, families and communities to promote health, prevent disease, maintain health and cope with illness and disability with or without the support of a health worker — has increasingly been regarded by health-care professionals as an important way to expand access to critical services. "Self-care interventions are among the most promising and exciting approaches to improve health and well-being, both from a health systems perspective and for the users of these interventions," the WHO noted in 2021 (WHO, 2021).

During the COVID-19 pandemic, as family planning programmes were suspended and travel was restricted, this approach proved even more vital. This led some researchers to call for "expanding self-care approaches to de-medicalize contraception" and "expanding the mix of self-administered contraceptives" in order to "increase an individual's agency in determining what method they use, when they use it, and where they obtain it" (Haddad and others, 2021).

WHO self-care guidelines from 2021 include the following recommendations for family planning (WHO, 2021):
* *Self-administered injectable contraception should be made available as an additional approach to deliver injectable contraception for individuals of reproductive age.*
* *Over-the-counter oral contraceptive pills (OCPs) should be made available without a prescription for individuals using OCPs.*
* *Over-the-counter emergency contraceptive pills should be available without a prescription to individuals who wish to use emergency contraception.*

Legal barriers

Legal barriers include laws, policies and practices that forbid adolescents or unmarried women from obtaining contraception. But they also include factors that are adjacent to legal restrictions, such as poor funding for sexual and reproductive health services.

Unequal gender norms and other social barriers

Addressing harmful social norms, including discriminatory gender norms, is a critical part of creating an enabling environment. The connection between gender equality and avoiding unintended pregnancy is clear (see page 23, Chapter 2), and when women have agency and choice, contraceptive use tends to be higher (United Nations, 2020). Much resistance to contraception is rooted in gender inequality, such as religious opposition; the medically inaccurate conflation of contraception and abortion; intimate partner violence in the form of reproductive coercion; social or family pressure to have children, have a large family, or continue childbearing until a son is born (son preference); as well as stigmas, myths and misinformation. When women face resistance from their community or their partners regarding use of contraception, they often are forced to go without, or resort to covert usage to reassert their bodily autonomy.

A study in Kenya found that 12.2 per cent of women were using contraception covertly (Akoth and others, 2021), and interviews with 300 women in Ghana found that 34 per cent were using contraceptives covertly (Baiden and others, 2016). (In both studies, injectables were the preferred method.) These relatively high rates of clandestine use are a clear indication that contraceptive non-use and disuse do not represent a lack of demand for contraception. They also highlight how a woman's choice in methods may be constrained by the need to use covertly, a reflection on her lack of empowerment more broadly.

There is additionally a social expectation that women assume responsibility for family planning. Part of this is the distribution of risk: the individual who becomes pregnant assumes all of the anatomical and economic consequences of pregnancy, including the risk of maternal morbidity and mortality and any job or income losses related to pregnancy or childbirth. That individual is more incentivized to correctly and consistently use contraception. But this factor is greatly reinforced by social norms. For instance, the paucity of available contraceptive options for men (explored in the feature on page 70) reflects the decision-making of investors and policymakers and their expectations for market demand or lack thereof. Male contraceptive pills, long-acting reversible gels (that block sperm), and injectables are perennially in clinical trials but have not been launched commercially (Thirumalai and Amory, 2021; Costantino and others, 2007).

It is telling that with sterilization, a form of contraception that is less invasive and less risky when undertaken by men, there is a major discrepancy in levels of use worldwide, reflecting the comparatively greater emphasis on women as the focus of contraceptive methods and programmes. In 2015, some 30 million men obtained a vasectomy, compared to 237 million women who obtained a permanent

FIGURE 8

Trends in worldwide use of permanent contraceptive methods

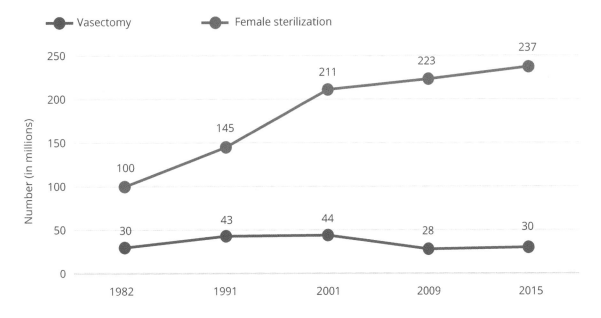

Source: Shelton and Jacobstein, 2016.

contraceptive method (UN DESA, 2015). "There is… longstanding international consensus on the importance of gender equity. From the standpoint of vasectomy (male sterilization), however, there has been a disconnect between stated commitments to choice and equity and programme realities," researchers have said (Jacobstein, 2015).

Comprehensive approaches needed

This research shows that misconceptions about contraception must be dispelled at every level. Individuals and health providers have assumptions and biases in need of

re-examination. But this is true in spheres of decision-making and budgeting, too, where the issue of unintended pregnancy is too often reduced to talking points about contraceptive supplies, last-mile service delivery or family planning counselling.

We see here that no single approach — however important it is — will be able to satisfy every need. Rather, a comprehensive package of interlinked efforts must be implemented from the ground up. Women and girls must have the space and knowledge to articulate their needs — to their partner and their health-care provider through to researchers and policymakers — and, most critically, they must be heard.

PLANNING FOR CHANGE

THE PHILIPPINES, 2021 — After her sixth birth, Rahma Samula, 40, in Maguindanao in the Philippines, was exhausted. She had already seen her mother raise eight children. "Seeing my mother struggle to care for my seven siblings helped me decide to try family planning, which my husband and I have both agreed to do." Most of her children were born just a year apart, but with the help of an injectable contraceptive, Rahma was able to delay her last pregnancy until 2021 – five years after her previous child was born. Rahma is quite sure that without the injections, there would have been two more in between. She and her husband are grateful to their local health workers, who advised them on the various family planning options available. In good health and with only some welcome weight gain as a side effect, she says birth spacing and using the contraceptive was better for her body and family, "so that the children don't have a hard time."

A generation ago, Rahma's story would not have been so simple. Government policy on family planning and reproductive health has fluctuated in the Philippines. Policies in the 1980s centred on limiting population growth through quotas and contraceptive incentives, then later aligned with Catholic teachings that prohibit modern methods of contraception. For decades, the tensions between pro- and anti-contraception camps led the country down a rocky middle road, in which family

> *"My husband and I agreed to use contraceptives because of how hard life is right now."*

planning was largely promoted as a maternal health and child survival intervention, an approach that marginalized adolescents and unmarried women (Alvarez, 1993). It wasn't until 2012, and the passage of the Responsible Parenthood and Reproductive Health Law, that the government settled on its current client- and reproductive-health-centred approach, committing the government to providing free family planning services for poor families. Still, influential religious leaders continue to oppose the use of any form of contraception other than so-called natural methods (fertility awareness methods).

Yet, for years, it was actually religious and community leaders, alongside non-profit organizations, who helped to provide contraceptives in remote areas and to families who could not afford to feed extra mouths. As one mother in an impoverished remote fishing village explained to UNFPA in 1998, "We have a parish priest who comes by, and he is the one who gives us access to [birth control pills]. We don't know where to get them."

The 2012 law and grassroots efforts, such as those by non-governmental groups, women's rights organizations and individuals like that parish priest, have had an enormous and positive cumulative impact on the state of contraception access in the Philippines. No single effort – by the health system, legal system or broader society – carried the momentum of this shift by itself. Rather, it was holistic and across-the-board work, over years, that brought about change.

Laws and grassroots efforts have contributed to change.
Jay Directo/AFP via Getty Images

The law helped to spur investment in clinics and reproductive services, and a health insurance programme now covers more than 90 per cent of municipalities in the country (FP2030, 2020a). Heated rhetoric around contraception has cooled, and a new conversation has emerged, one about choice and rights and long-term goals for individuals and families. Health workers, family planning counsellors and even religious leaders are proactively dispelling contraceptive misinformation.

"My husband and I agreed to use contraceptives because of how hard life is right now," says Theresa Batitits, a 36-year-old nutrition counsellor in a northern village. They want to spend their stretched resources on educating the four children they already have. Theresa had previously avoided hormonal contraceptives, partly out of fear over side effects, but when a local health worker talked about long-acting implants, she decided to try them. "Before they provide family planning to each woman, they offer information on what the methods are, how they work and how they are used, what are the side effects of the contraceptives, things like that," Theresa says.

Anisa T. Arab is one of 15 siblings in Maguindanao. She has always been strong-willed; she left home at age 20 rather than accept her father's plan for her to marry and curtail her education. She initially opposed family planning, believing it went against Islamic teachings, but "when I studied Islam, I saw in the community that our traditions regarding women were too far from what Islam actually says," Anisa explains.

Now 57, Anisa is a radio show host and teacher of Islamic studies (or Uztazah), and a vocal supporter of women's education and their rights to marry if, when and whom they want and to plan their families. She teaches her followers about the Fatwa on Family Planning, a legal opinion endorsed by Islamic scholars that clarifies contraception is not forbidden. Family planning is not bad, she says. Instead, "when our women learn to take care of their bodies, that is where the best family will emerge".

Where do laws and policies enable women to avoid unintended pregnancies?

The SDGs provide the first-ever attempt to comprehensively assess the extent to which countries' legal and regulatory frameworks support sexual and reproductive health and reproductive rights. SDG indicator 5.6.2 monitors laws and regulations across four components: maternity care, contraceptive services, sexuality education, and services to prevent and treat HIV and human papillomavirus (HPV).

Not all of the 13 components have a straightforward connection to the prevention of unintended pregnancy. But even those without an obvious link (such as HPV vaccine) still reflect the overall regulatory environment surrounding reproductive health and rights.

The indicator for each component assesses whether a supportive law exists and whether there are potential restrictions. It measures only the existence of laws and regulations, not implementation. It must be noted that significant variations are seen within regions. Country-level data are available at unstats.un.org/sdgs/dataportal.

SDG INDICATOR 5.6.2 measures 13 components (C1–C13) in four sections

Maternity Care

C1: Maternity Care
C2: Life-saving Commodities
C3: Abortion
C4: Post-abortion Care

Contraceptive Services

C5: Contraception
C6: Consent for Contraceptive Services
C7: Emergency Contraception

Sexuality Education

C8: Sexuality Education Curriculum Laws
C9: Sexuality Education Curriculum Topics

HIV and HPV

C10: HIV Testing and Counselling
C11: HIV Treatment and Care
C12: Confidentiality of Health Status for Men and Women Living with HIV
C13: HPV Vaccine

	MATERNITY CARE				CONTRACEPTIVE SERVICES				SEXUALITY EDUCATION			HIV AND HPV					SDG indicator 5.6.2 (overall)
	C1	C2	C3	C4	Section average	C5	C6	C7	Section average	C8	C9	Section average	C10	C11	C12	C13	Section average	
WORLD	**85**	**90**	**43**	**78**	**74**	**78**	**82**	**70**	**76**	**66**	**68**	**65**	**87**	**91**	**93**	**54**	**81**	**76**
More developed regions	94	88	71	81	85	84	92	76	84	89	88	88	91	94	95	81	90	87
Less developed regions	82	90	33	77	71	75	79	69	74	58	61	58	86	90	92	45	78	72
Least-developed countries	79	96	29	79	71	72	70	68	70	53	59	56	88	92	93	38	78	71

UNFPA REGIONS

	C1	C2	C3	C4	Section average	C5	C6	C7	Section average	C8	C9	Section average	C10	C11	C12	C13	Section average	SDG indicator 5.6.2 (overall)
Arab States	73	87	10	88	68	77	67	77	73	31	9	9	89	89	95	8	70	65
Asia and the Pacific	78	87	37	82	71	79	80	73	77	65	65	63	85	86	93	45	78	74
Eastern Europe and Central Asia	93	87	65	95	85	86	100	77	87	93	82	87	84	93	94	50	80	84
Latin America and the Caribbean	86	86	31	75	70	77	82	60	73	67	77	71	84	86	94	57	80	75
East and Southern Africa	84	97	28	87	73	69	72	69	70	53	69	61	84	88	90	61	81	72
West and Central Africa	83	98	34	65	70	76	77	72	75	52	55	54	89	97	91	35	79	70

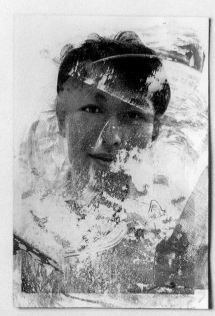

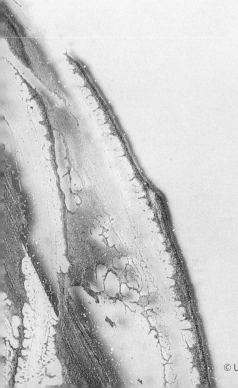

CHAPTER 5

Unveiling the costs of unintended pregnancy

The impacts of unintended pregnancy are clearly wide-ranging. The most obvious consequences are the direct outcomes of the pregnancies themselves, whether births, abortions or miscarriages. It may be tempting, therefore, to measure the impacts by weighing two possible scenarios: one in which a woman invests her time and resources in a baby, versus one in which she invests in herself — but that is a false dichotomy. A woman who obtains an abortion may do so to invest limited resources in the children she already has. A woman denied the agency to choose pregnancy may also lack the means to invest in either herself or a baby. And a woman with ample economic resources may incur other costs, such as continued exposure to a violent partner.

Nuance is also required when accounting for pregnancies that end in a birth. Many unintended pregnancies are undoubtedly met with delight, and even unintended pregnancies that cause fear and consternation can result, ultimately, in children who are deeply loved and a source of great joy. It must be stated firmly that any child born from an unintended pregnancy — no matter the circumstance — is a person with inherent value, dignity and human rights that must be upheld. None of these points is in conflict with the fact that unintended pregnancies can unleash ever-cascading consequences for the individuals and families that experience them.

Rather than investigate the outcomes of unintended pregnancies, then, we should look earlier, to the exercise or denial of choice that begins *before* pregnancy. This chapter attempts to grapple with those issues: What is the difference between a world in which pregnancies result from deliberate, informed choice and our current world, in which nearly half of all pregnancies take place without full volition? What are the consequences of losing bodily autonomy when it comes to pregnancy? Do societies that tolerate high rates of unintended pregnancy fully value the potential of women beyond their reproductive capacities?

The opportunity costs, framed this way, cannot all be calculated. But there are also concrete and quantifiable ways in which researchers have sought to understand some of the costs: costs to the health system for pregnancies that are unwanted whether they come to term or not; costs in terms of women's economic and educational contributions and opportunities; and the potential, if complex, risks to the mental

and physical health of both mothers and babies. There are also risks among those who choose to abort their pregnancies, particularly in places with restrictive abortion laws, where women resort to unsafe abortions, often experiencing avoidable maternal morbidity and even mortality.

These measures are only a starting point, but they begin the vital process of articulating more clearly how societies and economies are shaped by pregnancies that take place in the bodies of women who did not want or plan for them.

Counting the uncountable

There are many hypotheses about the consequences of unintended pregnancies that cannot be easily proved or disproved. Some people have proposed, for example, that higher rates of unintended births could lead to higher crime rates or to increased household stress (Yazdkhasti and others, 2015). These are controversial and provocative points that are reflective of real-world strains on communities and families that might be consequences of unintended pregnancy. There are other uncountable costs as well, such as stigma endured by unmarried women that can have life-long, even multi-generational, consequences.

One example of the rapid multiplication of consequences that are hard to tally is the consequences often borne by adolescents and younger persons who experience an unintended pregnancy. A girl may have to drop out of school (either because the school will not allow her to attend and/or because she needs to take care of her baby). Resuming school is challenging, and sometimes impossible, and few schools provide supportive environments for breastfeeding, childcare or flexible hours (Human Rights Watch, 2018). With an incomplete education, a girl faces reduced employment and earnings potential. If the baby is born outside of marriage, it can mean discrimination for herself and her child (Human Rights Watch, 2018).

Researchers overwhelmingly acknowledge these limitations. "The real damage to quality of life is incalculable," noted the authors of a 2015 literature review looking at different negative impacts of unintended pregnancy (Yazdkhasti and others, 2015). "Unintended pregnancies result in a range of adverse consequences… that have nothing to do with public balance sheets… Overall, the evidence suggests that unintended pregnancy is one of the most critical challenges facing the public health system and imposes significant financial and social costs on society" (Yazdkhasti and others, 2015).

Counting the countable

Labour force participation and earnings potential

Despite the challenges, there are discrete ways in which it is possible to measure some impacts of unintended pregnancy. One study in the United States, for instance, found that unplanned births reduce labour force participation by as much as 25 per cent. The study sought to account for the impacts of unwanted births, as well as mistimed births — such as when a woman intended to become pregnant at age 28 but instead had a

Unintended pregnancy opens the door to human rights violations

With the exception of pregnancies resulting from sexual violence and the various forms of reproductive coercion, most unintended pregnancies are not the direct result of human rights violations. But these pregnancies can lead to consequences that make women and girls vulnerable to human rights violations. Among the acknowledged negative effects, unintended pregnancy is associated with delayed prenatal care and thus potentially worse health outcomes for the pregnant woman (Khan and others, 2019) and, if she continues the pregnancy, with pre-term birth (Orr and others, 2000). Pregnancy, unintended or not, can lead to being forced to leave school (Human Rights Watch, 2018a) or discrimination in employment (ILO, 2012). This discrimination in turn can compound the already fragile socioeconomic circumstances that may underlie the unintended pregnancy in the first place (Aiken and others, 2015). In extreme cases, out-of-wedlock pregnancies may result in criminal penalties (Canada: Immigration and Refugee Board of Canada, 2013) or death sentences, extrajudicial deaths such as so-called "honour killings", or suicide (UN HRC, 2012; Mansur and others, n.d.).

Health, education, employment and non-discrimination are protected through international human rights instruments; when an unintended pregnancy compromises and diminishes the enjoyment of these rights by women and girls, governments, alone or in partnership with non-governmental organizations nationally and internationally, must take all measures — through law, policy, programmes, budgets, administration — to respect, protect and fulfil these rights (UN ECOSOC, 1990).

pregnancy at age 25 (Nuevo-Chiquero, 2014). The financial impact of unintended pregnancies on family well-being was found to be much greater in low-income families than it was in higher-income families, who are less dependent on wages, having savings and other assets to rely on (Nuevo-Chiquero, 2014).

Costs to the health system

The economic burden of events like pregnancy or abortion care can also be calculated. But there is a caveat: one cannot simply take a dollar value for the health-care costs of every woman who experiences an unintended pregnancy, then compare it to women who do not experience pregnancy at all. Many unintended pregnancies are mistimed rather than unwanted, meaning that the same woman might still have incurred pregnancy-related health-care costs but under other circumstances. But if it is presumed that women would prefer to start or expand a family under economically healthy conditions, we can start to derive some sense of cost.

Researchers in the United States found that unintended pregnancies among low-income and impoverished women resulted in very high public expenditure costs: "Government expenditures on unintended pregnancies nationwide totaled $21.0 billion in 2010" (Sonfield and Kost, 2015). Such costs in the United States have continued to rise in the meantime. Researchers also estimated potential gross savings that could have been realized if unintended pregnancies had been avoided — some $15.5 billion (Sonfield and Kost, 2015).

A study looking at 2010 data from Brazil estimated that the total costs of unintended pregnancies in that country amounted to approximately $2.33 billion (at the 2010 exchange rate). These costs were divided into a small percentage for caring for miscarriages (0.8 per cent), direct birth costs for the unintended pregnancies (30 per cent), and costs for paying for any infant complications that arose from the unintended pregnancies (about 70 per cent). Researchers excluded the costs of any induced abortions, and did not include the costs of maternal morbidity and absence from the labour force (Le and others, 2014).

These estimates are country-specific and limited in scope. Calculating similar costs for the world, or by regions, would be fraught with difficulties, and there is no agreed methodology for measuring costs, or which costs to measure. Still, it is clear that pregnancy and birth costs add up to very large numbers.

The other huge cost that is an indirect result of unintended pregnancies is that of providing abortions and post-abortion care. The Guttmacher Institute has done extensive research into these figures. Its most recent summary, *Adding It Up*, shows that, annually, low- and middle-income countries spend $2.8 billion on abortion and post-abortion care. This cost would be cut nearly in half, to $1.5 billion, if contraceptive needs in these countries were to be fully met (Sully and others, 2020).

Mental health impacts

It can be challenging to disentangle cause and effect when it comes to unintended pregnancy and mental health because both are drivers of, and driven by, many of the same vulnerabilities. Intimate partner violence, for example, can lead to the loss of agency

© UNFPA/Fidel Évora

that results in an unintended pregnancy and also degrades mental health and well-being (Gipson and others, 2008). Still, a number of studies have tried to tease out the relationships, and collectively they make a strong case that unintended pregnancy is often a causal factor in depression and worsened psychological well-being.

Postpartum depression

A recent meta-analysis covering 30 studies and more than 65,000 participants found that women who had become pregnant unintentionally were at a significantly higher risk of developing postpartum depression than women who had become pregnant by choice — an odds ratio of 1.53 (Qiu and others, 2020). This correlation has shown up in numerous studies in different countries and regions of the world (Steinberg and others, 2020; Brito and others, 2015).

As for high-income countries, one 21-year longitudinal study in Australia looked at factors associated with childbirth that influenced depression. Among the women in the study, 21 per cent experienced "high-escalating"

depression at some point following birth. The most prominent predictors of depression were partner relationship conflict, anxiety and stress during pregnancy, having many pregnancy symptoms and poor social networking; a less prominent predictor, but still statistically significant, was uncertainty about the desirability of having a child (Kingsbury and others, 2015).

Women who seek out, but are unable to obtain, an abortion may be particularly at risk. A 2011 cohort study in Brazil looked at depression among 1,057 women, and found a higher incidence of postnatal depression among women who had attempted, unsuccessfully, to abort their pregnancies, relative to a comparison group of women who had not attempted an abortion; this relationship persisted after controlling for other potential predictors of postnatal depression, such as mental health before the pregnancy (Ludermir and others, 2011). Similarly, a 2017 analysis of longitudinal data in the United States found that women who were turned away from having an abortion were at greater risk of adverse psychological outcomes than women who succeeded in obtaining an abortion (Biggs and others, 2017).

The Turnaway Study

Landmark research in the United States, "The Turnaway Study", was designed to understand how pregnant people who were denied an abortion fared over time compared to those who had an abortion (Foster, 2020). About 950 women who had requested an abortion were followed over five years, some of whom had been "turned away" because they requested the abortion after they exceeded the gestational limits. "We find no evidence that abortion hurts women ... Women who received an abortion were either the same or, more frequently, better off than women who were denied an abortion," the researchers said. This included their physical health, their employment and financial situations, and their mental health. The study also found that the women who had undergone an abortion "had a greater chance of having a wanted pregnancy and being in a good, romantic relationship years down the road."

Of those women in the study who were denied an abortion, two died from childbirth-related causes, and others experienced complications from delivery, with increased chronic pain and hypertension, and poorer overall health lasting years. In the period immediately after they were denied an abortion, many women reported increased anxiety and lower self-esteem. Women denied abortions were less able to extricate themselves from violent partners, and many reported economic hardship.

This seminal study and the dozens of academic papers resulting from it have received a lot of attention over the years because of its groundbreaking study design and the results showing that not only was abortion *not* harmful but it resulted in improved well-being for many women. "Women understand the wide-ranging consequences of carrying an unwanted pregnancy to term," Professor Diana Greene Foster, the study's lead researcher, told UNFPA. "All of their concerns — finances, health, responsibilities and future plans — are areas where women who were unable to get a wanted abortion had worse outcomes than those who received one."

Physical health consequences

Risks associated with unintended births

While the link between unintended pregnancies and risk of maternal morbidity and mortality remains understudied, correlations have been found in the existing literature (Tsui and others, 2010; Gipson and others, 2008; Mohllajee and others, 2007) and further indicated by the original analysis offered in Chapter 2 of this report. One of the reasons for the association between unintended pregnancy and higher maternal mortality is a simple correlation: the larger the number of pregnancies and births, the larger the number of women who die in pregnancy and childbirth. That is why every public health programme designed to reduce the number of maternal deaths incorporates contraception as one of the pillars of action. The more it is possible to reduce unintended pregnancies, the more it is possible to reduce the number of women who are injured or die from maternal causes.

A second reason for the impact of unintended pregnancy on maternal death is that, as has been explored in several contexts, the characteristics that put women at greater risk for unintended pregnancies, such as poverty, lack of access to health-care services, lower education levels, etc. also put them at greater risk for complications from childbirth, including maternal death and morbidity. This is true of older women and women of higher parity as well (Bauserman and others, 2020; Gipson and others, 2008; Campbell and Graham, 2006).

Additionally, a multi-country analysis of DHS data showed that women with unintended pregnancies tended to start receiving antenatal care later, and had fewer antenatal care visits, than women with planned pregnancies, on average (Amo-Adjei and Tuoyire, 2016). Some studies in developing countries have shown that unintended pregnancy is associated with such conditions as preeclampsia, postpartum haemorrhage and postpartum preeclampsia. This was the case in a large-scale study in India, where the prevalence of these conditions was seen as contributing to the high maternal mortality ratio (MMR) in the state of Uttar Pradesh (Dehingia and others, 2020); this study found that the association between unintended pregnancy and maternal morbidity outcomes was partly explained by the lower level of antenatal care that the mothers with unintended pregnancies received before giving birth (Dehingia and others, 2020).

Among adolescent mothers, the health risks are often heightened. Pregnant adolescents aged 10 to 19 years face higher risks of eclampsia, puerperal endometritis and systemic infections than women aged 20 to 24 years (WHO, 2020a). Pregnancy and childbirth complications are the leading cause of death among girls aged 15 to 19 years globally (WHO, 2019).

Still, a direct causal relationship is difficult to pin down because so many of the factors that affect maternal health (including poverty, lack of education and lack of access to health facilities) are factors that are also predictive of higher rates of unintended pregnancy. This reinforces the conclusions of Chapter 3 that reducing levels of unintended pregnancy is closely linked with reaching overall development goals, especially those relating to health, education and gender equality.

Risks from unsafe abortion

One negative impact of unintended pregnancy stands out for its clear causal relationship to poor maternal health and for its sheer magnitude globally: unsafe abortion. Researchers estimate that, of approximately 121 million unintended pregnancies occurring each year between 2015 and 2019, some 61 per cent ended in abortion (Bearak and others, 2020). Each year, an estimated 73.3 million abortions take place, and this corresponds to a rate of 39 abortions per 1,000 women aged 15 to 49 years (Bearak and others, 2020). Data from 2010 to 2014 suggest that approximately 45 per cent of all abortions performed globally are unsafe (Ganatra and others, 2017).

Almost all unsafe abortions take place in developing countries, with over half of all estimated unsafe abortions occurring in Asia, most of them in South and Central Asia, given the large populations in these areas. On the other hand, a higher proportion of abortions

Contraception and safe abortion are key tools in preventing maternal death

Researchers at the Guttmacher Institute estimate that fully meeting women's contraceptive needs in low- and middle-income countries, and providing antenatal and neonatal care at WHO-recommended levels, would reduce unsafe abortion by 72 per cent and reduce maternal deaths by 62 per cent (Sully and others, 2020). While these improvements would go a long way towards reducing mortality and morbidity, a substantial number of preventable maternal injuries and deaths are almost certain to continue to take place in settings with barriers to safe abortion care. This is because, as discussed in the preceding chapters, it is impossible to completely eliminate the risk of an unintended pregnancy under current real-world conditions.

reduce unsafe abortion (by 72%)

When abortion is carried out in quality health-care settings, by skilled health-care providers, the risks of complication are much lower than the risks associated with birth from an unintended pregnancy (Gerdts and others, 2016) and births in general (Raymond and Grimes, 2012). Medical abortion — an early-pregnancy abortion option that can be provided in primary care settings, via telemedicine or self-managed — offers an option for safe abortion (Gambir and others, 2020), if correctly administered early enough in a pregnancy. But availability of medical abortion is limited in many low- and middle-income settings where abortion is legal (Zhou and others, 2020). Effectively eliminating the catastrophic harms of unsafe abortion requires across-the-board improvements to abortion services, including equipping health professionals with the right skills, ensuring health-care settings are hygienic and private, and ensuring that the right supplies are affordable and available — conditions that can be met with public health regulations and investment. These are among the reasons that the WHO and various human rights bodies have recommended removing legal barriers to safe abortion, especially where health and life are at risk (UN CCPR, 2019; WHO, 2015).

are unsafe in other parts of the world: three out of four abortions that occurred in Africa and Latin America were unsafe, and the risk of dying from an unsafe abortion was highest in Africa (Ganatra and others, 2017).

Unsafe abortion is one of the leading causes of maternal death globally (Say and others, 2014). As highlighted, an estimated 4.7 to 13.2 per cent of maternal deaths each year can be attributed to unsafe abortion (WHO, 2020). This represents a persistent obstacle to achieving SDG 3, specifically undermining target 3.1 to reduce the global MMR to 70 per 100,000 live births by 2030.

An even greater number of women suffer illness and disability because of the consequences of unsafe abortion; data from 2012 show that about 7 million women are admitted to hospitals every year in developing countries for this reason, and the annual cost of treating major complications from unsafe abortion is estimated at $553 million (WHO, 2020).

Maternal morbidity shows up as both a short- and long-term consequence of unsafe abortion. Two recent studies by the WHO looked at the results of more than 20,000 unsafe abortions in sub-Saharan Africa and Latin America and the Caribbean; a small percentage had resulted in the "near miss" or death of the pregnant woman (2.3 per cent in Africa and 1.3 per cent in Latin America) while life-threatening complications had affected 7 per cent of the African women and 3.1 per cent of those in Latin America (Qureshi and others, 2021; Romero and others, 2021). Approximately half of the women studied had experienced at least moderate complications, potentially affecting

© UNFPA/Fidel Évora

their health for years (58.2 per cent in Africa and 49.5 per cent in Latin America) (Qureshi and others, 2021; Romero and others, 2021). A 2006 study found that morbidity and mortality from unsafe abortion resulted in the loss of 5 million disability-adjusted life-years (a measure of the loss of an individual's productive life) per year among women of reproductive age, and researchers cautioned that even this staggering figure was likely an underestimate (Grimes and others, 2006). By any standard, these numbers represent a public health emergency for millions of vulnerable women of reproductive age.

Impacts on children born from unintended pregnancies

As indicated above, many studies find unintended pregnancies are associated with delayed use of antenatal care and/or decreased frequency of care. Antenatal visits are not only an important health intervention for women; they also reduce the risk of neonatal death

The negative consequences of unintended pregnancy would not have occurred if the women experiencing them had been empowered to make conscious and deliberate choices over their fertility and reproductive futures in the first place.

(Wondemagegn and others, 2018) and improve nutritional outcomes for a baby, among other benefits (WHO, 2016).

Studies across Western countries show that unmarried women who reported that their pregnancy was unintended were significantly less likely to have an antenatal care visit during the first eight weeks of pregnancy, and they were twice as likely to wait to seek antenatal care until after the first trimester (Vanden Broek and others, 2016; Heaman and others, 2013; Korenman and others, 2002; Kost and others, 1998). Most, but not all, studies in developing countries also find that unintended pregnancy affects both the timing of the initial antenatal care visits and their frequency. For example, unintended pregnancy was found to result in later and fewer antenatal care visits in multi-country DHS studies (Amo-Adjei and Tuoyire, 2016) and in research in Egypt, Peru and the Philippines (Gipson and others, 2008).

Unintended pregnancy may negatively affect rates of breastfeeding, a practice recommended by the WHO to improve child survival and promote healthy growth (WHO, 2021a). Decades of research in Europe and the United States show that babies born from unintended pregnancies are less likely to be breastfed at all or are more likely to be breastfed for a shorter period (Gipson and others, 2008). Some studies found that even among siblings in the same family, those who were the result of a planned pregnancy were more likely to be breastfed (Korenman and others, 2002). One analysis of DHS data from 18 countries found that, overall, women with unintended pregnancies were 10 per cent less likely to continue breastfeeding beyond one year, although this pattern was not consistent across countries (Hromi-Fiedler and Pérez-Escamilla, 2006).

Children born as a result of an unintended pregnancy may also be at a disadvantage in terms of vaccinations, illness and curative care; some studies have shown such an association (Gipson and others, 2008); however, this seems to be highly context-specific.

There have been many studies into whether babies born from unintended pregnancies are more likely to have a low birthweight, an important indicator of infant well-being, compared to babies from planned births, and whether there are longer-term consequences for unplanned children, including malnutrition and stunting. The results have been mixed, with some showing no such associations (Bitto and others, 1997). DHS studies found that unplanned children were at a statistically significant higher risk of not receiving all infant vaccinations by the age of 1 year in Egypt,

Kenya and Peru, but not in Bolivia and the Philippines (Marston and Cleland, 2003). The same analysis found that children who were born from unintended pregnancies were more likely to suffer from stunting in Peru and Bolivia, but this was not the case in Egypt (Marston and Cleland, 2003).

Other studies have shown an association between unintended pregnancies and low birthweight and stunting. In a series of studies in Bangladesh, for example, the researchers found that "women who reported their pregnancies as unintended were 3.19 times more likely to have a baby with low birthweight than women with intended pregnancies" (Rahman and others, 2019) and "maternal pregnancy intentions are associated with child stunting, wasting and underweight" (Rahman, 2015). In Bolivia and Ethiopia, children from unintended pregnancies were at roughly three times greater risk of stunting (Shaka and others, 2020; Shapiro-Mendoza and others, 2005). Certain children may face particular disadvantages, such as girls in societies with son preference or younger daughters in societies where dowries are common (Gipson and others, 2008).

One reason for discrepancies between studies is the definitional issue that has emerged repeatedly in this report: some of the studies used the terms "unintended" and "unwanted" interchangeably when in fact more negative effects might be seen following "unwanted" pregnancies rather than "unexpected but still wanted" or "mistimed" pregnancies. Ascertaining such differences is very difficult and has a bearing on the study outcomes. Establishing causality is even more difficult. Researchers in a Bangladesh study proposed that the stress of having an unwanted pregnancy influenced the birth outcomes (Rahman and others, 2019), while other studies suggest children from "unwanted" pregnancies might be raised in less-nurturing environments.

And it must be noted that other factors are also significantly associated with these various child health impacts. Predictors of stunting in Ethiopia, for example, included the educational status of the father and other factors (Shaka and others, 2020). As is the case with maternal health outcomes, it can be difficult to disentangle causalities. Still, it is clear that many of the factors that reduce a woman's exercise of agency — including poverty and education levels — are also known to contribute to poor health outcomes for mothers, babies and families.

A conclusion from these studies, often unstated, is that the negative consequences of unintended pregnancy would not have occurred if the women experiencing them had been empowered to make conscious and deliberate choices over their fertility and reproductive futures in the first place. A world without unintended pregnancy would not be free of every negative consequence, of course — but in empowering women to exercise full choice, societies could greatly mitigate these circumstances and their concomitant costs, while promoting human dignity, rights and agency to the benefit of everyone. An important step in that direction would come from expanding research on the multiple countable and uncountable consequences of unintended pregnancy, including those illustrated above, to increase understanding of the often-hidden costs of this neglected crisis.

Where and how contraceptive needs are unmet: Insights from UNFPA's family planning programmes

Together with Avenir Health, UNFPA analyses contraceptive need and use information from countries where UNFPA implements family planning programmes, where data are available. These data are used to design and strengthen interventions, but they also illustrate real-world conditions that affect contraceptive use.

Quality of care

Large proportions of women using modern contraceptives reported receiving insufficient information about methods and side effects.

FIGURE 9   Users receiving key contraceptive method information

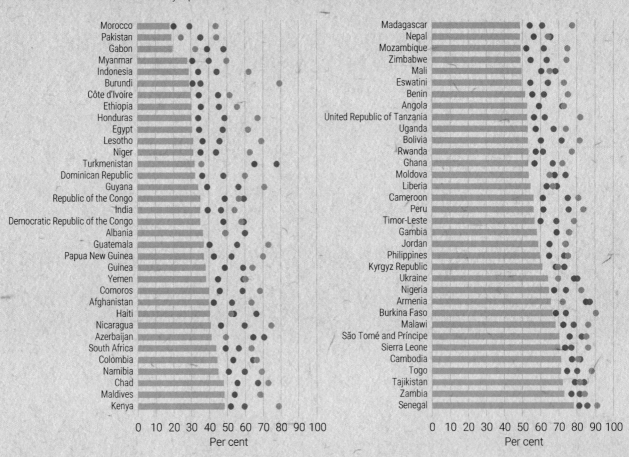

Source: ICF, 2015. The DHS Program STATcompiler, statcompiler.com. Accessed 10 February 2022 (data from national surveys ranging from 2000 to 2020: for women who started a new contraceptive method within the 5 years prior to the survey date).

Users not informed sterilization is permanent

In some countries surveyed, large proportions of women who were sterilized were not informed that the procedure was permanent (data from national surveys from 2000–2017), ranging from 0 per cent in Timor-Leste to 28 per cent in Lesotho. Lack of informed consent is a red flag that contraceptive counselling is not available or that it is failing to provide information in a way that users understand.

FIGURE 10 Users of female sterilization who were not informed the method is permanent

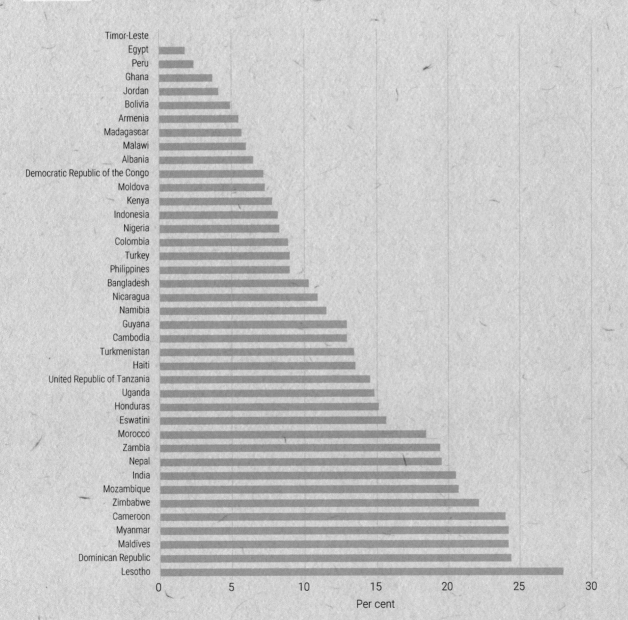

Source: ICF, 2015. The DHS Program STATcompiler, statcompiler.com. Accessed 10 February 2022 (data from national surveys ranging from 2000 to 2017).

Contraception discontinuation

Quality of care, lack of method availability, side effects, stigma and other factors contribute to users discontinuing a contraceptive method even while they still do not want to become pregnant. In places with high rates of method discontinuation, further analysis is needed to understand the reasons for discontinuation and whether users are able to switch to other reliable methods.

FIGURE 11 Users discontinuing contraception while still at risk of unintended pregnancy, by UNFPA region

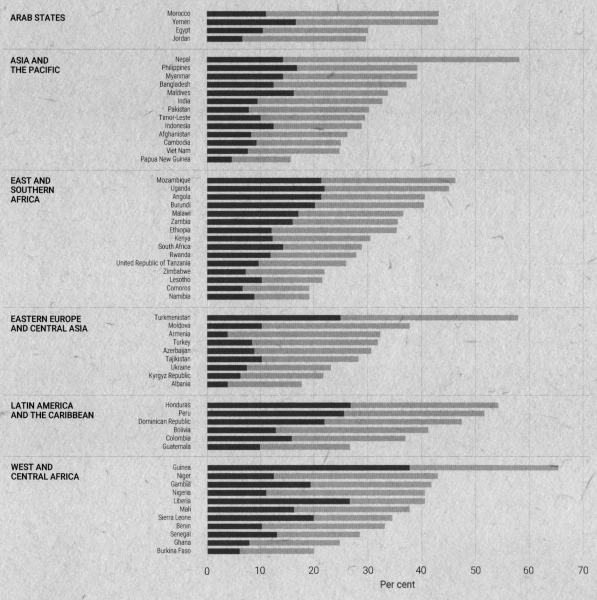

Source: UNFPA and Avenir Health. Family Planning Opportunities Database, updated October 2021 (in press). Compiled from DHS data.

Unmarried, sexually active youth

Young people who are unmarried and who engage in sexual activity sporadically are often not captured in survey-based estimates of unmet need for modern contraception. Unmet need estimates include only unmarried individuals who have been sexually active in the past 30 days, and in some contexts only married users are asked to respond to these questions or are comfortable doing so.

The graph below is an insight into the potential need for modern contraception among young, unmarried women and girls (aged 15 to 24 years); it shows those who have been sexually active in the past year but are not using a modern method of contraception.

FIGURE 12 Percentage of adolescent girls and young women who are unmarried, sexually active within past year and not using modern contraception, by UNFPA region

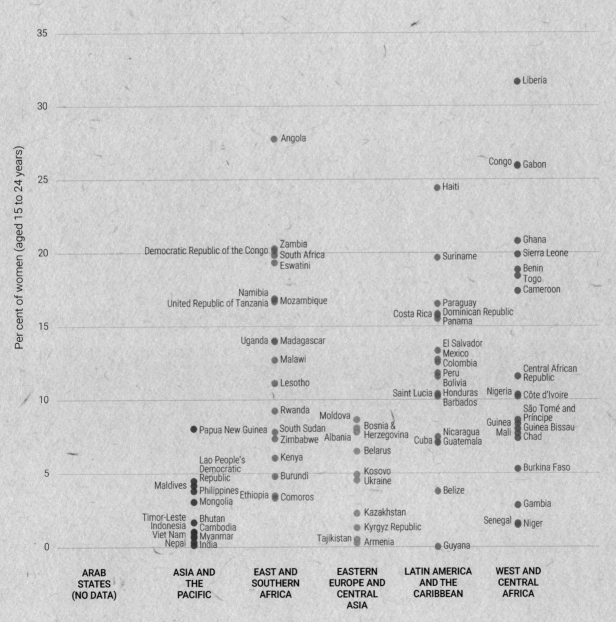

Source: UNFPA and Avenir Health. Family Planning Opportunities Database, updated October 2021 (in press).

STATE OF WORLD POPULATION 2022   105

© UNFPA/Fidel Évora

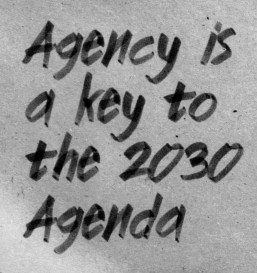

CHAPTER 6

Agency is a key to the 2030 Agenda

The facts of this report bear repeating: *Unintended pregnancy is a reality for millions each year, accounting for nearly half of all pregnancies.* Every year, about 6 per cent of women will experience one. Sixty per cent of these unintended pregnancies will end in abortion. Many unintended pregnancies occur because a woman has lost, or never had, autonomy over her own body. Together, these numbers point unequivocally to persistent levels of gender discrimination and to deficits in human rights and development. These must be addressed to achieve the SDGs.

The toll of these pregnancies is — and has long been — unseen. Though we can estimate health-care costs, monitor school drop-out rates and project levels of workforce attrition due to unintended pregnancies, these only scratch the surface. No number could adequately represent the loss of life, agency and human capital that result from unintended pregnancies. With populations, and their attendant need for sexual and reproductive health services, expected to rise most rapidly in the least developed countries (Starrs and others, 2018), these losses could potentially grow. COVID-19 has taught sharp lessons on the failure of many economic, political, social and other systems to support the sexual and reproductive health and rights of those who are most vulnerable (UNFPA, 2020c). Climate change promises to dramatically accelerate a variety of ills, alongside ongoing and escalating crises such as conflict and displacement.

The solution to so many of the world's biggest challenges is the realization of the full rights and potential of women and girls.

Yet the solution to so many of the world's biggest challenges is likely right in front of us: the realization of the full rights and potential of women and girls.

The 2030 Agenda for Sustainable Development is the agreed roadmap to a better future. But as this report shows, one of the keys to unlocking lasting development for all is agency. By prioritizing agency and the empowerment of all people — especially women, girls and the most marginalized — so they can finally exercise real, informed choice over their health, bodies and futures, we can unleash a powerful, reinforcing cycle of gains.

But efforts to realize agency must be comprehensive, focused on equity, and gender-transformative (UNFPA, 2020d). They must strive to eliminate root causes of gender inequality and accelerate the sharing of power, resources and opportunities — between women and men, between the powerful and the marginalized (UNFPA, 2020d). And these efforts must be reflected within economic, political and social systems, which are strengthened by the meaningful participation of women and limited by their exclusion.

Here is where to start.

Reframe the discourse

Unintended pregnancy must not be framed as solely a women's issue. Unintended pregnancy should not be seen as acceptable, inevitable or even desirable — as is at times suggested in places with concerns about falling population numbers. The discourse must not remain steeped in blame and shame.

This report offers both a human rights and a development case for abandoning such notions. It shows how unintended pregnancies result in additional social and fiscal burdens, including through greater demand for health care, unsafe abortion, loss of income and productivity, fewer resources for children in a family, and more fraught and unstable family relationships (Sonfield and others, 2013). These facts can and must be marshalled in the service of generating political will and community momentum to more vigorously address this issue.

Ensure policies support autonomy

No country or community is untouched by unintended pregnancies, which remain common in both rich and poor countries, even though the world has long possessed the tools and knowledge (imperfect, but largely effective) to prevent them. It is time for policies everywhere to address this issue in new terms and with greater urgency. The evidence in this report can be used to promote the creation of policies — across education, health care, labour, justice and other areas — that are rooted in strong support for individual bodily autonomy and broader social responsibility (Macleod, 2016), in line with the human rights obligations of States.

Recent moves at the United Nations Human Rights Council send an encouraging message of political accountability that could be amplified. The Universal Periodic Review, where countries review each other on their human rights records, has seen an uptick in questions about sexual and reproductive rights. This process

It is time for policies everywhere to address this issue in new terms and with greater urgency.

could highlight the issue of unintended pregnancies and recommend actions in line with human rights commitments.

Existing laws and regulations need to be revisited. A parliamentary review of unintended pregnancy, for example, could provide scope for public visibility and support better understanding of gaps. A review could probe whether current laws, regulatory policies and executive orders fully support individuals in avoiding unintended pregnancies. It might highlight legal barriers that still make sexual and reproductive health information and services difficult or impossible to obtain, such as barriers linked to age or marital status. It could define contradictions in current legislation that need to be resolved.

Other priorities could include examining how well contraceptive services are funded, and whether they have been identified as essential health services that must be sustained under all contingencies — an issue recently highlighted by the COVID-19 pandemic. These reviews could help reorient public discourse around a notion of sexuality that goes beyond the ability to reproduce (Luchsinger, 2021). This could open the door to more expansive services aimed at sexual health and well-being, including for people who are not trying to plan a family.

Invest in research

The causes and consequences of unintended pregnancy are still not well enough understood or measured, much less addressed. New research should generate robust evidence, for instance, on who is most vulnerable to unintended pregnancy and why, and what the most effective and rights-based responses might be. It should better define the differences between pregnancies that are unintended but wanted, those that are regarded with ambivalence, and those that are unwanted, to fully understand the drivers of those pregnancies.

Researchers must ask what contraceptive users want and need — questions that have not been asked loudly or often enough. If available options do not match the realities of many women's lives or how they think about their bodies, choice is not a choice at all. This process should involve close consultations with diverse groups of people who can become pregnant to understand their experiences and concerns. It should unpack assumptions that women who obtain contraceptives will automatically use and continue to use what has been provided. It should challenge preconceptions that some categories of people, like the young, the older, the disabled, the married and the gender-diverse, are not at risk of unintended pregnancy and have no need for targeted services. New data, such as on the percentage of men who support their partner's reproductive health practices, could shed light on gender dynamics in the intimate

spaces where unintended pregnancy begins (Measure Evaluation, 2017).

For many years, the contraceptive market has been considered relatively stagnant, even though new options are in clinical trials, including some with reduced side effects and some more suitable for infrequent use (Svoboda, 2020). The recent experience with the COVID-19 vaccine demonstrates the power of public research and development funds in propelling large-scale progress, a lesson that could be applied here. Countries with greater public research and development finances should commit to pursuing a variety of new contraceptive options, including for men, based on a comprehensive sampling of user demands. Similarly, the pandemic has highlighted gross inequities in access to advances in health care. Since public research and development funding comes from public sources like taxpayers, new contraceptive research should include a commitment to help all countries gain access, in line with human rights obligations.

Make health services comprehensive

Health systems can take a number of measures to better support the agency of individuals. At the top of the list is providing a comprehensive package of sexual and reproductive health services across the life-course, addressing issues from STI prevention and prenatal care to maternity care, prevention of stigma and violence, and respect for bodily autonomy. These comprehensive services should be free from mandated parental or spousal notification or consent (ACOG, 2017). They can signal their openness to adolescents by "rebranding" from family planning to contraceptive services, given that many adolescents and young people do not identify with the idea of planning a family (Paul and others, 2019). They can take steps such as not requiring routine pelvic examination or cervical cytology before initiating hormonal contraception, which may be particularly off-putting for adolescents (ACOG, 2017).

Interventions must also serve other neglected groups (e.g., LGBTI individuals and those with disabilities) and ensure equity in access, quality of care and accountability (UNFPA, 2019). This requires advocacy, training, gender-based budgeting and other tools to counter gender biases and other discriminatory assumptions.

Contraception is another key area for action and investment — one with a significant return on investment. One estimate indicates that every dollar spent on contraceptive services beyond current levels could reduce pregnancy and newborn care costs by three dollars (Sully and others, 2020). Contraceptives should therefore be included in all health benefits packages or defined lists of health services that are publicly or privately funded (Kaufman and Silverman, 2021), with adequate budgetary allocations. Funds should be sufficient to dismantle barriers related to location or operating hours, for example (WHO, 2019a). If choices are made to consolidate or restructure health facilities, contraceptive access should be part of evaluating the costs and benefits (ACOG, 2017).

Contraceptive services themselves must be comprehensive, including screening for pregnancy intentions; counselling around

> **Contraception is another key area for action and investment – one with a significant return on investment.**

options, side effects and other potential consequences; insertion, removal, replacement or reinsertion of long-acting reversible contraceptives or other contraceptive devices; and regular follow-up that includes a prompt response to women who want to change methods (CDC, 2015). Where health-care providers do not provide contraceptives, including for religious reasons, they should be directed to provide referrals for patients seeking them (ACOG, 2017).

Universal health coverage is a fundamental piece of the puzzle. In the SDGs, almost all countries pledged to achieve universal health coverage by 2030. Efforts to this end must address the sexual and reproductive health needs and rights of all people, while transforming discriminatory practices and norms. For example, systematically screening for gender disparities and discriminatory practices might detect – and correct — issues like unjustifiably high sterilization rates among women compared to men. Regular feedback from patients should be used to improve services, with surveys or other data disaggregated by gender to capture

Make health systems gender responsive

Health services must also be gender responsive. This means respectful, rights-based care that listens to patients and explores what they see as acceptable choices (explored further in Chapter 4). Skilled and compassionate care could become a place to talk about not just contraceptives but concepts like intentionality and bodily autonomy. It implies that patients would feel safe expressing worries or desires, and that providers would gauge if an individual has accurate information, faces pressure from a partner or has other concerns (WHO, 2019b; Johnson-Mallard and others, 2017). Providers should be trained and willing to treat everyone without discrimination, including women, men, young people and LGBTI populations (WHO, 2019a). Screening and referrals could be provided for survivors of gender-based violence (Hamberger and others, 2015).

And health systems can model gender equality, such as by closing the gender pay gap among health workers, still at 28 per cent in favour of men, and ensuring gender parity in health-care decision-making (WHO, 2019a). Greater deployment and use of midwives can support empowerment, since most midwives are women. Those from the same community as their clients may be better equipped to provide culturally sensitive care.

Finally, health systems must explore new ways to reach the most marginalized. The COVID-19 pandemic has demonstrated some innovative means to overcome distance and movement restrictions, such as through telemedicine and easier access to prescriptions. These could be continued and extended. In the United Kingdom, for instance, 80 per cent of women who used telemedicine to access early medical abortions said they would select this option in the future (FSRH, 2021; Luchsinger, 2021). The WHO recommends increasing the availability of self-care, such as greater access to self-administered injectable contraceptives and making oral contraceptive pills and emergency contraception available without prescription (WHO, 2021).

Extend social protections

The COVID-19 pandemic, as well as other crises such as climate change, have made universal social protection programmes a clearer imperative than ever before. Included in the commitments under the SDGs, these programmes are the final safety nets for people who would otherwise fall into poverty. The pandemic has demonstrated that many women do not have social protection, even where schemes exist, for reasons that include their disproportionate share of unpaid work at home and concentration in poor quality, poorly paid informal jobs.

Universal social protection schemes provide a powerful opportunity to reduce the multiple vulnerabilities that can lead to unintended pregnancies by closing gaps in income as well as education and health care (ILO, 2017). Countries such as Rwanda, Thailand and Viet Nam, for instance, have incorporated informal workers into social security systems. During the pandemic, Togo, one of the world's least-developed countries, introduced a six-month mobile cash transfer scheme for informal workers. It reached nearly 575,000 people, with women comprising 65 per cent of them. Women received larger benefits as both workers and household managers (UN Women, 2021).

Beyond reducing gaps in income, social protection programmes can adopt tools specific to contraceptive access, such as through vouchers for services. Well-designed programmes have increased access to contraceptives as well as contraceptive choice, and have been effective in reaching marginalized people, including those who are poor, young or lack education. Some programmes have established higher standards of care and provided a more consistent income flow that service providers have reinvested in improved services, yielding potential benefits on multiple fronts (HIP, 2020a).

End gender-based violence

Unintended pregnancy is often, tragically, linked to violence. Some 13 per cent of ever-partnered women and girls, aged 15 to 49 years, have been subjected to intimate partner violence in the past 12 months (United Nations, 2022). Surveys show many women are forced to yield decision-making around sex and pregnancy to a partner, and many believe violence is justifiable if they refuse to have sex (Hindin and others, 2008). Many experience forced sex and/or pregnancy. And across justice systems, there are low rates of reporting and prosecution of perpetrators, along with insufficient penalties.

Women must be able to readily obtain legal protections, including through free legal aid. They should be supported by high-quality,

survivor-centred services and respectful, unbiased legal personnel, from police to prosecutors and judges. Such initiatives must, in all countries, be backed by legal systems that fully recognize and address all forms of gender-based violence, and that eliminate discriminatory treatment of women. For example, the RESPECT Women Framework, published by the WHO, UNFPA and others in 2019, describes clear and scalable actions for policymakers to work towards ending gender-based violence (WHO, 2019c).

There has been progress. The United Arab Emirates, for instance, recently lifted a law requiring married women to obey their husbands (World Bank, 2021a). Yet discriminatory laws and legal gaps continue to affect women around the world. Recently published data from 95 countries found that 63 per cent of them lacked rape laws based on the principle of consent and half continue to restrict women from working in certain jobs or industries. Nearly a quarter of countries fail to grant women equal rights with men to enter into marriage or initiate divorce (United Nations, 2021).

The risk of sexual violence is exacerbated in humanitarian crises and fragile settings, where rape can be used as a weapon of war and a tool of genocide, and where intimate partner violence continues to take place while many community protection mechanisms fracture or disappear. In these settings, women face additional barriers to sexual and reproductive health services (Tran and others, 2021), including contraceptives (Women's Refugee Commission and others, 2012), elevating their vulnerability to unintended pregnancy. Access to a full range of sexual and reproductive health services, including emergency contraception and post-rape treatment, as well as safe spaces and protections that avert sexual violence, must be non-negotiable and essential components of any humanitarian response.

Change harmful social norms

Efforts to reduce unintended pregnancy will not succeed unless harmful social norms — everywhere — are revisited and revised. Taboos and gendered norms too often silence the voices of those most affected, yet this issue is perhaps the area where frank, factual conversations are most needed, and where the diverse experiences of people must rise to the surface.

We have seen how stigmas around contraception lead many to avoid, or quietly discontinue, its use. Adolescent girls may default to pregnancy because alternatives have never been mentioned. Older women may assume they cannot get pregnant. Women of all ages and backgrounds are reluctant to report partner violence or coercive behaviours.

Greater social awareness is needed, calling attention to everyone's right to bodily autonomy and what is required to achieve it. Eliminating the taboo around these discussions is essential to enabling perhaps the most important conversation of all: the open dialogue about desires, choices and plans that must take place between sexual partners to ensure both parties are able to exercise agency and autonomy.

Gendered norms and expectations must also be addressed, proactively and simultaneously. Unintended pregnancy is rooted in the disempowerment of women and girls in every sphere. UNFPA research shows that, at current rates of change, it will take 160 years to end motherhood in childhood (UNFPA, 2022). In developing countries, nearly one in three young women aged 20 to 24 years gave birth in adolescence, defined as ages 10 to 19. Even when adolescent pregnancy is self-identified as an individual choice, girls face limited autonomy, social pressures and a lack of information and services. Measures like school-based dating violence interventions, community-based interventions to form gender-equitable attitudes among boys and girls, and parenting interventions (Lundgren and Amin, 2015) can be effective not only in addressing gender-based violence but also in raising the value of women and girls. Public advocacy campaigns (Thomas, 2012), closely tailored to diverse audiences and contexts, can raise awareness about rights and autonomy.

Comprehensive sexuality education is a key ingredient for success. This information, grounded in medical evidence and guided by principles of rights and empowerment, can give people the space and vocabulary to discuss their bodies and relationships without shame. Done properly, this education can combat myths and misperceptions, and it can promote communication, consent and respectful relationships. It can address gender and power and teach adolescents about confidential contraceptive care. Where child marriage and early pregnancy are common, comprehensive sexuality education can be a place to involve adolescents, parents and the broader community in examining these norms and imagining alternatives. It also advances humanity towards the achievement of SDG target 4.7, which calls for all learners to acquire the skills and knowledge to promote gender equality, human rights and a culture of non-violence.

Although sexuality education is generally associated with adolescents, experts suggest it should begin, in an age-appropriate way,

in early childhood and continue through a person's life-course (ACOG, 2020), covering all stages of sexuality and reproduction. This can prompt people to rethink rigid gender norms and stereotypes well beyond their school years.

> **Pregnancy should not be the result of a breach of bodily autonomy but an affirmative choice.**

Investing in their empowerment is related to — but also distinct from — changing harmful norms. Empowered women and girls can be drivers of norms change, but they do not hold sole responsibility for raising up their own status in an unequal world. Efforts to reform harmful norms must take place *alongside* investments in women's and girls' empowerment and measures to give them entry into decision-making spaces.

There must be asset-building and mentorship programmes, for example. There must be broader efforts to keep girls in school and to reduce gender discrimination and pay gaps in the labour market. Tailored efforts are important for reaching women and girls with overlapping forms of marginalization, such as poverty and racial disparities. Messages about empowerment can be woven into programmes designed to reach these women and girls, such as job training and economic empowerment initiatives.

Investment in, and alliances with, women's rights organizations will help — particularly when these groups are led by women. These organizations often have detailed insights about the private lives of women and girls, including variations across diverse communities. They may be among those best positioned to understand the causes of unintended pregnancy and the solutions most in line with rights and individual preferences. As advocates and watchdogs, these groups have driven national policies that advance gender equality in every part of the world (UN Women, 2021).

And finally, men and boys must benefit from information and social norms that promote healthy models of masculinity. Such masculinities should reject gender-based violence, embrace the values of equality and equity, and allow for the expression of emotion, sensitivity and nuance when discussing the reproductive desires of their partners and themselves.

Invest in the empowerment of women and girls

Girls everywhere must be empowered to see and achieve a future beyond early pregnancy. That means investing in their empowerment, and the empowerment of women who can become role models for future generations.

© UNFPA/Fidel Évora

These organizations must not only be sufficiently funded; they must also be defended against ideologically driven forces that push back against gender equality, and clearly differentiated from groups working through civil society and service delivery to pursue agendas that are anti-gender equality or anti-democratic (UN Women, 2021).

Towards affirmative choice and justice

Pregnancy should not be the result of a breach of bodily autonomy but an affirmative choice. That is what human rights obligations require and what human and social well-being demand. Affirmative choice is a matter of justice. It leads to a more resilient world.

People vary widely in what they need to make affirmative choices. But everyone benefits when all are empowered to make these choices with information and dignity. We must work towards reducing the number of unintended pregnancies, if not to zero then to as close to zero as possible. Doing so will bring us closer to our professed shared vision for humanity: a world in which every pregnancy is wanted and every person enjoys the full realization of their rights and potential.

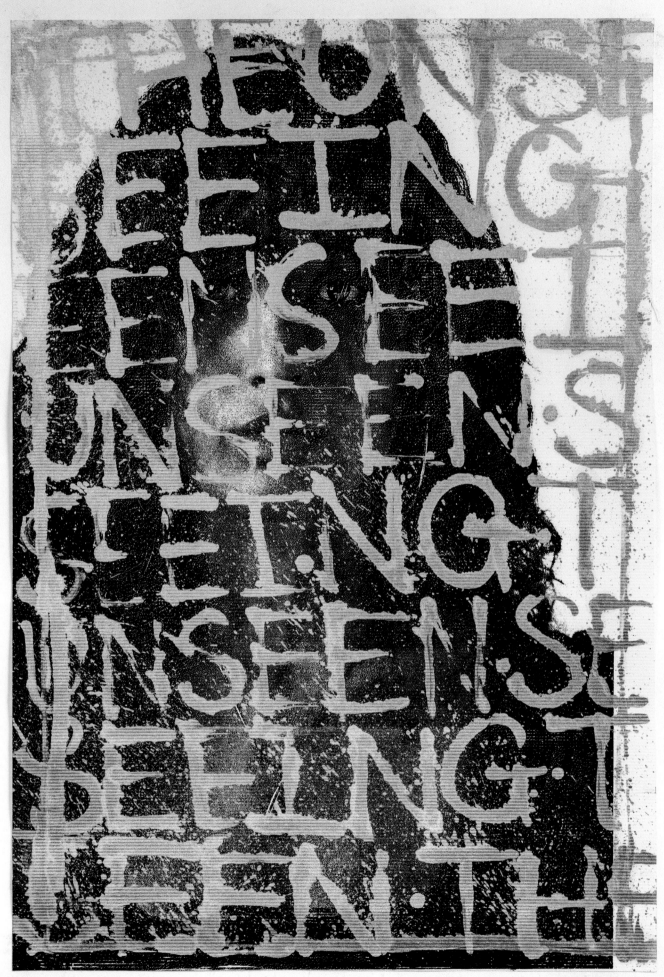

Indicators

SEXUAL AND REPRODUCTIVE HEALTH

	Maternal mortality ratio (MMR) (deaths per 100,000 live births)[a]	Range of MMR uncertainty (UI 80%), lower estimate[a]	Range of MMR uncertainty (UI 80%), upper estimate[a]	Births attended by skilled health personnel, per cent	Number of new HIV infections, all ages, per 1,000 uninfected population	Contraceptive prevalence rate, women aged 15–49, per cent				Unmet need for family planning, women aged 15–49, per cent		Proportion of demand satisfied with modern methods, all women aged 15–49	Laws and regulations that guarantee access to sexual and reproductive health care, information and education, per cent	Universal health coverage (UHC) service coverage index
						Any method		Modern method						
						All	Married or in union	All	Married or in union	All	Married or in union			
World and regional areas	2017	2017	2017	2014–2020	2020	2022		2022		2022		2022	2022	2019
World	**211**	**199**	**243**	**82**	**0.19**	**49**	**63**	**44**	**57**	**9**	**11**	**77**	**76**	**68**
More developed regions	12	11	13	99	0.14	58	70	51	62	7	9	79	87	–
Less developed regions	232	219	268	81	0.20	47	62	43	56	9	12	77	72	–
Least developed countries	415	396	477	65	0.44	32	42	29	37	16	20	60	71	–
UNFPA regions														
Arab States	151	121	208	86	0.03	34	53	29	45	10	15	66	65	61
Asia and the Pacific	120	108	140	86	0.06	52	67	47	62	7	9	81	74	68
Eastern Europe and Central Asia	20	18	22	99	0.15	46	64	36	49	8	11	67	84	74
Latin American and Caribbean	74	70	80	95	0.18	59	75	56	70	8	9	83	75	74
East and Southern Africa	391	361	463	70	1.20	35	44	32	40	16	21	63	72	47
West and Central Africa	717	606	917	55	0.41	20	23	17	19	17	22	46	70	43
Countries, territories, other areas	2017	2017	2017	2004–2020	2020	2022		2022		2022		2022	2022	2019
Afghanistan	638	427	1,010	59	0.04	20	27	18	24	17	24	48	56	37
Albania	15	8	26	100	0.03	31	44	5	5	11	16	11	79	62
Algeria	112	64	206	99	0.04	36	65	32	57	6	9	76	–	75
Angola	241	167	346	50	0.69	16	17	15	16	27	35	35	62	39
Antigua and Barbuda	42	24	69	100	–	45	63	43	61	10	13	78	–	72
Argentina	39	35	43	100	0.13	60	72	58	68	8	10	85	92	73
Armenia	26	21	32	100	0.11	39	60	21	32	8	12	45	87	69
Aruba	–	–	–	–	–	–	–	–	–	–	–	–	–	–
Australia	6	5	8	99	0.03	58	67	56	64	8	11	86	–	87
Austria	5	4	7	98	–	66	73	64	70	5	7	89	–	82
Azerbaijan	26	21	32	99	0.04	37	57	15	23	9	14	33	–	65
Bahamas	70	48	110	99	0.28	45	67	43	65	9	12	80	–	70
Bahrain	14	10	21	100	–	29	63	20	43	6	12	58	73	71
Bangladesh	173	131	234	59	–	52	63	46	55	10	12	74	–	51
Barbados	27	17	39	99	–	50	63	47	61	12	14	76	44	75
Belarus	2	1	4	100	0.13	61	70	52	59	5	8	79	83	74
Belgium	5	4	7	–	–	59	67	58	67	5	8	91	–	86
Belize	36	26	48	94	0.53	45	57	42	54	14	18	71	43	67
Benin	397	291	570	78	0.19	17	19	14	15	24	31	34	91	38
Bhutan	183	127	292	96	0.09	39	61	38	59	8	13	80	83	62
Bolivia (Plurinational State of)	155	113	213	81	0.08	48	68	36	49	12	16	60	94	67
Bosnia and Herzegovina	10	5	16	100	–	38	50	19	21	9	13	40	70	65
Botswana	144	124	170	100	4.39	58	70	57	69	8	10	87	64	54
Brazil	60	58	61	99	0.23	65	80	63	77	6	8	89	–	75
Brunei Darussalam	31	21	45	100	–	–	–	–	–	–	–	–	41	77
Bulgaria	10	6	14	100	–	66	80	50	58	5	6	71	62	70
Burkina Faso	320	220	454	80	0.1	29	32	28	31	20	24	57	81	43
Burundi	548	413	728	85	0.15	20	32	18	29	17	28	48	65	44
Cambodia	160	116	221	89	0.07	43	63	32	47	7	11	64	98	61
Cameroon, Republic of	529	376	790	69	0.6	23	23	19	17	16	21	49	–	44
Canada	10	8	14	98	–	73	82	71	80	3	4	93	–	89
Cape Verde	58	45	75	97	–	44	58	43	57	13	16	76	84	69
Central African Republic	829	463	1,470	40	–	21	23	16	18	23	25	37	77	33
Chad	1,140	847	1,590	24	0.22	7	8	7	7	19	24	25	59	28

SEXUAL AND REPRODUCTIVE HEALTH

Countries, territories, other areas	Maternal mortality ratio (MMR) (deaths per 100,000 live births)[a]	Range of MMR uncertainty (UI 80%), lower estimate[a]	Range of MMR uncertainty (UI 80%), upper estimate[a]	Births attended by skilled health personnel, per cent	Number of new HIV infections, all ages, per 1,000 uninfected population	Contraceptive prevalence rate, women aged 15–49, per cent — Any method — All	Married or in union	Modern method — All	Married or in union	Unmet need for family planning, women aged 15–49, per cent — All	Married or in union	Proportion of demand satisfied with modern methods, all women aged 15–49	Laws and regulations that guarantee access to sexual and reproductive health care, information and education, per cent	Universal health coverage (UHC) service coverage index
	2017	2017	2017	2014–2020	2020	2022	2022	2022	2022	2022	2022	2022	2022	2019
Chile	13	11	14	100	0.26	64	78	59	72	6	8	85	–	80
China	29	22	35	100	–	69	85	68	84	4	3	92	–	82
China, Hong Kong SAR	–	–	–	–	–	48	70	45	67	8	9	81	–	–
China, Macao SAR	–	–	–	–	–	–	–	–	–	–	–	–	–	–
Colombia	83	71	98	99	0.18	64	82	61	77	5	7	87	96	78
Comoros	273	167	435	82	0.01	20	27	16	22	19	29	42	–	44
Congo, Democratic Republic of the	473	341	693	85	0.18	26	30	16	16	21	25	33	–	39
Congo, Republic of the	378	271	523	91	1.94	43	45	29	28	15	18	51	55	41
Costa Rica	27	24	31	99	0.34	56	74	55	72	9	11	84	84	78
Côte d'Ivoire	617	426	896	74	0.24	26	26	23	23	21	26	49	64	45
Croatia	8	6	11	100	0.02	50	71	35	46	5	8	64	98	73
Cuba	36	33	40	100	0.18	69	72	68	71	8	9	88	–	80
Curaçao	–	–	–	–	–	–	–	–	–	–	–	–	–	–
Cyprus	6	4	10	99	–	–	–	–	–	–	–	–	72	79
Czechia	3	2	5	100	–	63	85	56	76	3	4	84	79	78
Denmark	4	3	5	95	0.02	64	77	60	73	5	6	88	87	85
Djibouti	248	116	527	87	0.13	17	29	16	29	15	26	51	–	48
Dominica	–	–	–	100	–	–	–	–	–	–	–	–	–	–
Dominican Republic	95	88	102	100	0.32	57	73	55	70	8	10	84	–	66
Ecuador	59	53	65	96	0.12	60	82	54	74	6	6	82	92	80
Egypt	37	27	47	92	0.03	45	61	43	60	9	12	81	–	70
El Salvador	46	36	57	100	0.13	52	73	49	69	8	10	82	92	76
Equatorial Guinea	301	181	504	68	–	18	18	15	15	23	31	38	–	43
Eritrea	480	327	718	34	0.07	9	14	9	13	18	29	33	–	50
Estonia	9	5	13	100	0.16	56	65	51	58	7	11	80	98	78
Eswatini	437	255	792	88	5.28	54	68	53	67	10	13	83	98	58
Ethiopia	401	298	573	50	0.12	30	42	30	42	14	21	67	73	38
Fiji	34	27	43	100	0.16	35	52	30	44	11	16	65	–	61
Finland	3	2	4	100	–	79	82	74	77	3	5	90	98	83
France	8	6	9	98	–	65	78	63	76	4	4	92	–	84
French Guiana	–	–	–	–	–	–	–	–	–	–	–	–	–	–
French Polynesia	–	–	–	–	–	–	–	–	–	–	–	–	–	–
Gabon	252	165	407	89	0.48	38	38	30	27	18	23	54	58	49
Gambia	597	440	808	84	0.93	14	19	13	19	16	25	44	–	48
Georgia	25	21	29	100	0.17	32	47	23	34	13	18	52	94	65
Germany	7	5	9	99	0.03	55	68	54	67	7	9	88	87	86
Ghana	308	223	420	79	0.63	27	36	23	32	19	27	51	66	45
Greece	3	2	4	100	0.09	53	75	38	50	4	7	66	72	78
Grenada	25	15	39	100	–	46	66	43	61	9	12	77	–	70
Guadeloupe	–	–	–	–	–	46	60	41	54	11	15	73	–	–
Guam	–	–	–	–	–	41	66	36	56	7	10	74	–	–
Guatemala	95	86	104	70	0.05	43	64	36	54	9	13	71	–	57
Guinea	576	437	779	55	0.42	14	14	13	13	17	23	42	79	37
Guinea–Bissau	667	457	995	54	0.88	33	23	31	22	16	20	64	80	37
Guyana	169	132	215	96	0.43	35	47	33	45	17	25	64	87	74
Haiti	480	346	680	42	0.45	28	39	26	36	23	34	50	65	47

SEXUAL AND REPRODUCTIVE HEALTH

Countries, territories, other areas	Maternal mortality ratio (MMR) (deaths per 100,000 live births)[a]	Range of MMR uncertainty (UI 80%), lower estimate[a]	Range of MMR uncertainty (UI 80%), upper estimate[a]	Births attended by skilled health personnel, per cent	Number of new HIV infections, all ages, per 1,000 uninfected population	Contraceptive prevalence rate, women aged 15–49, per cent — Any method, All	Any method, Married or in union	Modern method, All	Modern method, Married or in union	Unmet need for family planning, women aged 15–49, per cent, All	Married or in union	Proportion of demand satisfied with modern methods, all women aged 15–49	Laws and regulations that guarantee access to sexual and reproductive health care, information and education, per cent	Universal health coverage (UHC) service coverage index
	2017	2017	2017	2014–2020	2020	2022	2022	2022	2022	2022	2022	2022	2022	2019
Honduras	65	55	76	74	0.07	53	76	47	68	7	9	79	80	63
Hungary	12	9	16	100	–	49	70	44	62	6	9	80	93	73
Iceland	4	2	6	98	0.04	–	–	–	–	–	–	–	–	87
India	145	117	177	81	0.04	44	57	39	51	9	12	74	74	61
Indonesia	177	127	254	95	0.10	44	62	42	60	8	11	81	77	59
Iran (Islamic Republic of)	16	13	20	99	0.03	58	82	47	66	3	4	77	63	77
Iraq	79	53	113	96	–	38	56	27	40	8	12	58	59	55
Ireland	5	3	7	100	0.08	66	70	63	66	6	9	88	–	83
Israel	3	2	4	–	–	39	73	30	56	5	8	68	–	84
Italy	2	1	2	100	0.04	59	67	48	51	5	9	74	–	83
Jamaica	80	67	98	100	0.53	44	73	42	70	9	9	80	76	70
Japan	5	3	6	100	0.00	46	51	39	41	12	17	68	85	85
Jordan	46	31	65	100	0.01	31	54	22	39	8	14	57	56	60
Kazakhstan	10	8	12	100	0.19	43	54	40	51	11	15	76	65	76
Kenya	342	253	476	70	0.72	44	60	43	59	13	16	75	48	56
Kiribati	92	49	158	92	–	23	32	19	26	16	23	49	–	51
Korea, Democratic People's Republic of	89	38	203	100	–	58	74	55	71	8	9	84	83	68
Korea, Republic of	11	9	13	100	–	56	81	51	74	6	5	82	–	87
Kuwait	12	8	17	100	–	40	59	33	49	9	13	67	–	70
Kyrgyzstan	60	50	76	100	0.11	29	42	28	39	12	17	67	73	70
Lao People's Democratic Republic	185	139	253	64	0.13	38	61	34	54	10	14	71	96	50
Latvia	19	15	26	100	–	60	72	53	62	6	9	81	70	72
Lebanon	29	22	40	98	0.03	29	62	22	46	6	13	62	–	72
Lesotho	544	391	788	87	4.91	52	66	51	66	10	14	83	–	48
Liberia	661	481	943	84	0.29	26	27	25	26	27	32	47	–	42
Libya	72	30	164	100	0.05	26	40	17	25	17	25	39	–	60
Lithuania	8	5	12	100	–	48	71	39	57	7	8	72	87	70
Luxembourg	5	3	8	100	–	–	–	–	–	–	–	–	–	87
Madagascar	335	229	484	46	0.22	42	51	37	45	14	16	67	–	35
Malawi	349	244	507	90	1.21	49	65	48	64	13	15	78	79	48
Malaysia	29	24	36	100	0.19	35	57	25	41	9	15	57	83	76
Maldives	53	35	84	100	–	16	22	12	18	21	30	34	93	69
Mali	562	419	784	67	0.27	18	20	18	20	21	24	46	–	42
Malta	6	4	11	100	–	60	79	48	63	4	5	75	–	81
Martinique	–	–	–	–	–	47	62	43	57	11	14	75	–	–
Mauritania	766	528	1,140	69	–	14	22	13	20	18	28	41	65	40
Mauritius	61	46	85	100	0.8	43	67	29	44	8	10	57	75	65
Mexico	33	32	35	97	0.16	56	74	53	70	9	10	82	86	74
Micronesia (Federated States of)	88	40	193	100	–	–	–	–	–	–	–	–	–	48
Moldova, Republic of	19	15	24	100	0.24	55	63	44	50	11	13	67	–	67
Mongolia	45	36	56	99	0.01	41	57	37	51	13	15	70	–	63
Montenegro	6	3	10	99	0.04	23	27	15	16	15	21	41	52	67
Morocco	70	54	91	87	0.02	43	71	37	61	7	11	74	–	73
Mozambique	289	206	418	73	3.5	27	30	26	29	19	22	58	–	47
Myanmar	250	182	351	60	–	34	58	33	56	8	14	79	91	61
Namibia	195	144	281	88	2.44	52	61	52	61	10	15	83	88	62

Countries, territories, other areas	Maternal mortality ratio (MMR) (deaths per 100,000 live births)[a]	Range of MMR uncertainty (UI 80%), lower estimate[a]	Range of MMR uncertainty (UI 80%), upper estimate[a]	Births attended by skilled health personnel, per cent	Number of new HIV infections, all ages, per 1,000 uninfected population	Contraceptive prevalence rate, women aged 15–49, per cent — Any method — All	Contraceptive prevalence rate, women aged 15–49, per cent — Any method — Married or in union	Contraceptive prevalence rate — Modern method — All	Contraceptive prevalence rate — Modern method — Married or in union	Unmet need for family planning, women aged 15–49, per cent — All	Unmet need for family planning — Married or in union	Proportion of demand satisfied with modern methods, all women aged 15–49	Laws and regulations that guarantee access to sexual and reproductive health care, information and education, per cent	Universal health coverage (UHC) service coverage index
	2017	2017	2017	2014–2020	2020	2022	2022	2022	2022	2022	2022	2022	2022	2019
Nepal	186	135	267	77	0.03	42	53	37	47	17	22	63	48	53
Netherlands	5	4	7	–	0.02	63	72	61	71	5	7	89	100	86
New Caledonia	–	–	–	–	–	–	–	–	–	–	–	–	–	–
New Zealand	9	7	11	96	0.02	65	81	61	75	4	5	88	95	86
Nicaragua	98	77	127	96	0.11	53	82	51	79	5	6	88	75	70
Niger	509	368	724	39	0.05	17	19	16	18	15	18	50	–	37
Nigeria	917	658	1,320	43	0.42	18	21	14	15	15	19	42	–	45
North Macedonia	7	5	10	100	–	43	54	19	19	9	13	37	–	68
Norway	2	2	3	99	0.01	67	85	62	79	4	4	89	100	86
Oman	19	16	22	99	–	21	36	15	25	15	26	41	70	69
Pakistan	140	85	229	71	0.12	26	38	20	29	11	17	53	69	45
Palestine[1]	–	–	–	100	–	41	62	30	46	7	11	64	68	–
Panama	52	45	59	93	0.44	48	60	45	56	14	17	73	72	77
Papua New Guinea	145	67	318	56	0.39	28	39	23	32	18	25	51	–	33
Paraguay	84	72	96	98	0.13	59	73	55	67	8	9	82	76	61
Peru	88	69	110	94	0.13	55	77	43	58	5	7	70	85	78
Philippines	121	91	168	84	0.15	36	57	27	43	10	16	59	80	55
Poland	2	2	3	100	–	54	74	43	58	6	8	73	89	74
Portugal	8	6	11	100	0.07	60	74	51	62	4	7	79	95	84
Puerto Rico	21	16	29	–	–	57	82	52	74	6	5	83	–	–
Qatar	9	6	14	100	0.07	31	49	26	41	9	15	64	71	74
Réunion	–	–	–	–	–	49	72	48	71	8	9	84	–	–
Romania	19	14	25	95	0.04	54	72	45	58	5	8	75	98	72
Russian Federation	17	13	23	100	–	49	68	42	57	6	9	76	70	75
Rwanda	248	184	347	94	0.34	34	58	32	54	11	16	70	82	54
Saint Kitts and Nevis	–	–	–	100	–	–	–	–	–	–	–	–	–	–
Saint Lucia	117	71	197	100	–	49	61	46	57	12	15	76	33	72
Saint Vincent and the Grenadines	68	44	100	99	–	50	67	48	65	10	12	80	81	73
Samoa	43	20	97	89	–	12	19	11	18	26	46	29	22	53
San Marino	–	–	–	–	–	–	–	–	–	–	–	–	–	–
São Tomé and Príncipe	130	73	217	97	–	38	51	35	47	21	25	60	46	60
Saudi Arabia	17	10	30	99	0.05	19	30	15	24	15	25	46	–	73
Senegal	315	237	434	75	0.08	21	30	20	28	15	21	56	75	49
Serbia	12	9	17	100	0.02	47	58	28	28	6	11	53	99	71
Seychelles	53	26	109	99	–	–	–	–	–	–	–	–	–	70
Sierra Leone	1,120	808	1,620	87	0.7	27	25	26	25	20	24	56	65	39
Singapore	8	5	13	100	0.01	40	68	35	60	6	10	77	46	86
Sint Maarten	–	–	–	–	–	–	–	–	–	–	–	–	–	–
Slovakia	5	4	7	98	–	56	79	48	66	4	6	79	86	77
Slovenia	7	5	9	100	0.01	53	79	44	66	3	5	79	–	80
Solomon Islands	104	70	157	86	–	24	32	20	27	13	17	54	–	50
Somalia	829	385	1,590	32	0.02	6	10	2	2	15	26	9	–	27
South Africa	119	96	153	97	4.6	51	58	51	58	11	14	82	95	68
South Sudan	1,150	789	1,710	19	1.37	6	8	6	7	20	29	21	16	32
Spain	4	3	5	100	0.08	60	63	58	61	8	13	85	–	86
Sri Lanka	36	31	41	100	0.01	45	67	37	55	5	7	74	86	67

SEXUAL AND REPRODUCTIVE HEALTH

Countries, territories, other areas	Maternal mortality ratio (MMR) (deaths per 100,000 live births)[a]	Range of MMR uncertainty (UI 80%), lower estimate[a]	Range of MMR uncertainty (UI 80%), upper estimate[a]	Births attended by skilled health personnel, per cent	Number of new HIV infections, all ages, per 1,000 uninfected population	Contraceptive prevalence rate, women aged 15–49, per cent				Unmet need for family planning, women aged 15–49, per cent		Proportion of demand satisfied with modern methods, all women aged 15–49	Laws and regulations that guarantee access to sexual and reproductive health care, information and education, per cent	Universal health coverage (UHC) service coverage index
						Any method		Modern method						
						All	Married or in union	All	Married or in union	All	Married or in union			
	2017	2017	2017	2014–2020	2020	2022		2022		2022		2022	2022	2019
Sudan	295	207	408	78	0.09	11	16	10	15	17	27	36	57	44
Suriname	120	96	144	98	0.3	34	47	33	47	15	22	69	–	67
Sweden	4	3	6	–	–	60	71	57	68	6	8	87	100	87
Switzerland	5	3	7	–	–	73	73	68	69	4	7	89	94	87
Syrian Arab Republic	31	20	50	96	0	38	62	28	46	8	13	62	81	56
Tajikistan	17	10	26	95	0.09	24	33	22	30	16	22	55	–	66
Tanzania, United Republic of	524	399	712	64	1.26	37	45	33	40	15	19	62	–	46
Thailand	37	32	44	99	0.1	53	77	52	75	4	6	90	–	83
Timor–Leste, Democratic Republic of	142	102	192	57	0.1	19	32	17	29	13	23	53	–	53
Togo	396	270	557	69	0.45	24	27	22	25	22	30	48	–	44
Tonga	52	24	116	98	–	18	33	16	28	13	25	49	–	56
Trinidad and Tobago	67	50	90	100	0.07	41	49	36	45	14	20	67	27	73
Tunisia	43	33	54	100	0.03	31	59	27	51	7	13	70	–	70
Turkey	17	14	20	97	–	48	71	34	49	6	9	61	78	79
Turkmenistan	7	5	10	100	–	35	53	33	50	8	12	76	94	73
Turks and Caicos Islands	–	–	–	–	–	–	–	–	–	–	–	–	–	–
Tuvalu	–	–	–	93	–	–	–	–	–	–	–	–	–	–
Uganda	375	278	523	74	0.95	36	46	33	42	18	24	61	–	50
Ukraine	19	14	26	100	0.21	53	68	44	55	6	9	75	95	73
United Arab Emirates	3	2	5	99	0.13	36	51	29	41	12	17	61	–	78
United Kingdom	7	6	8	–	–	72	76	66	69	5	7	86	96	88
United States of America	19	17	21	99	–	62	76	54	67	5	6	81	–	83
United States Virgin Islands	–	–	–	–	–	52	75	49	70	8	8	81	–	–
Uruguay	17	14	21	100	0.19	57	79	55	77	6	7	87	97	79
Uzbekistan	29	23	37	100	0.08	50	70	46	66	6	8	84	92	71
Vanuatu	–	–	–	89	–	36	49	31	41	15	19	61	–	52
Venezuela (Bolivarian Republic of)	125	97	170	99	0.08	56	76	52	71	8	10	83	–	70
Viet Nam	43	32	61	94	0.06	59	80	50	67	4	5	79	54	70
Western Sahara	–	–	–	–	–	–	–	–	–	–	–	–	–	–
Yemen	164	109	235	45	0.04	28	44	21	33	14	23	49	65	44
Zambia	213	159	289	80	3.64	38	53	36	50	15	18	68	91	55
Zimbabwe	458	360	577	86	1.74	49	69	49	69	8	10	86	73	55

SEXUAL AND REPRODUCTIVE HEALTH

NOTES

- Data not available.
- a The MMR has been rounded according to the following scheme: <1,000, rounded to nearest 1; and ≥1,000, rounded to nearest 10.
- I On 29 November 2012, the United Nations General Assembly passed Resolution 67/19, which accorded Palestine "non-member observer State status in the United Nations..."

DEFINITIONS OF THE INDICATORS

Maternal mortality ratio: Number of maternal deaths during a given time period per 100,000 live births during the same time period (SDG indicator 3.1.1).

Births attended by skilled health personnel: Percentage of births attended by skilled health personnel (doctor, nurse or midwife) (SDG indicator 3.1.2).

Number of new HIV infections, all ages, per 1,000 uninfected population: Number of new HIV infections per 1,000 person-years among the uninfected population (SDG indicator 3.3.1).

Contraceptive prevalence rate: Percentage of women aged 15 to 49 years who are currently using any method of contraception.

Contraceptive prevalence rate, modern method: Percentage of women aged 15 to 49 years who are currently using any modern method of contraception.

Unmet need for family planning: Percentage of women aged 15 to 49 years who want to stop or delay childbearing but are not using a method of contraception.

Proportion of demand satisfied with modern methods: Percentage of total demand for family planning among women aged 15 to 49 years that is satisfied by the use of modern contraception (SDG indicator 3.7.1).

Laws and regulations that guarantee access to sexual and reproductive health care, information and education: The extent to which countries have national laws and regulations that guarantee full and equal access to women and men aged 15 years and older to sexual and reproductive health care, information and education (SDG indicator 5.6.2).

Universal health coverage (UHC) service coverage index: Average coverage of essential services based on tracer interventions that include reproductive, maternal, newborn and child health, infectious diseases, non-communicable diseases and service capacity and access, among the general and the most disadvantaged population (SDG indicator 3.8.1).

MAIN DATA SOURCES

Maternal mortality ratio: United Nations Maternal Mortality Estimation Inter-agency Group (WHO, UNICEF, UNFPA, The World Bank and the United Nations Population Division), 2019.

Births attended by skilled health personnel: Joint global database on skilled attendance at birth, 2021, United Nations Children's Fund (UNICEF) and World Health Organization (WHO). Regional aggregates calculated by UNFPA based on data from the joint global database.

Number of new HIV infections, all ages, per 1,000 uninfected population: UNAIDS 2021 HIV Estimates.

Contraceptive prevalence rate: United Nations Population Division, 2021.

Contraceptive prevalence rate, modern method: United Nations Population Division, 2021.

Unmet need for family planning: United Nations Population Division, 2021.

Proportion of demand satisfied with modern methods: United Nations Population Division, 2021.

Laws and regulations that guarantee access to sexual and reproductive health care, information and education: UNFPA, 2022.

Universal health coverage (UHC) service coverage index: WHO, 2021.

GENDER, RIGHTS AND HUMAN CAPITAL

	Adolescent birth rate per 1,000 girls aged 15–19	Unintended pregnancies per 1,000 women aged 15–49[2]	Child marriage by age 18, per cent	Female genital mutilation prevalence among women aged 15–49, per cent	Intimate partner violence, past 12 months, per cent	Decision-making on sexual and reproductive health and reproductive rights, per cent	Total net enrolment rate, primary education, per cent	Gender parity index, total net enrolment rate, primary education	Total net enrolment rate, lower secondary education, per cent	Gender parity index, total net enrolment rate, lower secondary education	Total net enrolment rate, upper secondary education, per cent	Gender parity index, total net enrolment rate, upper secondary education
World and regional areas	2020–2025	2015–2019	2005–2020	2004–2020	2018	2021	2020	2020	2020	2020	2020	2020
World	**40**	**64**	**26**	**–**	**13**	**57**	**91**	**0.98**	**84**	**1.00**	**66**	**1.01**
More developed regions	11	34	–	–	–	–	99	1.01	98	1.00	95	1.00
Less developed regions	44	70	27	–	–	56	90	0.98	82	1.00	63	1.01
Least developed countries	88	85	38	46	22	54	83	0.96	66	0.98	44	0.90
UNFPA regions												
Arab States	45	87	21	65	15	–	94	0.99	87	1.02	66	1.06
Asia and the Pacific	21	64	25	–	13	61	85	–	82	0.95	60	0.92
Eastern Europe and Central Asia	26	54	11	–	9	76	96	1.00	98	0.99	84	0.99
Latin America and the Caribbean	59	69	24	–	8	74	97	1.01	93	1.02	79	1.03
East and Southern Africa	92	101	31	35	24	52	86	0.98	66	0.95	44	0.84
West and Central Africa	104	76	41	28	15	36	76	0.91	60	0.97	40	0.87
Countries, territories, other areas	2004–2020	2015–2019	2005–2020	2004–2020	2018	2007–2020	2010–2020	2010–2020	2010–2020	2010–2020	2010–2020	2010–2020
Afghanistan	62	–	28	–	35	–	–	–	–	–	44	0.56
Albania	14	16	12	–	6	69	96	1.04	96	1.04	81	1.09
Algeria	12	–	4	–	–	–	–	–	–	–	–	–
Angola	163	120	30	–	25	62	82	0.78	76	0.76	18	0.71
Antigua and Barbuda	28	–	–	–	–	–	99	1.02	99	0.99	87	1.02
Argentina	50	69	–	–	5	–	100	–	99	0.99	89	1.09
Armenia	19	53	5	–	5	66	90	1.00	90	1.02	92	1.14
Aruba	21	–	–	–	–	–	100		–	–	–	–
Australia	9	37	–	–	3	–	99	1.00	98	1.00	94	1.03
Austria	6	–	–	–	4	–	100	1.00	99	1.01	90	1.02
Azerbaijan	48	93	11	–	5	–	90	1.04	99	1.00	100	1.00
Bahamas	29	–	–	–	–	–	–	–	78	1.02	73	1.07
Bahrain	13	–	–	–	–	–	98	0.99	96	1.07	87	1.14
Bangladesh	74	59	51	–	23	64	95	–	74	1.10	63	1.11
Barbados	50	77	29	–	–	–	97	0.99	96	1.00	94	1.04
Belarus	12	19	5	–	6	–	99	0.98	99	1.00	99	1.02
Belgium	6	21	–	–	5	–	99	1.01	100	1.00	98	1.00
Belize	58	71	34	–	8	–	100	0.99	85	0.98	69	1.11
Benin	108	86	31	9	15	36	93	0.94	58	0.87	34	0.75
Bhutan	59	48	26	–	9	–	96	1.03	88	1.15	72	1.16
Bolivia (Plurinational State of)	71	105	20	–	18	–	95	1.00	93	0.97	78	1.01
Bosnia and Herzegovina	10	20	4	–	3	–	–	–	–	–	81	1.04
Botswana	52	97	–	–	17	–	89	1.01	–	–	–	–
Brazil	49	67	26	–	7	–	99	1.00	98	1.02	85	1.02
Brunei Darussalam	10	–	–	–	–	–	98	1.00	100	1.00	83	1.07
Bulgaria	39	29	–	–	6	–	85	1.00	85	0.99	84	0.95
Burkina Faso	132	75	52	76	11	20	76	1.00	53	1.10	33	1.08
Burundi	58	98	19	–	22	44	90	1.04	70	1.10	38	1.16
Cambodia	30	69	19	–	9	76	89	1.00	85	1.06	45	0.95
Cameroon, Republic of	122	83	30	1	22	49	92	0.91	63	0.89	46	0.83
Canada	7	31	–	–	3	–	100	–	100	1.00	88	1.00
Cape Verde	12	102	18	–	11	–	92	0.99	87	0.98	73	1.08
Central African Republic	229	90	61	22	21	–	67	0.80	44	0.61	16	0.48

GENDER, RIGHTS AND HUMAN CAPITAL

Countries, territories, other areas	Adolescent birth rate per 1,000 girls aged 15–19	Unintended pregnancies per 1,000 women aged 15–49[2]	Child marriage by age 18, per cent	Female genital mutilation prevalence among women aged 15–49, per cent	Intimate partner violence, past 12 months, per cent	Decision-making on sexual and reproductive health and reproductive rights, per cent	Total net enrolment rate, primary education, per cent	Gender parity index, total net enrolment rate, primary education	Total net enrolment rate, lower secondary education, per cent	Gender parity index, total net enrolment rate, lower secondary education	Total net enrolment rate, upper secondary education, per cent	Gender parity index, total net enrolment rate, upper secondary education
	2004–2020	2015–2019	2005–2020	2004–2020	2018	2007–2020	2010–2020	2010–2020	2010–2020	2010–2020	2010–2020	2010–2020
Chad	179	60	61	34	16	27	74	0.79	38	0.68	22	0.51
Chile	23	70	–	–	6	–	100	0.99	96	0.99	95	1.00
China	9	65	–	–	8	–	–	–	–	–	–	–
China, Hong Kong SAR	2	28	–	–	3	–	98	–	99	1.00	100	1.00
China, Macao SAR	3	–	–	–	–	–	96	0.98	99	1.02	91	1.03
Colombia	58	63	23	–	12	–	99	1.01	97	1.01	81	1.03
Comoros	70	95	32	–	8	21	82	1.00	81	1.02	50	1.07
Congo, Democratic Republic of the	109	117	29	–	36	31	–	–	–	–	–	–
Congo, Republic of the	111	106	27	–	–	27	84	0.98	–	–	–	–
Costa Rica	41	52	21	–	7	–	100	1.00	96	1.01	92	1.03
Côte d'Ivoire	123	96	27	37	16	25	96	0.93	58	0.88	42	0.77
Croatia	9	33	–	–	4	–	98	1.02	99	1.02	88	1.05
Cuba	53	72	29	–	5	–	100	1.00	88	1.01	85	1.05
Curaçao	23	–	–	–	–	–	93	0.99	85	1.01	77	1.08
Cyprus	8	–	–	–	3	–	99	1.00	99	1.00	93	0.97
Czechia	11	35	–	–	4	–	99	1.01	100	1.00	96	1.00
Denmark	2	30	–	–	3	–	99	1.01	100	0.99	91	1.01
Djibouti	21	50	5	94	–	–	67	0.93	60	1.02	47	0.99
Dominica	47	–	–	–	–	–	99	1.00	97	1.02	80	0.85
Dominican Republic	54	84	36	–	10	77	96	1.01	91	1.01	74	1.04
Ecuador	64	80	22	–	8	87	99	–	98	1.03	79	1.02
Egypt	52	–	17	87	15	–	99	–	98	1.02	77	0.98
El Salvador	70	58	26	–	6	–	84	1.01	78	1.01	60	0.97
Equatorial Guinea	176	–	30	–	29	–	45	1.02	–	–	–	–
Eritrea	76	53	41	83	–	–	53	0.91	64	0.88	51	0.86
Estonia	10	38	–	–	4	–	98	1.01	99	1.01	98	1.00
Eswatini	87	111	5	–	18	49	85	0.98	97	1.00	84	0.96
Ethiopia	80	79	40	65	27	45	87	0.91	53	0.92	26	0.91
Fiji	23	–	–	–	23	–	99	0.99	96	–	74	1.09
Finland	4	33	0	–	8	–	98	1.01	100	1.00	96	0.98
France	9	29	–	–	5	–	100	1.00	100	1.00	96	1.01
French Guiana	76	71	–	–	–	–	–	–	–	–	–	–
French Polynesia	32	–	–	–	–	–	–	–	–	–	–	–
Gabon	91	112	22	–	22	48	–	–	–	–	–	–
Gambia	68	54	26	76	10	23	87	1.13	69	1.03	–	–
Georgia	29	94	14	–	3	82	99	1.01	99	1.01	95	1.03
Germany	7	21	–	–	–	–	99	1.01	96	1.02	85	0.98
Ghana	78	102	19	2	10	52	94	1.02	92	1.04	75	1.00
Greece	9	33	–	–	5	–	99	1.01	97	0.99	99	0.98
Grenada	36	–	–	–	8	–	99	–	97	–	97	1.00
Guadeloupe	9	68	–	–	–	–	–	–	–	–	–	–
Guam	35	–	–	–	–	–	–	–	–	–	–	–
Guatemala	77	63	30	–	7	65	89	1.01	65	0.94	37	0.94
Guinea	120	70	47	95	21	29	86	0.85	49	0.70	33	0.59
Guinea–Bissau	84	99	26	52	–	–	73	0.95	–	–	–	–
Guyana	74	76	30	–	11	71	98	0.97	93	1.02	70	1.11

GENDER, RIGHTS AND HUMAN CAPITAL

Countries, territories, other areas	Adolescent birth rate per 1,000 girls aged 15–19	Unintended pregnancies per 1,000 women aged 15–49[2]	Child marriage by age 18, per cent	Female genital mutilation prevalence among women aged 15–49, per cent	Intimate partner violence, past 12 months, per cent	Decision-making on sexual and reproductive health and reproductive rights, per cent	Total net enrolment rate, primary education, per cent	Gender parity index, total net enrolment rate, primary education	Total net enrolment rate, lower secondary education, per cent	Gender parity index, total net enrolment rate, lower secondary education	Total net enrolment rate, upper secondary education, per cent	Gender parity index, total net enrolment rate, upper secondary education
	2004–2020	2015–2019	2005–2020	2004–2020	2018	2007–2020	2010–2020	2010–2020	2010–2020	2010–2020	2010–2020	2010–2020
Haiti	55	107	15	–	12	59	–	–	–	–	–	–
Honduras	89	68	34	–	7	70	84	1.02	57	1.06	42	1.15
Hungary	22	27	–	–	6	–	95	1.00	97	1.00	88	1.01
Iceland	5	33	–	–	3	–	100	1.00	100	1.00	84	1.04
India	12	62	27	–	18	–	95	1.02	85	1.04	58	1.04
Indonesia	36	40	16	–	9	–	94	0.95	84	1.07	77	1.01
Iran (Islamic Republic of)	31	–	17	–	18	–	100	0.99	95	0.97	74	0.97
Iraq	70	–	28	7	–	–	–	–	–	–	–	–
Ireland	6	–	–	–	3	–	100	–	99	–	98	1.01
Israel	8	–	–	–	6	–	100	–	100	–	98	–
Italy	4	28	–	–	4	–	97	1.00	98	1.00	94	1.01
Jamaica	52	87	8	–	7	–	–	–	76	1.06	54	1.57
Japan	3	21	–	–	4	–	98	1.00	98	1.00	99	1.02
Jordan	27	–	10	–	14	61	80	0.99	72	1.00	57	1.10
Kazakhstan	23	57	7	–	6	–	90	1.01	100	–	99	–
Kenya	96	113	23	21	23	56	81	1.04	–	–	–	–
Kiribati	51	–	18	–	25	–	97	–	–	–	–	–
Korea, Democratic People's Republic of	1	–	0	–	–	–	–	–	–	–	–	–
Korea, Republic of	1	35	–	–	8	–	100	1.00	95	1.00	93	1.00
Kuwait	5	–	–	–	–	–	97	1.04	94	1.05	82	1.03
Kyrgyzstan	38	40	13	–	13	77	100	0.99	99	0.99	73	1.06
Lao People's Democratic Republic	83	51	33	–	8	–	92	0.98	70	1.00	53	0.92
Latvia	12	34	–	–	6	–	99	1.01	98	1.01	95	1.02
Lebanon	12	–	6	–	–	–	–	–	–	–	–	–
Lesotho	91	99	16	–	17	61	98	1.01	83	1.11	66	1.15
Liberia	128	106	36	44	27	62	79	1.01	79	0.90	74	0.86
Libya	11	–	–	–	–	–	–	–	–	–	–	–
Lithuania	11	26	0	–	5	–	100	–	100	–	97	1.02
Luxembourg	5	–	–	–	4	–	99	1.00	98	0.98	81	1.04
Madagascar	151	95	40	–	–	74	98	–	70	1.03	36	0.97
Malawi	138	115	42	–	17	47	98	–	81	1.01	31	0.64
Malaysia	9	–	–	–	–	–	99	1.00	88	1.04	64	1.14
Maldives	9	60	2	13	6	58	98	1.03	91	–	–	–
Mali	164	68	54	89	18	8	59	0.90	47	0.86	25	0.74
Malta	12	–	–	–	4	–	100	–	98	–	92	1.03
Martinique	17	50	–	–	–	–	–	–	–	–	–	–
Mauritania	84	68	37	67	–	–	77	1.05	72	1.08	39	1.12
Mauritius	23	–	–	–	–	–	100	1.02	97	1.03	78	1.12
Mexico	62	60	21	–	10	–	99	–	92	1.03	73	1.06
Micronesia (Federated States of)	44	–	–	–	21	–	83	1.02	87	1.06	–	–
Moldova, Republic of	21	26	12	–	9	73	99	–	99	–	88	1.01
Mongolia	31	31	12	–	12	63	99	0.99	92	1.01	88	1.07
Montenegro	10	11	6	–	4	–	100	1.00	94	1.00	88	1.03
Morocco	19	–	14	–	11	–	100	1.00	93	0.97	75	0.96
Mozambique	180	88	53	–	16	49	99	0.97	57	0.87	31	0.76

GENDER, RIGHTS AND HUMAN CAPITAL

Countries, territories, other areas	Adolescent birth rate per 1,000 girls aged 15–19	Unintended pregnancies per 1,000 women aged 15–49[2]	Child marriage by age 18, per cent	Female genital mutilation prevalence among women aged 15–49, per cent	Intimate partner violence, past 12 months, per cent	Decision–making on sexual and reproductive health and reproductive rights, per cent	Total net enrolment rate, primary education, per cent	Gender parity index, total net enrolment rate, primary education	Total net enrolment rate, lower secondary education, per cent	Gender parity index, total net enrolment rate, lower secondary education	Total net enrolment rate, upper secondary education, per cent	Gender parity index, total net enrolment rate, upper secondary education
	2004–2020	2015–2019	2005–2020	2004–2020	2018	2007–2020	2010–2020	2010–2020	2010–2020	2010–2020	2010–2020	2010–2020
Myanmar	28	35	16	–	11	67	98	0.99	79	1.03	57	1.16
Namibia	64	104	7	–	16	71	98	1.03	–	–	–	–
Nepal	63	60	33	–	11	48	96	–	97	1.03	81	1.18
Netherlands	3	18	–	–	5	–	100	1.01	97	1.01	99	1.01
New Caledonia	15	–	–	–	–	–	–	–	–	–	–	–
New Zealand	13	41	–	–	4	–	100	1.01	100	1.00	99	1.03
Nicaragua	103	56	35	–	6	–	96	1.03	88	1.03	64	1.08
Niger	154	49	76	2	13	7	59	0.88	35	0.79	14	0.67
Nigeria	106	68	43	20	13	46	66	0.84	–	–	–	–
North Macedonia	15	23	8	–	4	88	99	1.00	–	–	–	–
Norway	3	34	–	–	4	–	100	1.00	100	0.99	92	1.01
Oman	8	–	4	–	–	–	98	1.02	97	0.99	90	0.90
Pakistan	54	71	18	–	16	40	–	–	–	–	–	–
Palestine[1]	43	–	13	–	19	–	95	1.00	97	1.04	77	1.21
Panama	74	73	26	–	8	79	89	1.02	76	0.97	69	1.06
Papua New Guinea	68	80	27	–	31	57	98	0.94	72	0.90	45	0.80
Paraguay	72	67	22	–	6	–	80	1.00	76	1.01	70	1.05
Peru	44	90	17	–	11	–	98	–	98	1.00	96	0.94
Philippines	36	71	17	–	6	81	97	0.99	89	1.07	80	1.09
Poland	10	29	–	–	3	–	99	1.00	97	0.98	98	1.00
Portugal	7	21	–	–	4	–	100	0.99	100	1.00	100	0.99
Puerto Rico	22	54	–	–	–	–	87	1.04	90	1.07	76	1.05
Qatar	7	–	4	–	–	–	98	1.03	93	0.94	–	–
Réunion	28	52	–	–	–	–	–	–	–	–	–	–
Romania	36	44	–	–	7	–	87	1.00	89	0.99	80	1.03
Russian Federation	22	64	–	–	–	–	100	1.01	100	1.01	98	1.01
Rwanda	41	98	7	–	24	63	94	1.00	96	1.04	50	1.02
Saint Kitts and Nevis	46	–	–	–	–	–	99	–	–	–	96	0.99
Saint Lucia	25	69	24	–	–	–	97	1.06	91	0.99	84	0.95
Saint Vincent and the Grenadines	52	–	–	–	–	–	97	–	98	–	85	1.02
Samoa	39	66	7	–	18	–	100	–	–	–	90	1.11
San Marino	1	–	–	–	–	–	96	0.97	92	1.00	43	0.81
São Tomé and Príncipe	86	130	28	–	18	46	94	1.00	90	1.06	83	1.03
Saudi Arabia	9	–	–	–	–	–	95	1.00	98	0.98	96	0.94
Senegal	68	61	31	25	12	7	75	1.14	40	1.19	20	1.13
Serbia	12	21	6	–	4	96	97	1.00	97	1.00	86	1.03
Seychelles	68	–	–	–	–	–	99	–	97	–	86	1.13
Sierra Leone	102	88	30	86	20	36	98	–	51	0.99	35	0.93
Singapore	2	19	0	–	2	–	100	–	100	1.00	100	1.00
Sint Maarten	–	–	–	–	–	–	97	–	88	1.06	78	0.95
Slovakia	26	27	–	–	6	–	97	1.00	95	1.00	89	1.00
Slovenia	4	33	–	–	3	–	100	1.01	99	1.01	99	1.00
Solomon Islands	78	114	21	–	28	–	93	1.05	–	–	–	–
Somalia	118	100	36	99	–	–	–	–	–	–	–	–
South Africa	41	81	4	–	13	65	89	1.02	90	1.01	79	1.01

GENDER, RIGHTS AND HUMAN CAPITAL

Countries, territories, other areas	Adolescent birth rate per 1,000 girls aged 15–19	Unintended pregnancies per 1,000 women aged 15–49[2]	Child marriage by age 18, per cent	Female genital mutilation prevalence among women aged 15–49, per cent	Intimate partner violence, past 12 months, per cent	Decision–making on sexual and reproductive health and reproductive rights, per cent	Total net enrolment rate, primary education, per cent	Gender parity index, total net enrolment rate, primary education	Total net enrolment rate, lower secondary education, per cent	Gender parity index, total net enrolment rate, lower secondary education	Total net enrolment rate, upper secondary education, per cent	Gender parity index, total net enrolment rate, upper secondary education
	2004–2020	2015–2019	2005-2020	2004–2020	2018	2007–2020	2010–2020	2010–2020	2010–2020	2010–2020	2010–2020	2010–2020
South Sudan	158	54	52	–	27	–	38	0.77	44	0.72	36	0.65
Spain	6	20	–	–	3	–	97	1.00	100	–	99	1.01
Sri Lanka	21	39	10	–	4	–	99	–	100	1.00	84	1.06
Sudan	87	–	34	87	17	–	67	0.93	66	0.97	48	1.08
Suriname	54	67	36	–	8	–	88	1.04	85	1.09	62	1.15
Sweden	4	36	–	–	6	–	100	–	100	–	99	0.99
Switzerland	2	20	–	–	2	–	100	–	99	0.99	81	0.96
Syrian Arab Republic	22	–	13	–	–	–	72	0.98	62	0.97	34	1.00
Tajikistan	54	37	9	–	14	33	99	0.99	94	0.94	61	0.74
Tanzania, United Republic of	139	105	31	10	24	47	84	1.04	28	–	14	0.76
Thailand	23	38	20	–	9	–	–	–	–	–	79	1.00
Timor–Leste, Democratic Republic of	42	50	15	–	28	40	95	1.04	90	1.04	76	1.07
Togo	79	100	25	3	13	30	99	0.98	79	0.85	44	0.64
Tonga	30	49	10	–	17	–	99	–	89	1.15	59	1.33
Trinidad and Tobago	32	84	11	–	8	–	99	0.99	–	–	–	–
Tunisia	7	–	2	–	10	–	99	–	–	–	–	–
Turkey	19	–	15	–	12	–	95	0.99	97	0.99	82	0.97
Turkmenistan	22	23	6	–	–	59	–	–	–	–	–	–
Turks and Caicos Islands	21	–	–	–	–	–	99	–	80	1.06	68	0.90
Tuvalu	27	–	10	–	20	–	83	1.03	67	0.92	35	1.21
Uganda	111	145	34	0	26	62	96	1.03	–	–	–	–
Ukraine	18	27	9	–	9	81	92	1.02	96	1.01	94	1.03
United Arab Emirates	4	–	–	–	–	–	100	–	99	–	98	1.01
United Kingdom	12	36	0	–	4	–	99	1.00	100	1.00	97	1.01
United States of America	17	35	–	–	6	–	99	1.00	100	1.02	96	0.98
United States Virgin Islands	39	–	–	–	–	–	–	–	–	–	–	–
Uruguay	36	41	25	–	4	–	99	1.01	99	1.01	89	1.06
Uzbekistan	19	29	7	–	–	–	99	0.98	99	0.98	86	0.99
Vanuatu	51	87	21	–	29	–	97	0.99	75	1.04	44	1.14
Venezuela (Bolivarian Republic of)	95	–	–	–	9	–	90	1.00	86	1.02	77	1.12
Viet Nam	35	86	11	–	10	–	99	–	–	–	–	–
Western Sahara	–	–	–	–	–	–	–	–	–	–	–	–
Yemen	67	–	32	19	–	–	84	0.88	72	0.85	44	0.59
Zambia	135	123	29	–	28	49	85	1.05	–	–	–	–
Zimbabwe	108	74	34	–	18	60	86	1.02	98	0.95	52	0.90

NOTES

- – Data not available.
- [1] On 29 November 2012, the United Nations General Assembly passed Resolution 67/19, which accorded Palestine "non-member observer State status in the United Nations…"
- [2] Data provided by Guttmacher Institute.

DEFINITIONS OF THE INDICATORS

Adolescent birth rate: Number of births per 1,000 adolescent girls aged 15–19 (SDG indicator 3.7.2).

Unintended pregnancy rate: Estimated annual number of unintended pregnancies per 1,000 women aged 15–49.

Child marriage by age 18: Proportion of women aged 20 to 24 years who were married or in a union before age 18 (SDG indicator 5.3.1).

Female genital mutilation prevalence among women aged 15–49: Proportion of girls aged 15 to 49 years who have undergone female genital mutilation (SDG indicator 5.3.2).

Intimate partner violence, past 12 months: Percentage of ever-partnered women and girls aged 15 to 49 who have experienced physical and/or sexual partner violence in the previous 12 months (SDG indicator 5.2.1).

Decision-making on sexual and reproductive health and reproductive rights: Percentage of women aged 15 to 49 years who are married (or in union), who make their own decisions on three areas – their healthcare, use of contraception, and sexual intercourse with their partners (SDG indicator 5.6.1).

Total net enrolment rate, primary education: Total number of students of the official age group for primary education who are enrolled in any level of education, expressed as a percentage of the corresponding population.

Gender parity index, total net enrolment rate, primary education: Ratio of female to male values of total net enrolment rate for primary education.

Total net enrolment rate, lower secondary education: Total number of students of the official age group for lower secondary education who are enrolled in any level of education, expressed as a percentage of the corresponding population.

Gender parity index, total net enrolment rate, lower secondary education: Ratio of female to male values of total net enrolment rate for lower secondary education.

Total net enrolment rate, upper secondary education: Total number of students of the official age group for upper secondary education who are enrolled in any level of education, expressed as a percentage of the corresponding population.

Gender parity index, total net enrolment rate, upper secondary education: Ratio of female to male values of total net enrolment rate for upper secondary education.

MAIN DATA SOURCES

Adolescent birth rate: United Nations Population Division, 2021.

Unintended pregnancy rate: Bearak, Jonathan and others, 2022. "Country-Specific Estimates of Unintended Pregnancy and Abortion Incidence: A Global Comparative Analysis of Levels in 2015–2019." BMJ Global Health, in press. Methodology information available at https://data.guttmacher.org/countries

Child marriage by age 18: UNICEF, 2021. Regional aggregates calculated by UNFPA based on data from UNICEF.

Female genital mutilation prevalence among women aged 15–49: UNICEF, 2021. Regional aggregates calculated by UNFPA based on data from UNICEF.

Intimate partner violence, past 12 months: Violence Against Women Inter-Agency Group on Estimation and Data (WHO, UN Women, UNICEF, United Nations Statistics Division, United Nations Office on Drugs and Crime, and UNFPA), 2021.

Decision-making on sexual and reproductive health and reproductive rights: UNFPA, 2022.

Total net enrolment rate, primary education: UNESCO Institute for Statistics, 2022.

Gender parity index, total net enrolment rate, primary education: UNESCO Institute for Statistics, 2022.

Total net enrolment rate, lower secondary education: UNESCO Institute for Statistics, 2022.

Gender parity index, total net enrolment rate, lower secondary education: UNESCO Institute for Statistics, 2022.

Total net enrolment rate, upper secondary education: UNESCO Institute for Statistics, 2022.

Gender parity index, total net enrolment rate, upper secondary education: UNESCO Institute for Statistics, 2022.

DEMOGRAPHIC INDICATORS

	POPULATION	POPULATION CHANGE	POPULATION COMPOSITION					FERTILITY	LIFE EXPECTANCY	
	Total population in millions	Average annual rate of population change, per cent	Population aged 0–14, per cent	Population aged 10–19, per cent	Population aged 10–24, per cent	Population aged 15–64, per cent	Population aged 65 and older, per cent	Total fertility rate, per woman	Life expectancy at birth, years, 2022	
World and regional areas	2022	2020–2025	2022	2022	2022	2022	2022	2022	male	female
World	**7,954**	**1.0**	**25**	**16**	**24**	**65**	**10**	**2.4**	**71**	**76**
More developed regions	1,277	0.1	16	11	17	64	20	1.6	77	83
Less developed regions	6,677	1.1	27	17	25	65	8	2.5	70	74
Least developed countries	1,107	2.2	38	22	32	58	4	3.8	64	68
UNFPA regions										
Arab States	393	2.0	34	19	28	61	5	3.2	70	74
Asia and the Pacific	4,149	0.8	23	16	23	68	9	2.1	71	75
Eastern Europe and Central Asia	251	0.5	23	15	21	66	11	2.1	71	78
Latin America and the Caribbean	661	0.8	23	16	24	67	9	2.0	73	79
East and Southern Africa	649	2.5	41	23	32	56	3	4.1	62	67
West and Central Africa	483	2.6	43	23	32	55	3	4.8	58	60
Countries, territories, other areas	2022	2020–2025	2022	2022	2022	2022	2022	2022	male	female
Afghanistan	40.8	2.2	41	25	35	57	3	3.9	64	67
Albania	2.9	-0.3	17	12	19	67	16	1.6	77	80
Algeria	45.4	1.6	31	16	23	62	7	2.8	76	79
Angola	35.0	3.2	46	24	33	52	2	5.2	59	65
Antigua and Barbuda	0.1	0.8	22	14	21	68	10	2.0	76	79
Argentina	46.0	0.9	24	16	23	64	12	2.2	74	80
Armenia	3.0	0.1	21	13	19	67	13	1.8	72	79
Aruba[1]	0.1	0.4	17	13	19	67	16	1.9	74	79
Australia[2]	26.1	1.1	19	12	19	64	17	1.8	82	86
Austria	9.1	0.2	15	10	15	66	20	1.6	80	84
Azerbaijan[3]	10.3	0.7	23	14	20	69	8	2.0	71	76
Bahamas	0.4	0.9	21	16	24	71	8	1.7	72	76
Bahrain	1.8	1.8	18	11	18	79	3	1.9	77	79
Bangladesh	167.9	0.9	26	18	27	69	6	1.9	72	75
Barbados	0.3	0.1	16	12	19	66	18	1.6	78	81
Belarus	9.4	-0.1	18	11	15	66	17	1.7	70	80
Belgium	11.7	0.3	17	12	17	63	20	1.7	80	84
Belize	0.4	1.7	28	19	29	66	5	2.2	72	78
Benin	12.8	2.6	42	23	32	55	3	4.6	61	64
Bhutan	0.8	1.0	24	17	26	69	7	1.9	72	73
Bolivia (Plurinational State of)	12.0	1.3	29	19	28	63	8	2.6	69	75
Bosnia and Herzegovina	3.2	-0.4	14	11	17	67	19	1.2	75	80
Botswana	2.4	1.8	33	20	29	63	5	2.7	67	73
Brazil	215.4	0.6	20	14	22	70	10	1.7	73	80
Brunei Darussalam	0.4	0.8	22	15	22	72	6	1.8	75	78
Bulgaria	6.8	-0.8	15	10	15	63	22	1.6	72	79
Burkina Faso	22.1	2.8	44	24	33	54	2	4.9	62	64
Burundi	12.6	2.9	45	23	32	53	3	5.1	61	64
Cambodia	17.2	1.3	30	19	27	65	5	2.4	68	73
Cameroon, Republic of	27.9	2.5	42	23	33	56	3	4.3	59	62
Canada	38.4	0.8	16	11	17	65	19	1.5	81	85
Cape Verde	0.6	1.0	27	18	26	68	5	2.2	70	77
Central African Republic	5.0	2.0	43	26	36	55	3	4.4	52	57
Chad	17.4	2.9	46	25	34	52	3	5.4	54	57
Chile	19.3	0.1	19	13	20	68	13	1.6	78	83

Countries, territories, other areas	POPULATION Total population in millions 2022	POPULATION CHANGE Average annual rate of population change, per cent 2020–2025	POPULATION COMPOSITION Population aged 0–14, per cent 2022	Population aged 10–19, per cent 2022	Population aged 10–24, per cent 2022	Population aged 15–64, per cent 2022	Population aged 65 and older, per cent 2022	FERTILITY Total fertility rate, per woman 2022	LIFE EXPECTANCY Life expectancy at birth, years, 2022 male	female
China[4]	1,448.5	0.3	18	12	17	70	13	1.7	75	80
China, Hong Kong SAR[5]	7.6	0.7	13	8	12	67	20	1.4	82	88
China, Macao SAR[6]	0.7	1.3	15	8	12	72	14	1.3	82	88
Colombia	51.5	0.4	22	15	24	69	10	1.7	75	80
Comoros	0.9	2.1	39	22	31	58	3	4.0	63	67
Congo, Democratic Republic of the	95.2	3.0	45	24	32	52	3	5.5	60	63
Congo, Republic of the	5.8	2.4	41	23	32	57	3	4.2	64	67
Costa Rica	5.2	0.8	20	14	21	69	11	1.7	78	83
Côte d'Ivoire	27.7	2.5	41	23	33	56	3	4.4	57	60
Croatia	4.1	-0.5	14	10	16	64	22	1.4	76	82
Cuba	11.3	-0.1	16	11	17	68	16	1.6	77	81
Curaçao[1]	0.2	0.4	18	13	19	64	19	1.7	76	82
Cyprus[7]	1.2	0.6	16	12	19	69	15	1.3	79	83
Czechia	10.7	0.1	16	10	15	64	21	1.7	77	82
Denmark[8]	5.8	0.4	16	11	18	63	21	1.8	79	83
Djibouti	1.0	1.3	28	18	27	67	5	2.5	66	70
Dominica	0.1	0.2	–	–	–	–	–	–	–	–
Dominican Republic	11.1	0.9	27	18	26	65	8	2.2	72	78
Ecuador	18.1	1.2	27	17	26	65	8	2.3	75	80
Egypt	106.2	1.8	34	19	27	61	6	3.2	70	75
El Salvador	6.6	0.5	26	17	27	65	9	2.0	69	78
Equatorial Guinea	1.5	3.1	37	20	29	61	2	4.2	59	61
Eritrea	3.7	1.7	40	25	33	56	4	3.8	65	70
Estonia	1.3	-0.3	16	11	15	63	21	1.6	75	83
Eswatini	1.2	1.1	36	24	33	60	4	2.8	57	66
Ethiopia	120.8	2.4	39	23	33	57	4	3.9	66	70
Fiji	0.9	0.7	29	18	26	65	6	2.7	66	70
Finland[9]	5.6	0.1	15	11	17	61	23	1.4	80	85
France[10]	65.6	0.2	17	12	18	61	21	1.8	80	86
French Guiana[11]	0.3	2.4	32	19	27	63	6	3.2	78	83
French Polynesia[11]	0.3	0.6	22	15	23	69	10	1.9	76	80
Gabon	2.3	2.2	37	19	27	59	4	3.8	65	69
Gambia	2.6	2.8	44	23	32	54	3	4.9	62	65
Georgia[12]	4.0	-0.3	20	12	18	64	16	2.0	70	79
Germany	83.9	-0.1	14	9	15	64	22	1.6	80	84
Ghana	32.4	2.0	37	21	30	60	3	3.7	64	66
Greece	10.3	-0.5	13	10	15	64	23	1.3	80	85
Grenada	0.1	0.4	24	15	22	66	10	2.0	70	75
Guadeloupe[11]	0.4	0.0	18	14	21	62	21	2.1	79	86
Guam[13]	0.2	0.8	23	16	24	65	11	2.2	78	84
Guatemala	18.6	1.8	33	21	31	62	5	2.7	72	78
Guinea	13.9	2.7	42	24	34	55	3	4.4	62	63
Guinea-Bissau	2.1	2.3	41	23	32	56	3	4.2	57	61
Guyana	0.8	0.5	27	18	27	65	8	2.4	67	73
Haiti	11.7	1.2	32	20	30	63	5	2.8	63	67
Honduras	10.2	1.5	30	20	30	65	5	2.3	73	78
Hungary	9.6	-0.3	14	10	15	65	21	1.5	74	81
Iceland	0.3	0.6	19	13	20	65	17	1.7	82	85

DEMOGRAPHIC INDICATORS

Countries, territories, other areas	POPULATION Total population in millions	POPULATION CHANGE Average annual rate of population change, per cent	POPULATION COMPOSITION Population aged 0–14, per cent	Population aged 10–19, per cent	Population aged 10–24, per cent	Population aged 15–64, per cent	Population aged 65 and older, per cent	FERTILITY Total fertility rate, per woman	LIFE EXPECTANCY Life expectancy at birth, years, 2022 male	female
	2022	2020–2025	2022	2022	2022	2022	2022	2022	male	female
India	1,406.6	0.9	25	18	27	68	7	2.1	69	72
Indonesia	279.1	1.0	25	17	25	68	7	2.2	70	75
Iran (Islamic Republic of)	86.0	1.1	25	14	21	68	7	2.1	76	78
Iraq	42.2	2.3	37	22	31	60	4	3.5	69	73
Ireland	5.0	0.7	20	14	20	65	15	1.8	81	84
Israel	8.9	1.5	28	17	24	60	13	2.9	82	85
Italy	60.3	-0.2	13	10	14	64	24	1.3	82	86
Jamaica	3.0	0.4	23	15	24	68	10	1.9	73	77
Japan	125.6	-0.4	12	9	14	59	29	1.4	82	88
Jordan	10.3	0.3	31	21	31	64	4	2.6	73	77
Kazakhstan	19.2	1.0	29	16	21	63	8	2.6	70	78
Kenya	56.2	2.2	37	24	33	60	3	3.3	65	70
Kiribati	0.1	1.6	36	20	29	60	5	3.4	65	73
Korea, Democratic People's Republic of	26.0	0.4	20	13	21	70	10	1.9	69	76
Korea, Republic of	51.3	0.0	12	9	15	71	17	1.1	80	86
Kuwait	4.4	1.1	21	14	19	76	4	2.0	75	77
Kyrgyzstan	6.7	1.4	33	18	25	62	5	2.8	68	76
Lao People's Democratic Republic	7.5	1.3	31	20	29	64	5	2.5	67	71
Latvia	1.8	-1.0	17	10	14	62	21	1.7	71	80
Lebanon	6.7	-1.3	24	16	24	68	8	2.0	77	81
Lesotho	2.2	0.8	32	20	29	63	5	3.0	52	59
Liberia	5.3	2.4	40	23	32	57	3	4.1	64	66
Libya	7.0	1.1	27	18	25	68	5	2.1	71	76
Lithuania	2.7	-1.0	16	9	14	63	22	1.7	71	82
Luxembourg	0.6	1.1	16	11	17	69	15	1.4	81	85
Madagascar	29.2	2.6	40	23	32	57	3	3.9	66	70
Malawi	20.2	2.7	42	25	34	55	3	3.9	62	69
Malaysia[14]	33.2	1.2	23	15	24	69	8	1.9	75	79
Maldives	0.5	-0.7	20	12	19	76	4	1.8	78	81
Mali	21.5	2.9	46	25	34	51	3	5.5	60	61
Malta	0.4	0.3	15	9	15	63	22	1.5	81	85
Martinique[11]	0.4	-0.2	15	12	19	62	23	1.8	80	86
Mauritania	4.9	2.6	39	22	31	57	3	4.3	64	67
Mauritius[15]	1.3	0.1	16	13	20	70	14	1.3	72	79
Mexico	131.6	1.0	25	17	25	67	8	2.0	73	78
Micronesia (Federated States of)	0.1	1.0	31	20	29	64	5	2.9	67	70
Moldova, Republic of[16]	4.0	-0.3	16	11	16	71	14	1.3	68	76
Mongolia	3.4	1.4	31	16	23	64	5	2.8	66	75
Montenegro	0.6	0.0	18	12	19	66	17	1.7	75	80
Morocco	37.8	1.1	26	17	24	66	8	2.3	76	79
Mozambique	33.1	2.8	44	24	34	54	3	4.6	59	65
Myanmar	55.2	0.8	25	18	26	69	7	2.1	65	71
Namibia	2.6	1.8	37	21	30	60	4	3.2	62	68
Nepal	30.2	1.7	27	20	30	67	6	1.8	70	73
Netherlands[17]	17.2	0.2	15	11	17	64	21	1.7	81	84
New Caledonia[11]	0.3	0.9	21	15	23	68	10	1.9	76	81
New Zealand[18]	4.9	0.8	19	13	19	64	17	1.8	81	84

	POPULATION	POPULATION CHANGE	POPULATION COMPOSITION					FERTILITY	LIFE EXPECTANCY	
	Total population in millions	Average annual rate of population change, per cent	Population aged 0–14, per cent	Population aged 10–19, per cent	Population aged 10–24, per cent	Population aged 15–64, per cent	Population aged 65 and older, per cent	Total fertility rate, per woman	Life expectancy at birth, years, 2022	
Countries, territories, other areas	2022	2020–2025	2022	2022	2022	2022	2022	2022	male	female
Nicaragua	6.8	1.1	29	19	27	65	6	2.3	72	79
Niger	26.1	3.7	49	25	33	48	3	6.6	62	65
Nigeria	216.7	2.5	43	23	32	54	3	5.1	55	57
North Macedonia	2.1	-0.1	16	11	17	69	15	1.5	74	78
Norway[19]	5.5	0.8	17	12	18	65	18	1.7	81	85
Oman	5.3	1.7	23	12	18	74	3	2.6	77	81
Pakistan	229.5	1.8	34	20	30	61	5	3.3	67	69
Palestine[20]	5.3	2.3	38	22	31	59	3	3.4	73	76
Panama	4.4	1.4	26	17	25	65	9	2.4	76	82
Papua New Guinea	9.3	1.9	35	21	31	62	4	3.4	64	67
Paraguay	7.3	1.2	28	18	27	65	7	2.3	73	77
Peru	33.7	0.9	25	15	23	66	9	2.2	75	80
Philippines	112.5	1.3	29	19	28	65	6	2.4	68	76
Poland	37.7	-0.2	15	10	15	65	20	1.5	75	83
Portugal	10.1	-0.3	13	10	15	64	24	1.3	80	85
Puerto Rico[13]	2.8	0.3	14	14	20	64	22	1.2	77	84
Qatar	3.0	1.6	14	9	17	84	2	1.8	80	82
Réunion[11]	0.9	0.7	22	15	23	65	14	2.2	78	84
Romania	19.0	-0.5	15	11	16	65	20	1.6	73	80
Russian Federation	145.8	-0.1	19	11	16	65	17	1.8	68	78
Rwanda	13.6	2.4	39	22	31	58	3	3.8	68	72
Saint Kitts and Nevis	0.1	0.6	–	–	–	–	–	–	–	–
Saint Lucia	0.2	0.4	18	13	21	72	11	1.4	75	78
Saint Vincent and the Grenadines	0.1	0.2	21	15	24	68	10	1.8	71	76
Samoa	0.2	1.1	37	21	30	58	5	3.7	72	76
San Marino	0.0	0.2	–	–	–	–	–	–	–	–
São Tomé and Príncipe	0.2	1.9	41	25	34	56	3	4.1	68	73
Saudi Arabia	35.8	1.4	24	14	21	72	4	2.2	74	77
Senegal	17.7	2.6	42	23	32	55	3	4.4	67	71
Serbia[21]	8.7	-0.5	15	11	17	65	20	1.4	74	79
Seychelles	0.1	0.5	24	15	21	68	9	2.4	70	78
Sierra Leone	8.3	2.0	40	23	33	57	3	3.9	55	57
Singapore	5.9	0.8	12	8	14	72	15	1.2	82	86
Sint Maarten[1]	0.0	1.2	–	–	–	–	–	–	–	–
Slovakia	5.5	0.0	16	10	15	67	18	1.6	75	81
Slovenia	2.1	-0.1	15	10	14	63	22	1.6	79	84
Solomon Islands	0.7	2.4	40	22	31	57	4	4.2	72	75
Somalia	16.8	2.9	46	25	34	51	3	5.7	57	60
South Africa	60.8	1.1	28	18	26	66	6	2.3	61	68
South Sudan	11.6	2.1	41	23	33	56	3	4.4	57	60
Spain[22]	46.7	-0.1	14	10	15	65	21	1.4	81	87
Sri Lanka	21.6	0.3	23	16	23	65	12	2.1	74	81
Sudan	46.0	2.4	39	23	32	57	4	4.2	64	68
Suriname	0.6	0.8	26	17	25	66	7	2.3	69	75
Sweden	10.2	0.6	18	11	17	62	21	1.8	82	85
Switzerland	8.8	0.6	15	10	15	65	20	1.6	82	86
Syrian Arab Republic	19.4	5.5	31	18	26	65	5	2.7	72	79
Tajikistan	10.0	2.0	37	19	27	59	4	3.4	69	74

DEMOGRAPHIC INDICATORS

	POPULATION	POPULATION CHANGE	POPULATION COMPOSITION					FERTILITY	LIFE EXPECTANCY	
	Total population in millions	Average annual rate of population change, per cent	Population aged 0–14, per cent	Population aged 10–19, per cent	Population aged 10–24, per cent	Population aged 15–64, per cent	Population aged 65 and older, per cent	Total fertility rate, per woman	Life expectancy at birth, years, 2022	
Countries, territories, other areas	2022	2020–2025	2022	2022	2022	2022	2022	2022	male	female
Tanzania, United Republic of[23]	63.3	2.9	43	24	33	54	3	4.7	65	68
Thailand	70.1	0.2	16	12	18	70	14	1.5	74	81
Timor-Leste, Democratic Republic of	1.4	1.9	36	22	32	59	4	3.7	68	72
Togo	8.7	2.3	40	23	32	57	3	4.1	61	63
Tonga	0.1	0.9	34	22	31	60	6	3.4	69	73
Trinidad and Tobago	1.4	0.2	20	14	20	68	12	1.7	71	77
Tunisia	12.0	0.9	24	14	21	66	10	2.1	75	79
Turkey	85.6	0.6	23	16	24	67	10	2.0	75	81
Turkmenistan	6.2	1.3	31	17	25	64	5	2.6	65	72
Turks and Caicos Islands	0.0	1.3	–	–	–	–	–	–	–	–
Tuvalu	0.0	1.1	–	–	–	–	–	–	–	–
Uganda	48.4	2.7	45	25	35	53	2	4.5	62	67
Ukraine[24]	43.2	-0.6	16	11	15	67	18	1.4	68	77
United Arab Emirates	10.1	0.9	15	9	17	83	2	1.3	78	80
United Kingdom[25]	68.5	0.4	18	12	17	63	19	1.7	80	83
United States of America[26]	334.8	0.6	18	13	19	65	17	1.8	77	82
United States Virgin Islands[13]	0.1	-0.3	19	14	20	60	22	2.0	79	83
Uruguay	3.5	0.3	20	14	21	64	16	1.9	75	82
Uzbekistan	34.4	1.2	29	17	24	66	5	2.3	70	74
Vanuatu	0.3	2.3	38	22	30	59	4	3.6	69	73
Venezuela (Bolivarian Republic of)	29.3	2.0	26	18	26	66	8	2.2	69	76
Viet Nam	99.0	0.8	23	14	21	68	9	2.0	72	80
Western Sahara	0.6	2.2	27	16	25	69	4	2.3	69	73
Yemen	31.2	2.1	38	23	32	59	3	3.5	65	68
Zambia	19.5	2.8	43	25	34	55	2	4.4	62	68
Zimbabwe	15.3	1.6	41	25	34	56	3	3.3	60	64

DEMOGRAPHIC INDICATORS

NOTES

– Data not available.

[1] For statistical purposes, the data for Netherlands do not include this area.

[2] Including Christmas Island, Cocos Keeling Islands and Norfolk Island.

[3] Including Nagorno-Karabakh.

[4] For statistical purposes, the data for China do not include Hong Kong and Macao, Special Administrative Regions (SAR) of China, or Taiwan Province of China.

[5] As of 1 July 1997, Hong Kong became a Special Administrative Region (SAR) of China. For statistical purposes, the data for China do not include this area.

[6] As of 20 December 1999, Macao became a Special Administrative Region (SAR) of China. For statistical purposes, the data for China do not include this area.

[7] Refers to the whole country.

[8] For statistical purposes, the data for Denmark do not include Faroe Islands or Greenland.

[9] Including Åland Islands.

[10] For statistical purposes, the data for France do not include French Guiana, French Polynesia, Guadeloupe, Martinique, Mayotte, New Caledonia, Réunion, Saint Pierre and Miquelon, Saint Barthélemy, Saint Martin (French part) or Wallis and Futuna Islands.

[11] For statistical purposes, the data for France do not include this area.

[12] Including Abkhazia and South Ossetia.

[13] For statistical purposes, the data for United States of America do not include this area.

[14] Including Sabah and Sarawak.

[15] Including Agalega, Rodrigues and Saint Brandon.

[16] Including Transnistria.

[17] For statistical purposes, the data for Netherlands do not include Aruba, Bonaire, Sint Eustatius and Saba, Curaçao or Sint Maarten (Dutch part).

[18] For statistical purposes, the data for New Zealand do not include Cook Islands, Niue or Tokelau.

[19] Including Svalbard and Jan Mayen Islands.

[20] Including East Jerusalem.

[21] Including Kosovo.

[22] Including Canary Islands, Ceuta and Melilla.

[23] Including Zanzibar.

[24] Refers to the territory of the country at the time of the 2001 census.

[25] Refers to the United Kingdom of Great Britain and Northern Ireland. For statistical purposes, the data for United Kingdom do not include Anguilla, Bermuda, British Virgin Islands, Cayman Islands, Channel Islands, Falkland Islands (Malvinas), Gibraltar, Isle of Man, Montserrat, Saint Helena or Turks and Caicos Islands.

[26] For statistical purposes, the data for United States of America do not include American Samoa, Guam, Northern Mariana Islands, Puerto Rico or United States Virgin Islands.

DEFINITIONS OF THE INDICATORS

Total population: Estimated size of national populations at mid-year.

Average annual rate of population change: Average exponential rate of growth of the population over a given period, based on a medium variant projection.

Population aged 0–14, per cent: Proportion of the population between age 0 and age 14.

Population aged 10–19, per cent: Proportion of the population between age 10 and age 19.

Population aged 10–24, per cent: Proportion of the population between age 10 and age 24.

Population aged 15–64, per cent: Proportion of the population between age 15 and age 64.

Population aged 65 and older, per cent: Proportion of the population aged 65 years and older.

Total fertility rate: Number of children who would be born per woman if she lived to the end of her childbearing years and bore children at each age in accordance with prevailing age-specific fertility rates.

Life expectancy at birth: Number of years newborn children would live if subject to the mortality risks prevailing for the cross section of population at the time of their birth.

MAIN DATA SOURCES

Total population: United Nations Population Division, 2019.

Average annual rate of population change: United Nations Population Division, 2019.

Population aged 0–14, per cent: UNFPA calculation based on data from United Nations Population Division, 2019.

Population aged 10–19, per cent: UNFPA calculation based on data from United Nations Population Division, 2019.

Population aged 10–24, per cent: UNFPA calculation based on data from United Nations Population Division, 2019.

Population aged 15–64, per cent: UNFPA calculation based on data from United Nations Population Division, 2019.

Population aged 65 and older, per cent: UNFPA calculation based on data from United Nations Population Division, 2019.

Total fertility rate: United Nations Population Division, 2019.

Life expectancy at birth: United Nations Population Division, 2019.

Technical notes

The statistical tables in the *State of World Population 2022* include indicators that track progress toward the goals of the Framework of Actions for the follow-up to the Programme of Action of the International Conference on Population and Development (ICPD), and the Sustainable Development Goals (SDGs) in the areas of maternal health, access to education, reproductive and sexual health. In addition, these tables include a variety of demographic indicators. The statistical tables support UNFPA's focus on progress and results towards delivering a world where every pregnancy is wanted, every birth is safe, and every young person's potential is fulfilled.

Different national authorities and international organizations may employ different methodologies in gathering, extrapolating or analyzing data. To facilitate the international comparability of data, UNFPA relies on the standard methodologies employed by the main sources of data. In some instances, therefore, the data in these tables differ from those generated by national authorities. Data presented in the tables are not comparable to the data in previous *State of the World Population* reports due to regional classifications updates, methodological updates, and revisions of time series data.

The statistical tables draw on nationally representative household surveys such as Demographic and Health Surveys (DHS) and Multiple Indicator Cluster Surveys (MICS), United Nations organizations estimates, and inter-agency estimates. They also include the latest population estimates and projections from *World Population Prospects: The 2019 Revision*, and *Model-based Estimates and Projections of Family Planning Indicators 2021* (United Nations Department of Economic and Social Affairs, Population Division). Data are accompanied by definitions, sources and notes. The statistical tables in the *State of World Population 2022* generally reflect information available as of February 2022.

Tracking Progress Towards ICPD Goals
Sexual and Reproductive Health

Maternal mortality ratio (MMR) (deaths per 100,000 live births) and range of MMR uncertainty (UI 80%), lower and upper estimates. Source: United Nations Maternal Mortality Estimation Inter-agency Group (WHO, UNICEF, UNFPA, The World Bank and the United Nations Population Division), 2019. This indicator presents the number of maternal deaths during a given time period per 100,000 live births during the same time period. The estimates are produced by the Maternal Mortality Estimation Inter-agency Group (MMEIG) using data from vital registration systems, household surveys and population censuses. Estimates and methodologies are reviewed regularly by MMEIG and other agencies and academic institutions and are revised where necessary, as part of the ongoing process of improving maternal mortality data. Estimates should not be compared with previous inter-agency estimates (SDG indicator 3.1.1).

Births attended by skilled health personnel, per cent. Source: Joint global database on skilled attendance at birth, 2021, UNICEF and WHO. Regional aggregates calculated by UNFPA based on data from the joint global database. Percentage of births attended by skilled health personnel (doctors, nurses or midwives) is the percentage of deliveries attended by health personnel trained in providing life-saving obstetric care, including giving the necessary supervision, care and advice to women during pregnancy, labour and the post-partum period; conducting deliveries on their own; and caring for newborns (SDG indicator 3.1.2). Traditional birth attendants, even if they receive a short training course, are not included.

Number of new HIV infections, all ages, per 1,000 uninfected population. Source: UNAIDS 2021 HIV Estimates. Number of new HIV infections per 1,000 person-years among the uninfected population (SDG indicator 3.3.1).

Contraceptive prevalence rate, women aged 15–49, per cent, any method. Source: United Nations Population Division, 2021. Percentage of women aged 15 to 49 years who are currently using any method of contraception. Model-based estimates are based on data that are derived from sample survey reports. Survey data estimate the proportion of all women of reproductive age, and married women (including women in consensual unions), currently using any method of contraception.

Contraceptive prevalence rate, women aged 15–49, per cent modern methods. Source: United Nations Population Division, 2021. Percentage of women aged 15 to 49 years who are currently using any modern method of contraception. Model-based estimates are based on data that are derived from sample survey reports. Survey data estimate the proportion of all women of reproductive age, and married women (including women in consensual unions), currently using any modern methods of contraception. Modern methods of contraception include female and male sterilization, the intrauterine device (IUD), the implant, injectables, oral contraceptive pills, male and female condoms, vaginal barrier methods (including the diaphragm, cervical cap and spermicidal foam, jelly, cream and sponge), lactational amenorrhea method (LAM), emergency contraception and other modern methods not reported separately (e.g., the contraceptive patch or vaginal ring).

Unmet need for family planning, women aged 15–49, per cent. Source: United Nations Population Division, 2021. Percentage of women aged 15 to 49 years who want to stop or delay childbearing but are not using a method of contraception. Model-based estimates are based on data that are derived from sample survey reports. Women who are using a traditional method of contraception are not considered as having an unmet need for family planning. All women or all married and in-union women are assumed to be sexually active and at risk of pregnancy. The assumption of universal exposure among all women or all married or in-union women may lead to lower estimates compared to the actual risks among the exposed. It might be possible, in particular at low levels of contraceptive prevalence that, when contraceptive prevalence increases, unmet need for family planning also increases. Both indicators, therefore, need to be interpreted together.

Proportion of demand for family planning satisfied with modern methods, all women aged 15-49. Source: United Nations Population Division, 2021. Percentage of total demand for family planning among women aged 15 to 49 years that is satisfied by the use of modern contraception (SDG indicator 3.7.1). This number is calculated by dividing modern contraceptive prevalence by total demand for family planning. Total demand for family planning is the sum of contraceptive prevalence and unmet need for family planning.

Laws and regulations that guarantee access to sexual and reproductive health care, information and education, per cent.
Source: UNFPA, 2022. The extent to which countries have national laws and regulations that guarantee full and equal access to women and men aged 15 years and older to sexual and reproductive health care, information and education (SDG indicator 5.6.2).

Universal health coverage (UHC) service coverage index.
Source: WHO, 2021. Average coverage of essential services based on tracer interventions that include reproductive, maternal, newborn and child health, infectious diseases, non-communicable diseases and service capacity and access, among the general and the most disadvantaged population (SDG indicator 3.8.1).

Gender, Rights and Human Capital

Adolescent birth rate per 1,000 girls aged 15-19.
Source: United Nations Population Division, 2021. Number of births per 1,000 adolescent girls aged 15 to 19 years (SDG indicator 3.7.2). The adolescent birth rate represents the risk of childbearing among adolescent women aged 15 to 19 years. For civil registration, rates are subject to limitations which depend on the completeness of birth registration, the treatment of infants born alive but which die before registration or within the first 24 hours of life, the quality of the reported information relating to the age of the mother and the inclusion of births from previous periods. The population estimates may suffer from limitations connected to age misreporting and coverage. For survey and census data, both the numerator and denominator come from the same population. The main limitations concern age misreporting, birth omissions, misreporting the date of birth of the child and sampling variability in the case of surveys.

Unintended pregnancies per 1,000 women aged 15-49
Source: Bearak and others, 2022. As this report went to press, these estimates and methodology were planned for release at the Guttmacher Institute's Data Center, at https://data.guttmacher.org/countries.

Child marriage by age 18, per cent. Source: UNICEF, 2021. Regional aggregates calculated by UNFPA based on data from UNICEF. Proportion of women aged 20 to 24 years who were married or in a union before the age of 18 (SDG indicator 5.3.1).

Female genital mutilation prevalence among girls aged 15-49, per cent.
Source: UNICEF, 2021. Regional aggregates calculated by UNFPA based on data from UNICEF. Proportion of girls aged 15 to 49 years who have undergone female genital mutilation (SDG indicator 5.3.2).

Intimate partner violence, past 12 months, per cent.
Source: Violence Against Women Inter-Agency Group on Estimation and Data (WHO, UN Women, UNICEF, United Nations Statistics Division, United Nations Office on Drugs and Crime, and UNFPA), 2021. Percentage of ever-partnered women and girls aged 15 to 49 years who have experienced physical and/or sexual partner violence in the previous 12 months (SDG indicator 5.2.1).

Decision-making on sexual and reproductive health and reproductive rights, per cent.
Source: UNFPA, 2022. Percentage of women aged 15 to 49 years who are married (or in union), who make their own decisions on three areas — their health care, use of contraception, and sexual intercourse with their partners (SDG indicator 5.6.1).

Total net enrolment rate, primary education, per cent.
Source: UNESCO Institute for Statistics, 2022. Total number of students of the official age group for primary education who are enrolled in any level of education, expressed as a percentage of the corresponding population.

Gender parity index, total net enrolment rate, primary education.
Source: UNESCO Institute for Statistics, 2022. Ratio of female to male values of total net enrolment rate for primary education.

Total net enrolment rate, lower secondary education, per cent.
Source: UNESCO Institute for Statistics, 2022. Total number of students of the official age group for lower secondary education who are enrolled in any level of education, expressed as a percentage of the corresponding population.

Gender parity index, total net enrolment rate, lower secondary education.
Source: UNESCO Institute for Statistics, 2022. Ratio of female to male values of total net enrolment rate for lower secondary education.

Total net enrolment rate, upper secondary education, per cent.
Source: UNESCO Institute for Statistics, 2022. Total number of students of the official age group for upper secondary education who are enrolled in any level of education, expressed as a percentage of the corresponding population.

Gender parity index, total net enrolment rate, upper secondary education.
Source: UNESCO Institute for Statistics, 2022. Ratio of female to male values of total net enrolment rate for upper secondary education.

Demographic indicators

Population
Total population in millions.
Source: United Nations Population Division, 2019. Estimated size of national populations at mid-year.

Population change
Average annual rate of population change, per cent.
Source: United Nations Population Division, 2019. Average exponential rate of growth of the population over a given period, based on a medium variant projection.

Population composition

Population aged 0-14, per cent.
Source: UNFPA calculation based on data from the United Nations Population Division, 2019. Proportion of the population between age 0 and age 14.

Population aged 10-19, per cent.
Source: UNFPA calculation based on data from the United Nations Population Division, 2019. Proportion of the population between age 10 and age 19.

Population aged 10-24, per cent.
Source: UNFPA calculation based on data from the United Nations Population Division, 2019. Proportion of the population between age 10 and age 24.

Population aged 15-64, per cent.
Source: UNFPA calculation based on data from the United Nations Population Division, 2019. Proportion of the population between age 15 and age 64.

Population aged 65 and older, per cent.
Source: UNFPA calculation based on data from the United Nations Population Division, 2019. Proportion of the population aged 65 years and older.

Fertility

Total fertility rate, per woman.
Source: United Nations Population Division, 2019. Number of children who would be born per woman if she lived to the end of her childbearing years and bore children at each age in accordance with prevailing age-specific fertility rates.

Life expectancy

Life expectancy at birth, years.
Source: United Nations Population Division, 2019. Number of years newborn children would live if subject to the mortality risks prevailing for the cross section of population at the time of their birth.

Regional classifications

UNFPA regional aggregates presented at the end of the statistical tables are calculated using data from countries and areas as classified below.

Arab States Region
Algeria; Djibouti; Egypt; Iraq; Jordan; Lebanon; Libya; Morocco; Oman; Palestine; Somalia; Sudan; Syrian Arab Republic; Tunisia; Yemen

Asia and the Pacific Region
Afghanistan; Bangladesh; Bhutan; Cambodia; China; Cook Islands; Fiji; India; Indonesia; Iran (Islamic Republic of); Kiribati; Korea, Democratic People's Republic of; Lao People's Democratic Republic; Malaysia; Maldives; Marshall Islands; Micronesia (Federated States of); Mongolia; Myanmar; Nauru; Nepal; Niue; Pakistan; Palau; Papua New Guinea; Philippines; Samoa; Solomon Islands; Sri Lanka; Thailand; Timor-Leste, Democratic Republic of; Tokelau; Tonga; Tuvalu; Vanuatu; Viet Nam.

Eastern Europe and Central Asia Region
Albania; Armenia; Azerbaijan; Belarus; Bosnia and Herzegovina; Georgia; Kazakhstan; Kyrgyzstan; Moldova, North Macedonia; Republic of; Serbia; Tajikistan; Turkey; Turkmenistan; Ukraine; Uzbekistan.

East and Southern Africa Region
Angola; Botswana; Burundi; Comoros; Congo, Democratic Republic of the; Eritrea; Eswatini; Ethiopia; Kenya; Lesotho; Madagascar; Malawi; Mauritius; Mozambique; Namibia; Rwanda; South Africa; South Sudan; Tanzania, United Republic of; Uganda; Zambia; Zimbabwe.

Latin America and the Caribbean Region
Anguilla; Antigua and Barbuda; Argentina; Aruba; Bahamas; Barbados; Belize; Bermuda; Bolivia (Plurinational State of); Brazil; British Virgin Islands; Cayman Islands; Chile; Colombia; Costa Rica; Cuba; Curaçao; Dominica; Dominican Republic; Ecuador; El Salvador; Grenada; Guatemala; Guyana; Haiti; Honduras; Jamaica; Mexico; Montserrat; Nicaragua; Panama; Paraguay; Peru; Saint Kitts and Nevis; Saint Lucia; Saint Vincent and the Grenadines; Sint Maarten; Suriname; Trinidad and Tobago; Turks and Caicos Islands; Uruguay; Venezuela (Bolivarian Republic of).

West and Central Africa Region
Benin; Burkina Faso; Cameroon, Republic of; Cape Verde; Central African Republic; Chad; Congo, Republic of the; Côte d'Ivoire; Equatorial Guinea; Gabon; Gambia; Ghana; Guinea; Guinea-Bissau; Liberia; Mali; Mauritania; Niger; Nigeria; São Tomé and Príncipe; Senegal; Sierra Leone; Togo.

More developed regions are intended for statistical purposes and do not express a judgment about the stage reached by a particular country or area in the development process, comprising UNPD regions Europe, Northern America, Australia/New Zealand and Japan.

Less developed regions are intended for statistical purposes and do not express a judgment about the stage reached by a particular country or area in the development process, comprising all UNPD regions of Africa, Asia (except Japan), Latin America and the Caribbean plus Melanesia, Micronesia and Polynesia.

The least developed countries, as defined by the United Nations General Assembly in its resolutions (59/209, 59/210, 60/33, 62/97, 64/L.55, 67/L.43, 64/295 and 68/18) included 46 countries (as of January 2022): 33 in Africa, 8 in Asia, 4 in Oceania and one in Latin America and the Caribbean — Afghanistan, Angola, Bangladesh, Benin, Bhutan, Burkina Faso, Burundi, Cambodia, Central African Republic, Chad, Comoros, Democratic Republic of the Congo, Djibouti, Eritrea, Ethiopia, Gambia, Guinea, Guinea-Bissau, Haiti, Kiribati, Lao People's Democratic Republic, Lesotho, Liberia, Madagascar, Malawi, Mali, Mauritania, Mozambique, Myanmar, Nepal, Niger, Rwanda, São Tomé and Príncipe, Senegal, Sierra Leone, Solomon Islands, Somalia, South Sudan, Sudan, Democratic Republic of Timor-Leste, Togo, Tuvalu, Uganda, United Republic of Tanzania, Yemen and Zambia. These countries are also included in the less developed regions. Further information is available at https://www.un.org/en/conferences/least-developed-countries.

Note on correlations between GNI, educational attainment and unintended pregnancy rates (page 22)

Correlations in 2015–2019

		Human development index in 2019	Mean years of education (both sexes) in 2019	Gross national income per capita in 2019	Gender inequality index in 2019
Unintended pregnancy	Global	***	***	***	***
	LMIC	***	***	***	***
	HIC	***	*	***	***
	Sub-Saharan Africa	**	**		
% UP ending in abortion	Global				
	LMIC	*	*	*	***
	HIC	*	**		

***: p-value < 0.001
**: 0.001 <= p-value <0.01
* : 0.01 <= p-value <0.05

Red: negative correlation
Green: positive correlation
White: no significant correlation

1. Global observations: Globally, higher levels of social and economic development, as measured by HDI, GNI and education attainment, were strongly correlated with lower incidence of unintended pregnancy. One explanation is that countries with higher development scores are likely those where contraceptive services are more widely accessible and where women face fewer cultural barriers to managing their fertility preferences. A notably different pattern was observed in sub-Saharan Africa, where social and economic development were associated with higher unintended pregnancy rates. This suggests that access to, and use of, means to control fertility, including contraceptive services, have not kept pace with the social and economic development that may have led women and couples to want fewer children in these countries.

2. Pregnancy outcomes: While both low- to middle-income countries outside of sub-Saharan Africa and high-income countries saw a relationship between greater socioeconomic development and lower rates of unintended pregnancy, the pregnancy outcomes tended to differ. In high-income countries, stronger development scores were associated with a lower likelihood that pregnancies would be terminated, while lower development scores were linked to a greater likelihood of abortion. This finding might have been driven by former Soviet bloc countries, which score lower on development indicators and where abortion rates tend to be higher than in other countries with high incomes. However, the negative correlation persisted after removing former Soviet bloc countries from the analysis. An alternate hypothesis is that, in countries with higher levels of development, the women who are most strongly motivated to avoid having a child are better able to avoid pregnancy, including through the use of contraception. It is also possible that social and economic safety nets make it easier for women to carry an unintended pregnancy to term in more developed countries.

In low- and middle-income countries, higher levels of social and economic development were associated with a higher proportion of unintended pregnancies being aborted (even after controlling for differences in the legal status of abortion). This finding lends itself to the hypothesis that, as opportunity costs associated with childbearing increase, women who experience an unintended pregnancy are more strongly motivated to avoid having a child. The same pattern was true with respect to trends over the 30-year period between 1990 and 2019 in these countries: improvements in development scores at the country level were associated with increases in the proportion of unintended pregnancies that were terminated.

3. GNI and education by sex: Per capita GNI scores and levels of educational attainment among females were *not* more strongly correlated with the incidence of unintended pregnancy or the proportion aborted than were male scores for per capita GNI and educational attainment.

4. GII and adolescent birth rate: It must be noted that the GII includes adolescent birth rate as a component of its score, and because many adolescent pregnancies are unintended, this could lead to an overestimation of the strength of the correlation between GII and unintended pregnancy. However, it is also true that many adolescent births might not be classified as unintended pregnancies, because many adolescent births take place in the context of a marriage or union where pregnancy is often a social expectation, particularly in settings with high gender inequality.

5. GII and pregnancy outcome: In low- and middle-income countries, less gender equality was associated with smaller proportions of unintended pregnancies aborted. This correlation held despite wide variations in abortion laws across those countries. By contrast, in high-income countries, better scores in gender equality were slightly but non-significantly associated with lower proportions of unintended pregnancies aborted. (Nearly all high-income countries allow abortion on many grounds, so the legal status of abortion is not a plausible explanation for this finding.)

Note on correlations between maternal mortality and unintended pregnancy rates (page 26)

1. Higher maternal mortality is correlated to higher unintended pregnancy rates in all regions, regardless of income level, with the exception of sub-Saharan Africa.

2. In sub-Saharan Africa, countries with lower maternal mortality ratios tended to have higher unintended pregnancy rates. One hypothesis is that, in these countries, increasing development might lead to decreases in the maternal mortality ratio and rising opportunity costs for unintended pregnancy, but without a concomitant increased ability to avoid pregnancy.

Note on abortion trends (page 21)

	Rate per 1,000 Women of Reproductive Age			Per cent of ALL pregnancies ending in abortion	Per cent of UNINTENDED pregnancies ending in abortion
	pregnancy	unintended pregnancy	abortion		
1990-94	162	79	40	24.7	50.6
2014-19	133	64	39	29.3	60.9

Source: Bearak and others, 2020.

Note on adolescent pregnancy and choice (page 30)

Childbearing and marriage have become less common among adolescents. Adolescent birth rates have declined globally between 2000 and 2020 from 56 to 41 births per 1,000 women aged 15 to 19 years (UN DESA, 2019). Despite significant reductions, the adolescent birth rate in sub-Saharan Africa is 100 births per 1,000 adolescent women, more than twice as high as the global rate. Latin America and the Caribbean also continues to have relatively high levels of adolescent fertility (61 births per 1,000 women aged 15 to 19 years), despite experiencing substantial declines in total fertility. Over the last few decades, declining adolescent fertility has been accompanied by decreases in the proportion of adolescents aged 15 to 19 years who are married or in a cohabiting union (globally from 16 to 12 per cent between 2000 and 2020) and the most rapid changes have occurred in Central and Southern Asia and sub-Saharan Africa.

The sequence analysis of first births below age 18 and marriage reveals considerable diversity across regions and countries and calls for more detailed analyses of specific country settings to better understand how intentions and circumstances shape the early life course transitions linked to schooling, sexual initiation, contraceptive use, marriage and childbearing.

Findings from UN DESA (2013) and unpublished research by the same, based on further analysis of DHS data:
- The trends show an average increase in the proportions of adolescent women who have never had sex in sub-Saharan Africa, decreasing trends in Latin America and the Caribbean and high, stable levels in Asia.
- However, the context of sexual initiation is changing and a shift from sexual initiation within marriage to before marriage has taken place in many countries.
- Sexually active unmarried women often have different socio-economic and reproductive health challenges than their married peers, particularly where non-marital childbearing is a source of social stigma. Should they get pregnant, many young women in such settings marry earlier than they might have if they would not have become pregnant.
- Contraceptive prevalence among adolescents was less than 30 per cent in most countries; and even lower (less than 10 per cent) among those aged 15 to 17 years. Increases in contraceptive use were associated with declines in the adolescent birth rate among adolescent women aged 18 to 19 years in all regions (UN DESA, 2022).
- Married adolescent women tend to consistently have less education, less household and economic power, less mobility, and less exposure to modern media than unmarried adolescents and older women. They also tend to be isolated, lack the knowledge and skills to negotiate situations that are detrimental to their health and wellbeing and often face pressure to prove their fertility. Their husbands are usually much older than husbands of older married women (Haberland and others, 2004; UN DESA, 2022). Early sexual activity with an older partner has been linked to poor gender relations and poor reproductive health outcomes (Ryan and others, 2008).

Note on figure of first births by age 18 (page 33)

The underlying data used to produce the figure includes the most recent DHS survey for each country which had at least one DHS conducted since (and including) 2010.

The denominator population was defined as: (1) women aged 18 to 24 years (inclusive) at the time of the survey, (2) who had a recorded age at first birth below age 18, (3) and whose date of first birth was available. *Thus, the denominator reflects the total number of first births occurring before age 18 to women aged 18 to 24 years at the time of survey.* Four surveys had fewer than 50 births before age 18 and these were consequently excluded.

Births were classified into one of three mutually exclusive categories:
1. *First birth outside of marriage:* Date of first birth occurred before marriage date OR a woman has never been married.
2. *First birth within 7 months of marriage:* Date of first birth occurred on or after marriage date AND before the marriage date plus 7 months.
3. *First birth after 7 months and before age 18:* Date of first birth occurred after the marriage date plus 7 months.

All estimates were calculated using the provided sample weights. In total, 54 countries were included in the final graph. These represented 61,490 first births before age 18.

Data limitations: One country had fewer than 100 births prior to age 18. In addition, there were five countries that only sampled ever-married women, which may lead to an underestimate of the share of births occurring outside of marriage.

References

Acharya, Dev R. and others, 2010. "Women's Autonomy in Household Decision-Making: A Demographic Study in Nepal." *Reproductive Health* 7: 15.

ACOG (American College of Obstetricians and Gynecologists), 2020. "Comprehensive Sexuality Education." Committee Opinion Number 678. Website: acog. org/clinical/clinical-guidance/committee-opinion/articles/2016/11/comprehensive-sexuality-education, accessed 1 December 2021.

ACOG (American College of Obstetricians and Gynecologists), 2017. "Access to Contraception." Committee Opinion Number 615. Website: acog.org/clinical/clinical-guidance/committee-opinion/articles/2015/01/access-to-contraception, accessed 1 December 2021.

Ahrens, Katherine A and others, 2018. "Unintended Pregnancy and Interpregnancy Interval by Maternal Age." *Contraception* 98: 52-55.

Aiken, Abigail and others, 2016. "Comparison of a Timing-Based Measure of Unintended Pregnancy and the London Measure of Unplanned Pregnancy." *Perspectives on Sexual and Reproductive Health* 48(3): 139-146.

Aiken, Abigail and others, 2015. "A Blessing I Can't Afford: Factors Underlying the Paradox of Happiness about Unintended Pregnancy." *Social Science and Medicine* 132: 149-155.

Akoth, Catherine and others, 2021. "Prevalence and Factors Associated with Covert Contraceptive Use in Kenya: A Cross-Sectional Study." *BMC Public Health* 21: 1316.

Ali, Mohamed M. and others, 2012. "Causes and Consequences of Contraceptive Discontinuation: Evidence From 60 Demographic and Health Surveys." Geneva: WHO. Website: apps.who.int/iris/handle/10665/75429, accessed 26 November 2021.

Alio, Amina P. and others, 2009. "Intimate Partner Violence and Contraception Use among Women in Sub-Saharan Africa." *International Journal of Gynecology & Obstetrics* 107(1): 35-38.

Allotey, Pascale and others, 2021. "Trends in Abortion Policies in Low- and Middle-Income Countries." *Annual Review of Public Health* 42: 505-518.

Alvarez, R.O., 1993. "'We Will Not Rest.' Filipino Women Want a Fertility Management Program that Respects Women's Dignity, Women's Bodies and Women's Choices." *Integration* 35: 22-23.

Ameyaw, Edward Kwabena and others, 2019. "Prevalence and Determinants of Unintended Pregnancy in Sub-Saharan Africa: A Multi-Country Analysis of Demographic and Health Surveys." *PLOS ONE* 14(8): e0220970.

Amo-Adjei, Joshua and Derek Anamaale Tuoyire, 2016. "Effects of Planned, Mistimed and Unwanted Pregnancies on the Use of Prenatal Health Services in Sub-Saharan Africa: A Multicountry Analysis of Demographic and Health Survey Data." *Tropical Medicine & International Health* 21(12): 1552-1561.

Ampt, Frances H. and others, 2018. "Incidence of Unintended Pregnancy Among Female Sex Workers in Low-Income and Middle-Income Countries: A Systematic Review and Meta-Analysis." *BMJ Open* 8(9): e021779.

Ashburn-Nardo, Leslie, 2017. "Parenthood as a Moral Imperative? Moral Outrage and the Stigmatization of Voluntarily Childfree Women and Men." *Sex Roles* 76: 393-401.

Atake, Esso-Hanam and Pitaloumani Gnakou Ali, 2019. "Women's Empowerment and Fertility Preferences in High Fertility Countries in Sub-Saharan Africa." *BMC Women's Health* 19: 54.

Austin, Judya and others, 2008. "Reproductive Health: A Right for Refugees and Internally Displaced Persons." *Reproductive Health Matters* 16(31): 10-21.

Baiden, Frank and others, 2016. "Covert Contraceptive Use Among Women Attending a Reproductive Health Clinic in a Municipality in Ghana." *BMC Women's Health* 16: 31.

Bain, Luchuo Engelbert and others, 2020. "Prevalence and Determinants of Unintended Pregnancy in Sub-Saharan Africa: A Systematic Review." *African Journal of Reproductive Health* 24(2): 187-205.

Bakour, Shagaf H. and others, 2017. "Contraceptive Methods and Issues Around the Menopause: An Evidence Update." *The Obstetrician and Gynaecologist* 19(4): 289-297.

Baldwin, Maureen K. and Jeffrey T. Jensen, 2013. "Contraception During the Perimenopause." *Maturitas* 76(3): 235-242.

Bansode, Oshin M. and others, 2021. "Contraception." In: StatPearls [Internet]. Treasure Island, Florida: StatPeals Publishing. Website: ncbi.nlm.nih.gov/books/NBK536949/#_NBK536949_pubdet_, accessed 15 November 2021.

Bauserman, Melissa and others, 2020. "Maternal Mortality in Six Low and Lower-Middle Income Countries from 2010 to 2018: Risk Factors and Trends." *Reproductive Health* 17(Suppl 3): 173.

BBC (British Broadcasting Corporation), 2017. "Contraception Fails in Quarter of Abortions, Say Experts." BBC News, 7 July 2017. Website: bbc.co.uk/news/health-40520235, accessed 17 November 2021.

Bearak, Jonathan and others, 2022. "Country-Specific Estimates of Unintended Pregnancy and Abortion Incidence: A Global Comparative Analysis of Levels in 2015-2019." *BMJ Global Health*, in press.

Bearak, Jonathan and others, 2020. "Unintended Pregnancy and Abortion by Income, Region, and the Legal Status of Abortion: Estimates from a Comprehensive Model for 1990-2019." *Lancet Global Health* 8(9): e1152-e1161.

Behre, Hermann M., and others, 2016. "Efficacy and Safety of an Injectable Combination Hormonal Contraceptive for Men." *The Journal of Clinical Endocrinology & Metabolism* 101(12): 4779-4788,

Bellizzi, Saverio and others, 2020. "Reasons for Discontinuation of Contraception Among Women with a Current Unintended Pregnancy in 36 Low and Middle-Income Countries." *Contraception* 101(1): 26-33.

Bietsch, Kristin and Priya Emmart, 2022. *Couple Concordance Index: Construction of the Couple Concordance Index and its Relationship with Contraceptive Use.* Washington, DC: USAID MOMENTUM.

Biggs, M. Antonia and others, 2017. "Women's Mental Health and Well-Being 5 Years After Receiving or Being Denied an Abortion. A Prospective, Longitudinal Cohort Study." *JAMA Psychiatry* 74(2): 169-178.

Bitto, A. and others, 1997. "Adverse Outcomes of Planned and Unplanned Pregnancies among Users of Natural Family Planning: A Prospective Study." *American Journal of Public Health* 87(3): 338–343.

Boyce, Sabrina C. and others, 2020. "Women's and Girls' Experiences of Reproductive Coercion and Opportunities for Intervention in Family Planning Clinics in Nairobi, Kenya: A Qualitative Study." *Reproductive Health* 17(1): 1–12.

Bradley, Sarah E. K. and others, 2019. "Global Contraceptive Failure Rates: Who is Most at Risk?" *Studies in Family Planning* 50(1): 3-24.

Bradley, Sarah E. K. and others, 2009. *Levels, Trends, and Reasons for Contraceptive Discontinuation.* DHS Analytical Studies No. 20. Calverton: ICF Macro.

Brito, Cynthia Nunes de Oliveira and others, 2015. "Postpartum Depression among Women with Unintended Pregnancy." *Revista de Saúde Pública* 49: 33.

Brodsky, Alexandra, 2017. "Rape-Adjacent: Imagining Legal Responses to Nonconsensual Condom Removal." *Columbia Journal of Gender and Law* 32: 183–210.

Calliope, n.d. The Contraceptive Pipeline Database. Website: pipeline.ctiexchange.org, accessed 31 January 2022.

Campbell, Oona M. and Wendy J. Graham, 2006. "Strategies for Reducing Maternal Mortality: Getting On with What Works." *Lancet* 368(9543): 1284-1299.

Canada: Immigration and Refugee Board of Canada, 2013. "Tanzania: Consequences for a Woman who gets Pregnant out of Wedlock, Including the Possibility of Arrest and Criminal or Civil Proceedings; Whether the same Consequences Apply if the Woman Marries Before the Birth of the Child (2012–July 2013)." TZA104531.E. Website: refworld.org/docid/53e481264.html, accessed 18 December 2021.

Carter, Marion and Ilene S. Speizer, 2005. "Pregnancy Intentions Among Salvadoran Fathers: Results from the 2003 National Male Reproductive Health Survey." *International Perspectives on Sexual and Reproductive Health* 31(4): 179-182.

Castle, Sarah and Ian Askew, 2015. *Contraceptive Discontinuation: Reasons, Challenges, and Solutions.* New York: Population Council and FP2020.

Castle, Sarah and others, 1999. "A Qualitative Study of Clandestine Contraceptive Use in Urban Mali." *Studies in Family Planning* 30(3): 231-248.

CDC (Centers for Disease Control and Prevention), 2015. "The 6|18 Initiative. Evidence Summary, Prevent Unintended Pregnancy." Website: cdc.gov/sixeighteen/docs/6-18-evidence-summary-pregnancy.pdf, accessed 1 December 2021.

Chae, Sophia and others, 2017. "Characteristics of Women Obtaining Induced Abortions in Selected Low- and Middle-Income Countries." *PLOS ONE* 12(3): e0172976.

Chant, Sylvia, 2013. "Cities Through a 'Gender Lens': A Golden 'Urban Age' for Women in the Global South?" *Environment and Urbanization* 25(1): 9-29.

Chebet, Joy J. and others, 2015. "'Every Method Seems to have its Problems' – Perspectives on Side Effects of Hormonal Contraceptives in Morogoro Region, Tanzania." *BMC Womens Health* 15: 97.

Chung, Hye Won and others, 2018. "Comprehensive Understanding of Risk and Protective Factors Related to Adolescent Pregnancy in Low- and Middle-Income Countries: A Systematic Review." *Journal of Adolescence* 69: 180–188.

Clements, K. C., 2018. "Can Men Get Pregnant?" *Healthline*, 20 December 2018. Website: healthline.com/health/transgender/can-men-get-pregnant, accessed 18 November 2021.

Coker, Ann L., 2007. "Does Physical Intimate Partner Violence Affect Sexual Health? A Systematic Review." *Trauma, Violence, & Abuse* 8(2): 149–177.

Cook, Rebecca J. and Bernard M. Dickens, 2014. "Reducing Stigma in Reproductive Health." *International Journal of Gynecology & Obstetrics* 125(1): 89–92.

Costantino, Antonietta and others, 2007. "Current Status and Future Perspectives in Male Contraception." *Minerva Ginecologica* 59(3): 299–310.

Darteh, Eugene Kofuor Maafo and others, 2019. "Women's Reproductive Health Decision-Making: A Multi-Country Analysis of Demographic and Health Surveys in Sub-Saharan Africa." *PLOS ONE* 14(1): e0209985.

Dehingia, Nabamallika and others, 2020. "Unintended Pregnancy and Maternal Health Complications: Cross-Sectional Analysis of Data from Rural Uttar Pradesh, India." *BMC Pregnancy and Childbirth* 20(1): 188.

Dietz, Patricia M. and others, 1999. "Unintended Pregnancy Among Adult Women Exposed to Abuse or Household Dysfunction During Their Childhood." *Journal of the American Medical Association* 282(14): 1359–1364.

ECLAC (Economic Commission for Latin America and the Caribbean), 2020. Gender Equality Observatory for Latin America and the Caribbean. Website: oig.cepal.org/es/indicadores/matrimonio-infantil, accessed 1 March 2022.

ENDES (Encuesta Demográfica y de Salud Familiar), 2020. "ENDES Realizadas." Perú Instituto Nacional de Estadísticañ e Informática. Website: https://proyectos.inei.gob.pe/endes, accessed 17 November 2021.

Everett, Bethany G. and others, 2019. "Do Sexual Minorities Receive Appropriate Sexual and Reproductive Health Care and Counseling?" *Journal of Women's Health (Larchmont)* 28(1): 53–62.

Everett, Bethany G. and others, 2017. "Sexual Orientation Disparities in Mistimed and Unwanted Pregnancy Among Adult Women." *Perspectives on Sexual and Reproductive Health* 49(3): 157–165.

Faini, Diana and others, 2020. "'I Did Not Plan to Have a Baby. This is the Outcome of Our Work': A Qualitative Study Exploring Unintended Pregnancy Among Female Sex Workers." *BMC Women's Health* 20: 267.

Fanslow, Janet and others, 2008. "Pregnancy Outcomes and Intimate Partner Violence in New Zealand." *Australian and New Zealand Journal of Obstetrics and Gynaecology* 48(4): 391–397.

Festin, Mario Philip R. and others, 2016. "Moving Towards the Goals of FP2020 – Classifying Contraceptives." *Contraception* 94(4): 289–294.

Fine, Johanna and others, 2017. "The Role of International Human Rights Norms in the Liberalization of Abortion Laws Globally." *Health and Human Rights* 19(1): 69–80.

Finer, Lawrence B., 2010. "Unintended Pregnancy Among U. S. Adolescents: Accounting for Sexual Activity." *Journal of Adolescent Health* 47(3): 312–314.

Finer, Lawrence B. and Mia R. Zolna, 2016. "Declines in Unintended Pregnancy in the United States, 2008-2011." *New England Journal of Medicine* 374(9): 843–852.

Foster, Angel and others, 2017. "The 2018 Inter-Agency Field Manual on Reproductive Health in Humanitarian Settings: Revising the Global Standards." *Reproductive Health Matters* 25(51): 18–24.

Foster, Diana Greene, 2020. *The Turnaway Study: Ten Years, a Thousand Women, and the Consequences of Having – or Being Denied – an Abortion.* New York: Scribner.

Frederiksen, Line and others, 2018. "Risk of Adverse Pregnancy Outcomes at Advanced Maternal Age." *Obstetrics & Gynecology* 131(3): 457–463.

Friedman and others, 2019. *Interest Among U.S. Men for New Male Contraceptive Options Consumer Research Study.* Male Contraceptive Initiative.

Frost, Jennifer J. and Jacqueline E. Darroch, 2008. "Factors Associated With Contraceptive Choice and Inconsistent Method Use, United States, 2004." *Perspectives on Sexual and Reproductive Health* 40(2): 94–104.

FP2030, 2020. Sierra Leone Commitments. Website: fp2030.org/sierra-leone, accessed 31 January 2022.

FP2030, 2020a. Philippines Commitments. Website: fp2030.org/philippines, accessed 31 January 2022.

FSRH (The Faculty of Sexual and Reproductive Healthcare of the Royal College of Obstetricians and Gynaecologists). 2021. "FSRH statement: Home use of abortion medicines is safe, more accessible and preferred by women, new national study shows." Website: https://www.fsrh.org/news/fsrh-statement-new-study-telemedicine-abortion-2021/, accessed November 2021.

Gambir, Katherine and others, 2020. "Effectiveness, Safety and Acceptability of Medical Abortion at Home Versus in the Clinic: A Systematic Review and Meta-Analysis in Response to COVID-19." BMJ Global Health 5: e003934.

Ganatra, Bela and others, 2017. "Global, Regional, and Subregional Classification of Abortions by Safety, 2010-14: Estimates from a Bayesian Hierarchical Model." Lancet 390(10110): 2372-2381.

Garraza, Lucas Godoy and others, 2020. "Out-Of-Pocket Spending for Contraceptives in Latin America." Sexual and Reproductive Health Matters 28(2): 1833429.

Gerdts, Caitlin and others, 2016. "Side Effects, Physical Health Consequences, and Mortality Associated with Abortion and Birth after an Unwanted Pregnancy." Women's Health Issues 26(1): 55-59.

Gipson, Jessica D. and others, 2008. "The Effects of Unintended Pregnancy on Infant, Child, and Parental Health: A Review of the Literature." Studies in Family Planning 39(1): 18-38.

Gold, Rachel Benson and Kinsey Hasstedt, 2017. "Publicly Funded Family Planning Under Unprecedented Attack." American Journal of Public Health 107(12): 1895-1897.

Gottschall, Jonathan A. and Tiffani A. Gottschall, 2003. "Are Per-Incident Rape-Pregnancy Rates Higher than Per-Incident Consensual Pregnancy Rates?" Human Nature 14: 1-20.

Grace, Karen Trister and Jocelyn C. Anderson, 2018. "Reproductive Coercion: A Systematic Review." Trauma, Violence, & Abuse 19(4): 371-390.

Grimes, David and others, 2006. "Unsafe Abortion: The Preventable Pandemic." Lancet 368(9550): 1908-1919.

Haberland, Nicole and Deborah Rogow, 2015. "Sexuality Education: Emerging Trends in Evidence and Practice." Journal of Adolescent Health 56(1 Suppl): S15-S21.

Haberland, Nicole and others, 2004. "Married adolescents: An overview," paper prepared for the WHO/UNFPA/Population Council Technical Consultation on Married Adolescents. New York: Population Council.

Habib, Muhammad Ali and others, 2017. "Prevalence and Determinants of Unintended Pregnancies Amongst Women Attending Antenatal Clinics in Pakistan." BMC Pregnancy and Childbirth 17(1): 156.

Haddad, Lisa B. and others, 2021. "Addressing Contraceptive Needs Exacerbated by COVID-19: A Call for Increasing Choice and Access to Self-Managed Methods." Contraception 103: 377-379.

Hall, Jennifer Anne and others, 2017. "London Measure of Unplanned Pregnancy: Guidance for its Use as an Outcome Measure." Patient Related Outcome Measures 8: 43-56.

Hall, Jennifer Anne and others, 2016. "Prevalence and Determinants of Unintended Pregnancy in Mchinji District, Malawi: Using a Conceptual Hierarchy to Inform Analysis." PLOS One 11(10): e0165621.

Hamberger, L. Kevin and others, 2015. "Screening and Intervention for Intimate Partner Violence in Healthcare Settings: Creating Sustainable System-Level Programs." Journal of Women's Health 24(1): 86-91.

Hannaford, Philip C. and others, 2010. "Mortality Among Contraceptive Pill Users: Cohort Evidence from Royal College of General Practitioners' Oral Contraception Study." BMJ 340: c927.

Heaman, Maureen and others, 2013. "Migrant Women's Utilization of Prenatal Care: A Systematic Review." Maternal and Child Health Journal 17: 816-836.

Heidari, Shirin and others, 2019. "Sexual and Reproductive Health and Rights in Humanitarian Crises at ICPD25+ and Beyond: Consolidating Gains to Ensure Access to Services for All." Sexual and Reproductive Health Matters 27(1): 1676513.

Heinemann, Klaas and others, 2005. "Attitudes Toward Male Fertility Control: Results of a Multinational Survey on Four Continent." Human Reproduction 20(2): 549-556.

Hindin, Michelle J. and others, 2014. "Misperceptions, Misinformation and Myths About Modern Contraceptive Use in Ghana." Journal of Family Planning and Reproductive Health Care 40(1): 30-35.

Hindin, Michelle J. and others, 2008. Intimate Partner Violence Among Couples in 10 DHS Countries: Predictors and Health Outcomes." DHS Analytical Studies 18. Washington DC: USAID. Website: dhsprogram.com/pubs/pdf/AS18/AS18.pdf, accessed 10 February 2022.

HIP (High Impact Practices in Family Planning), 2020. "Supply Chain Management: Investing in Contraceptive Security and Strengthening Health Systems." Washington, DC: HIPs Partnership. Website: fphighimpactpractices.org/briefs/supply-chain-management/, accessed 26 November 2021.

HIP (High Impact Practices in Family Planning), 2020a. "Family Planning Vouchers: A Tool to Boost Contraceptive Method Access and Choice." Washington, DC: HIPs Partnership. Website: fphighimpactpractices.org/wp-content/uploads/2019/06/family-planning-vouchers-en-june-2020.pdf, accessed 1 December 2021.

Hodson, K. and others, 2016. "Lesbian and Bisexual Women's Likelihood of Becoming Pregnant: A Systematic Review and Meta-Analysis." *BJOG* 124(3): 393–402.

Horii, Hoko, 2021. "Child Marriage as a 'Solution' to Modern Youth in Bali." *Progress in Development Studies* 20(4): 282-295.

Horner-Johnson, Willi and others, 2020. "Pregnancy Intendedness by Maternal Disability Status and Type in the United States." *Perspectives on Sexual and Reproductive Health* 52(1): 31–38.

Hromi-Fiedler, Amber and Rafael Pérez-Escamilla, 2006. "Unintended Pregnancies Are Associated with Less Likelihood of Prolonged Breast-feeding: An Analysis of 18 Demographic and Health Surveys." *Public Health Nutrition* 9(3): 306–312.

Huda, Fauzia Achter and others, 2013. *Understanding Unintended Pregnancy in Bangladesh: Country Profiile Report.* STEP UP Research Report. Dhaka: icddr,b.

Human Rights Watch, 2018. "Africa: Pregnant Girls, Young Mothers Barred from School." Website: hrw.org/news/2018/06/14/africa-pregnant-girls-young-mothers-barred-school, accessed 18 November 2021.

Human Rights Watch, 2018a. "Leave No Girl Behind in Africa. Discrimination in Education against Pregnant Girls and Adolescent Mothers." Website: hrw.org/report/2018/06/14/leave-no-girl-behind-africa/discrimination-education-against-pregnant-girls-and#, accessed 1 December 2021.

ICRC (International Committee of the Red Cross), 1977. "Protocol Additional to the Geneva Conventions of 12 August 1949, and Relating to the Protection of Victims of International Armed Conflicts (Protocol I)." Website: refworld.org/docid/3ae6b37f40.html, accessed 26 November 2021.

Ikamari, Lawrence and others, 2013. "Prevalence and Determinants of Unintended Pregnancy Among Women in Nairobi, Kenya." *BMC Pregnancy and Childbirth* 13: 69.

Ilankoon, I. M. P. S. and others, 2021. "Menopause is a Natural Stage of Aging: A Qualitative Study." *BMC Women's Health* 21: 47.

ILO (International Labour Organization), 2017. *World Social Protection Report 2017–19: Universal Social Protection to Achieve the Sustainable Development Goals.* Website: ilo.org/wcmsp5/groups/public/---dgreports/---dcomm/---publ/documents/publication/wcms_604882.pdf, accessed 1 December 2021.

ILO (International Labour Organization), 2012. *Maternity Resource Protection Package: From Aspiration to Reality For All.* Website: mprp.itcilo.org/pages/en/introduction.html, accessed 1 December 2021.

Im, Eun-Ok and others, 2010. "Black Women in Menopausal Transition." *Journal of Obstetric, Gynecologic & Neonatal Nursing* 39(4): 435–443.

IRC (International Rescue Committee), 2020. "IRC Data Shows an Increase in Reports of Gender-Based Violence Across Latin America." Website: reliefweb.int/report/el-salvador/irc-data-shows-increase-reports-gender-based-violence-across-latin-america, accessed 8 February 2022.

Jackson, Ashley and Léonce Dossou, 2021. "The Appeal and Potential of On-Demand Contraceptive Options." Washington DC: PSI. Website: psi.org/2021/12/the-appeal-and-potential-of-on-demand-contraceptive-options, accessed 9 February 2022.

Jacobstein, Roy, 2015. "The Kindest Cut: Global Need to Increase Vasectomy Availability." *Lancet Global Health* 3(12): e733–e734.

Jain, Rakhi and Sumathi Muralidhar, 2011. "Contraceptive Methods: Needs, Options and Utilization." *Journal of Obstetrics and Gynaecology of India* 61(6): 626–634.

Jain, Aparna and others, 2021. "Not All Women Who Experience Side Effects Discontinue Their Contraceptive Method: Insights from a Longitudinal Study in India." Studies in Family Planning 52(2): 165–178.

Johnson-Mallard, Versie and others, 2017. "Unintended Pregnancy: A Framework for Prevention and Options for Midlife Women in the US." *Women's Midlife Health* 3: 8.

Kantorová, Vladmíra and others, 2021. "Contraceptive Use and Needs Among Adolescent Women Aged 15-19: Regional and Global Estimates and Projections from 1990 to 2030 from a Bayesian Hierarchical Modelling Study." *PLOS ONE* 16(3): e0247479.

Kaufman, Julia and Rachel Silverman, 2021. "Bridging the Gap Between Health Financing and Family Planning: How to Effectively Advocate for Contraception in UHC." Washington DC: Center for Global Development. Website: cgdev.org/blog/bridging-gap-between-health-financing-and-family-planning-how-effectively-advocate, accessed 1 December 2021.

Keogh, Sarah C. and others, 2021. "Hormonal Contraceptive Use in Ghana: The Role of Method Attributes and Side Effects in Method Choice and Continuation." *Contraception* 104(3): 235–245.

Khan, Md Nuruzzaman and others, 2019. "Effects of Unintended Pregnancy on Maternal Healthcare Services Utilization in Low- and Lower-Middle-Income Countries: Systematic Review and Meta-Analysis." *International Journal of Public Health* 64(5): 743-754.

Kholsa, Rajat and others, 2016. "International Human Rights and the Mistreatment of Women During Childbirth." *Health and Human Rights* 18(2): 131-143.

Kibira, Simon P. S. and others, 2020. "Covert Use of Contraception in Three Sub-Saharan African Countries: A Qualitative Exploration of Motivations and Challenges." *BMC Public Health* 20: 865.

Kimport, Katrina and others, 2017. "Patient-Provider Conversations About Sterilization: A Qualitative Analysis." *Contraception* 95(3): 227-233.

Kingsbury, Ann M. and others, 2015. "Trajectories and Predictors of Women's Depression Following the Birth of an Infant to 21 Years: A Longitudinal Study." *Maternal and Child Health Journal* 19: 877-888.

Korenman, Sanders and others, 2002. "Consequences for Infants of Parental Disagreement in Pregnancy Intention." *Perspectives in Sexual and Reproductive Health* 34(4): 198-205.

Kost, Kathryn and others, 1998. "Predicting Maternal Behaviors During Pregnancy: Does Intention Status Matter?" *Family Planning Perspectives* 23(1): 79-88.

Kupoluyi, Joseph Ayodeji, 2020. "Intimate Partner Violence as a Factor in Contraceptive Discontinuation among Sexually Active Married Women in Nigeria." *BMC Womens Health* 20(1): 128.

Le, Hoa H. and others, 2014. "The Burden of Unintended Pregnancies in Brazil: A Social and Public Health System Cost Analysis." *International Journal of Women's Health* 6: 663-670.

Le Guen, Mireille and others, 2021. "Reasons for Rejecting Hormonal Contraception in Western Countries: A Systematic Review." *Social Science and Medicine* 284: 114247.

Luchsinger, Gretchen, 2021. *No Exceptions, No Exclusions: Realizing Sexual and Reproductive Health, Rights and Justice for All.* High-Level Commission on the Nairobi Summit on ICPD25 Follow-up. Website: nairobisummiticpd.org/publication/no-exceptions-no-exclusions, accessed 24 November 2021.

Ludermir, Ana Bernarda and others, 2011. "Postnatal Depression in Women After Unsuccessful Attempted Abortion." *British Journal of Psychiatry* 198(3): 237-238.

Lundgren, Rebecka and Avni Amin, 2015. "Addressing Intimate Partner Violence and Sexual Violence Among Adolescents: Emerging Evidence of Effectiveness." *Journal of Adolescent Health* 56(1 Suppl): S42-S50.

Macleod, Catriona Ida, 2016. "Public Reproductive Health and 'Unintended' Pregnancies: Introducing the Construct 'Supportability'." *Journal of Public Health* 38(3): e384-e391.

Mansur, Yusuf and others, n.d. *The Economic Underpinnings of Honor Crimes in Jordan.* Information and Research Center, King Hussein Foundation. Website: tbinternet.ohchr.org/Treaties/CRC/Shared%20Documents/JOR/INT_CRC_NGO_JOR_15745_E.pdf, accessed 18 December 2021.

Marston, Cicely and John Cleland, 2003. "Do Unintended Pregnancies Carried to Term Lead to Adverse Outcomes for Mother and Child? An Assessment in Five Developing Countries." *Population Studies* 57(1): 77-93.

Maxwell, Lauren and others, 2018. "Intimate Partner Violence and Pregnancy Spacing: Results from a Meta-Analysis of Individual Participant Time-to-Event Data from 29 Low-and-Middle-Income Countries." *BMJ Global Health* 3: e000304.

Maxwell, Lauren and others, 2015. "Estimating the Effect of Intimate Partner Violence on Women's Use of Contraception: A Systematic Review and Meta-Analysis." *PLOS ONE* 10(2): e0118234.

Mbadu, Fidele Muanda and others, 2017. "Barriers to Modern Contraceptive Use in Rural Areas in DRC." *Culture, Health and Sexuality* 19(9): 1011-1023.

McCarraher, Donna R. and others, 2006. "The Influence of Method-Related Partner Violence on Covert Pill Use and Pill Discontinuation Among Women Living in La Paz, El Alto and Santa Cruz, Bolivia." *Journal of Biosocial Science* 38(2): 169-186.

Measure Evaluation, 2017. "The Importance of Gender in Family Planning and Reproductive Health Data." Website: measureevaluation.org/resources/publications/fs-17-205b/at_download/document, accessed 1 December 2021.

Melian, María Mercedes, 2013. ["Reproductive Intentions and Factors Related to Unplanned Births, Paraguay, 1995-2008."] *Revista Panamericana de Salud Pública* 33(4): 244-251. [In Spanish]

Miller, Elizabeth and Jay G. Silverman, 2010. "Reproductive Coercion and Partner Violence: Implications for Clinical Assessment of Unintended Pregnancy." *Expert Review of Obstetrics & Gynecology* 5: 511-515.

Miller, Elizabeth and others, 2010. "Reproductive Coercion: Connecting the Dots Between Partner Violence and Unintended Pregnancy." *Contraception* 81(6): 457-459.

Miller, Elizabeth and others, 2010a. "Pregnancy Coercion, Intimate Partner Violence and Unintended Pregnancy." *Contraception* 81(4): 316-322.

Moges, Yohannes and others, 2020. "Factors Associated with the Unplanned Pregnancy at Suhul General Hospital, Northern Ethiopia, 2018." *Journal of Pregnancy* 2020: 2926097.

Mohllajee, Anshu P. and others, 2007. "Pregnancy Intention and Its Relationship to Birth and Maternal Outcomes." *Obstetrics & Gynecology* 109(3): 678-686.

Molitoris, Joseph and others, 2019. "When and Where Birth Spacing Matters for Child Survival: An International Comparison Using the DHS." *Demography* 56(4): 1349-1370.

Moreau, Caroline and others, 2014. "Unplanned or Unwanted? A Randomized Study of National Estimates of Pregnancy Intentions." *Fertility and Sterility* 102(6): 1663-1670.

Moreira, Laísa Rodrigues and others, 2019. "Reasons for Nonuse of Contraceptive Methods by Women with Demand for Contraception Not Satisfied: An Assessment of Low and Middle-Income Countries using Demographic and Health Surveys." *Reproductive Health* 16: 148.

Moseson, Heidi and others, 2021. "Pregnancy Intentions and Outcomes Among Transgender, Nonbinary, and Gender-Expansive People Assigned Female or Intersex at Birth in the United States: Results From a National, Quantitative Survey." *International Journal of Transgender Health* 22(1-2): 30-41.

Mukasa, Bakali and others, 2017. "Contraception Supply Chain Challenges: A Review of Evidence from Low- and Middle-Income Countries." *European Journal of Contraception and Reproductive Health Care* 22(5): 384-390.

Müller, Alex and others, 2018. "The No-Go Zone: A Qualitative Study of Access to Sexual and Reproductive Health Services for Sexual and Gender Minority Adolescents in Southern Africa." *Reproductive Health* 15: 12.

Mwaisaka, Jefferson and others, 2020. "Exploring Contraception Myths and Misconceptions Among Young Men and Women in Kwale County, Kenya." *BMC Public Health* 20: 1694.

Napyo, Agnes and others, 2020. "Prevalence and Predictors for Unintended Pregnancy Among HIV-Infected Pregnant Women in Lira, Northern Uganda: A Cross-Sectional Study." *Scientific Reports* 10: 16319.

Neal, Sarah and others, 2020. "Trends in Adolescent First Births in Sub-Saharan Africa: A Tale of Increasing Inequity?" *International Journal for Equity in Health* 19: 151.

November, Lucy and Jane Sandall, 2018. "Just Because She's Young, It Doesn't Mean She Has to Die: Exploring the Contributing Factors to High Maternal Mortality in Adolescents in Eastern Freetown: A Qualitative Study." *Reproductive Health* 15(1): 31.

Nuevo-Chiquero, Ana, 2014. "The Labor Force Effects of Unplanned Childbearing." *Labour Economics* 29: 91-101.

Nyarko, Samuel H., 2019. "Unintended Pregnancy among Pregnant Women in Ghana: Prevalence and Predictors." *Journal of Pregnancy* 2019: 2920491.

OHCHR (Office of the High Commissioner for Human Rights), 2018. "Your Health, Your Choice, Your Rights: International and Regional Obligations on Sexual and Reproductive Health and Rights." Website: ohchr.org/Documents/Issues/Women/OHCHRFactsheetYourHealth.pdf, accessed 1 December 2021.

Oladeji, Olusola and others, 2021. "Sexual Violence-Related Pregnancy among Internally Displaced Women in an Internally Displaced Persons Camp in Northeast Nigeria." *Journal of Interpersonal Violence* 36(9-10): 4758-4770.

Orr, Suezanne and others, 2000. "Unintended Pregnancy and Preterm Birth." *Paediatric and Perinatal Epidemiology* 14(4): 309-313.

Paterno, Mary T. and others, 2021. "Exploring Reproductive Coercion in Relationship Contexts Among Young Adult, Primarily African American Women at Three Women's Health Clinics." *Journal of Interpersonal Violence* 36(3-4): NP2248-2271NP.

Paul, Mandira and others, 2019. "Contraception and Youth: Being Responsive to their Sexual and Reproductive Health Needs and Rights." Issue Paper. New York: UNFPA and Guttmacher Institute.

Petroni, Suzanne and others, 2017. "New Findings on Child Marriage in Sub-Saharan Africa." *Annals of Global Health* 83(5-6): 781-790.

Pierotti, Rachael S., 2013. "Increasing Rejection of Intimate Partner Violence: Evidence of Global Cultural Diffusion." American Sociological Review 78(2): 240-265.

Pile, John M. and Mark A. Barone, 2009. "Demographics of vasectomy – USA and international." Urologic Clinics of North America 36(3): 295-305.

Polis, Chelsea B. and others, 2018. "There Might be Blood: A Scoping Review on Women's Responses to Contraceptive-Induced Menstrual Bleeding Changes." *Reproductive Health* 15: 114.

Population Council, 2015. "Conceptualizing and Measuring Unintended Pregnancy and Birth: Moving the Field Forward". STEP UP Meeting Report. Accra: Population Council. Website: popcouncil. org/uploads/pdfs/2015STEPUP_ ConceptualizingMeasuringUP.pdf, accessed 24 November 2021.

Qiu, Xing and others, 2020. "Unintended Pregnancy and Postpartum Depression: A Meta-Analysis of Cohort and Case-Control Studies." *Journal of Psychosomatic Research* 138: 110259.

Qureshi, Zahida and others, 2021. "Understanding Abortion-Related Complications in Health Facilities: Results from WHO Multicountry Survey on Abortion (MCS-A) Across 11 Sub-Saharan African Countries." *BMJ Global Health* 6: e003702.

Rahman, Mosfequr, 2015. "Is Unwanted Birth Associated with Child Malnutrition in Bangladesh?" *International Perspectives on Sexual and Reproductive Health* 41(4): 80-88.

Rahman, Mosfequr and others, 2019. "Maternal Pregnancy Intention and Its Association with Low Birthweight and Pregnancy Complications in Bangladesh: Findings from a Hospital-Based Study." *International Health* 11(6): 447-454.

Raj, Anita and others, 2015. "Associations of Marital Violence with Different Forms of Contraception: Cross-Sectional Findings from South Asia." *International Journal of Gynecology & Obstetrics* 130(S3): E56-E61.

Ralph, Lauren J. and others, 2020. "Comparing Prospective and Retrospective Reports of Pregnancy Intention in a Longitudinal Cohort of U.S. Women." *Perspectives on Sexual and Reproductive Health* 52(1): 39-48.

Raymond, Elizabeth G. and David A. Grimes, 2012. "The Comparative Safety of Legal Induced Abortion and Childbirth in the United States." *Obstetrics & Gynecology* 119(2 pt 1): 215-219.

Riley, Taylor and others, 2020. "Estimates of the Potential Impact of the COVID-19 Pandemic on Sexual and Reproductive Health In Low- and Middle-Income Countries." *International Perspectives on Sexual and Reproductive Health* 46: 73-76.

Romero, Mariana and others, 2021. "Abortion-Related Morbidity in Six Latin American and Caribbean Countries: Findings of the WHO/HRP Multi-Country Survey on Abortion (MCS-A)." *BMJ Global Health* 6: e005618.

Rominski, Sarah D. and Rob Stephenson, 2019. "Toward a New Definition of Unmet Need for Contraception." *Studies in Family Planning* 50(2): 195-198.

Rothman, Emily F. and others, 2011. "The Prevalence of Sexual Assault Against People Who Identify as Gay, Lesbian or Bisexual in the United States: A Systematic Review." *Trauma, Violence, & Abuse* 12(2): 55-66.

Rothschild, Claire W. and others, 2021. "Incorporating Method Dissatisfaction into Unmet Need for Contraception: Implications for Measurement and Impact." *Studies in Family Planning* 52(1): 95-102.

Rowlands, Sam and Susan Walker, 2019. "Reproductive Control by Others: Means, Perpetrators and Effects." *BMJ Sexual and Reproductive Health* 45: 61-67.

Rutstein, Shea O., 2008. "Further Evidence of the Effects of Preceding Intervals on Neonatal, Infant, and Under-Five-Years Mortality and Nutritional Status in Developing Countries: Evidence from the Demographic and Health Surveys." Demographic and Health Surveys Working Paper No. 41. Calverton, Maryland: Macro International. Website: dhsprogram.com/pubs/pdf/WP41/WP41.pdf, accessed 25 November 2021.

Ryan, Suzanne and others, 2008. "Older Sexual Partners during Adolescence: Links to Reproductive Health Outcomes in Young Adulthood." Perspectives on Sexual and Reproductive Health 40(1): 17-26.

Sarder, Alamgir and others, 2021. "Prevalence of Unintended Pregnancy and its Associated Factors: Evidence from Six South Asian Countries." *PLOS ONE* 16(2): e0245923.

Say, Laie and others, 2014. "Global Causes of Maternal Death: A WHO Systematic Analysis." *Lancet Global Health* 2(6): e323-e333.

Sedgh, Gilda and others, 2016. *Unmet Need for Contraception in Developing Countries: Examining Women's Reasons for Not Using a Method.* New York: Guttmacher Institute. Website: guttmacher. org/report/unmet-need-for-contraception-in-developing-countries, accessed 17 November 2021.

Sedgh, Gilda and others, 2016a. "Abortion Incidence Between 1990 and 2014: Global, Regional, and Subregional Levels and Trends." *Lancet* 388(10041): 258-267.

Seifu, Canaan Negash and others, 2020. "Association of Husbands' Education Status with Unintended Pregnancy in their Wives in Southern Ethiopia: A Cross-Sectional Study." *PLOS ONE* 15(7): e0235675.

Senderowicz, Leigh, 2020. "Contraceptive Autonomy: Conceptions and Measurement of a Novel Family Planning Indicator." *Studies in Family Planning* 51(2): 161-176.

Shaka, Mohammad Fayesso and others, 2020. "Determinants of Undernutrition among Children under Five Years Old in Southern Ethiopia: Does Pregnancy Intention Matter? A Community-Based Unmatched Case-Control Study." *BMC Pediatrics* 20(1): 101.

Shapiro-Mendoza, Carrie and others, 2005. "Parental Pregnancy Intention and Early Childhood Stunting: Findings from Bolivia." *International Journal of Epidemiology* 34(2): 387-396.

Skovlund, Charlotte Wessel and others, 2016. "Hormonal Contraception With Depression." JAMA Psychiatry 73(11): 1154-1162.

Shelton, James and Roy Jacobstein, 2016. "Vasectomy: A Long, Slow Haul to Successful Takeoff." *Global Health: Science and Practice* 4(4): 514-517.

Silverman, Jay G. and Anita Raj, 2014. "Intimate Partner Violence and Reproductive Coercion: Global Barriers to Women's Reproductive Control." *PLoS Medicine* 11(9): e1001723.

Silverman, Jay and others, 2020. "Associations of Reproductive Coercion and Intimate Partner Violence with Overt and Covert Family Planning Use Among Married Adolescent Girls in Niger." *EClinicalMedicine* 22: 100359.

Silverman, Jay G. and others, 2019. "Reproductive Coercion in Uttar Pradesh, India: Prevalence and Associations with Partner Violence and Reproductive Health." *SSM – Population Health* 9: 100484.

Silverman, Jay G, and others, 2007. "Intimate Partner Violence and Unwanted Pregnancy, Miscarriage, Induced Abortion, and Still Births among a National Sample of Bangladeshi Women." *BJOG* 114(10): 1246-1252.

Singh, Susheela and Isaac Maddow-Zimet, 2016. "Facility-Based Treatment for Medical Complications Resulting From Unsafe Pregnancy Termination in the Developing World, 2012: A Review of Evidence from 26 Countries." *BJOG* 123: 1489-1498.

Skracic, Izidora and others, 2021. "Types of Lifetime Reproductive Coercion and Current Contraceptive Use." *Journal of Women's Health* 30(8): 1078-1085.

Smith, Julia, 2020. "Improving Adolescent Access to Contraception in Sub-Saharan Africa: A Review of the Evidence." *African Journal of Reproductive Health* 24(1): 152-164.

Solo, Julie and Mario Festin, 2019. "Provider Bias in Family Planning Services: A Review of Its Meaning and Manifestations." *Global Health: Science and Practice* 7(3): 371-385.

Sonfield, Adam and Kathryn Kost, 2015. *Public Costs from Unintended Pregnancies and the Role of Public Insurance Programs in Paying for Pregnancy-Related Care: National and State Estimates for 2010.* New York: Guttmacher Institute. Website: guttmacher.org/report/public-costs-unintended-pregnancies-and-role-public-insurance-programs-paying-pregnancy, accessed 18 November 2021.

Sonfield, Adam and others, 2013. *The Social and Economic Benefits of Women's Ability to Determine Whether and When to have Children.* New York: Guttmacher Institute. Website: guttmacher.org/sites/default/files/report_pdf/social-economic-benefits.pdf, accessed 1 December 2021.

Stamatakis, Caroline E. and others, 2020. "Sexual Violence Prevalence and Related Pregnancy Among Girls and Young Women: A Multicountry Analysis." *Journal of Interpersonal Violence* July 2020. 37: 3-4.

Starrs, Ann M. and others, 2018. "Accelerate Progress—Sexual and Reproductive Health and Rights for All: Report of the Guttmacher-*Lancet* Commission." *Lancet* 391: 2642-2692.

Stats SL (Statistics Sierra Leone) and ICF, 2020. *Sierra Leone Demographic and Health Survey 2019.* Freetown, Sierra Leone, and Rockville, Maryland, USA: Stats SL and ICF.

Steinberg, Julia R. and others, 2020. "Psychosocial Factors Associated with Postpartum Contraceptive Method Use after an Unintended Pregnancy." *Obstetrics & Gynecology* 135(4): 821-831.

Sully, Elizabeth A. and others, 2020. *Adding It Up: Investing in Sexual and Reproductive Health 2019.* New York: Guttmacher Institute. Website: guttmacher.org/report/adding-it-up- investing-in-sexual-reproductive-health-2019, accessed 28 November 2021.

Suttie, David, 2019. *Overview: Rural Poverty in Developing Countries: Issues, Policies and Challenges.* International Fund for Agricultural Development (IFAD). Website: un.org/development/desa/dspd/wp-content/uploads/sites/22/2019/03/Rural-poverty-EGM_IFAD-overview.pdf, accessed 16 November 2021.

Svoboda, Elizabeth, 2020. "Better Birth Control." *Nature* 588: S166–S167.

Tarzia, Laura and Kelsey Hegarty, 2021. "A Conceptual Re-Evaluation of Reproductive Coercion: Centring Intent, Fear and Control." *Reproductive Health* 18(1): 87.

Taylor, Diana and Evelyn Angel James, 2012. "Risks of Being Sexual in Midlife: What We Don't Know Can Hurt Us." *The Female Patient* 37: 17-20.

Thiel de Bocanegra, Heike and others, 2010. "Birth Control Sabotage and Forced Sex: Experiences Reported by Women in Domestic Violence Shelters." *Violence Against Women* 16: 601-612.

Thirumalai, Arthi and John K. Amory, 2021. "Emerging Approaches to Male Contraception." *Fertility and Sterility* 115(6): 1369-1376.

Thomas, Adam, 2012. "Policy Solutions for Preventing Unplanned Pregnancy." Washington DC: Brookings Institution. Website: brookings. edu/research/policy-solutions-for-preventing-unplanned-pregnancy/, accessed 1 December 2021.

Tran, Nguyen Toan and others, 2021. "Strengthening Health Systems in Humanitarian Settings: Multi-Stakeholder Insights on Contraception and Postabortion Care Programs in the Democratic Republic of Congo and Somalia." *Frontiers in Global Women's Health* 62

Tsui, Amy O. and others, 2010. "Family Planning and the Burden of Unintended Pregnancies." *Epidemiologic Reviews* 32(1): 152-174.

United Nations, Statistics Division, 2022. Global SDG Indicators Database. Website: unstats.un.org/sdgs/ dataportal, accessed 3 March 2022.

United Nations, 2021. *The Sustainable Development Goals Report 2021.* Website: unstats.un.org/sdgs/ report/2021/The-Sustainable-Development-Goals-Report-2021. pdf, accessed 1 December 2021.

United Nations, 2020. *Conflict-Related Sexual Violence: Report of the United Nations Secretary-General.* Website: undocs.org/en/S/2020/487, accessed 17 November 2021.

UN CCPR (United Nations Committee on Civil and Political Rights), 2019. "General Comment No. 36: Article 6, Right to Life: Human Rights Committee." CCPR/C/ GC/36. Website: digitallibrary. un.org/record/3884724?ln=en, accessed 26 November 2021.

UN CEDAW (United Nations Committee on the Elimination of Discrimination against Women), 2017. "General Recommendation No. 35 on Gender-Based Violence Against Women, Updating General Recommendation No. 19." Website: digitallibrary. un.org/record/1305057?ln=en, accessed 25 November 2021.

UN CESCR (United Nations Committee on Economic, Social and Cultural Rights), 2016. "General Comment No. 22: (2016) on the Right to Sexual and Reproductive Health (Article 12 of the International Covenant on Economic, Social and Cultural Rights)." Website: digitallibrary. un.org/record/832961?ln=en, accessed 25 November 2021.

UN CESCR (United Nations Committee on Economic, Social and Cultural Rights), 2000. "General Comment No. 14: The Right to the Highest Attainable Standard of Health (Article 12 of the International Covenant on Economic, Social and Cultural Rights)." Website: digitallibrary. un.org/record/425041?ln=en, accessed 25 November 2021.

UN CRC (United Nations Committee on the Rights of the Child), 2016. "General Comment No. 20 (2016) on the Implementation of the Rights of the Child during Adolescence." Website: digitallibrary. un.org/record/855544?ln=en, accessed 25 November 2021.

UN CRC (United Nations Committee on the Rights of the Child), 2003. "General Comment No. 4 (2003): Adolescent Health and Development in the Context of the Convention on the Rights of the Child." Website: digitallibrary. un.org/record/503074?ln=en, accessed 25 November 2021.

UN DESA (United Nations Department of Economic and Social Affairs), Population Division, 2022. Forthcoming

UN DESA (United Nations Department of Economic and Social Affairs), Population Division, 2021. Website: https://www.un.org/development/ desa/pd/data/family-planning-indicators Accessed 3 March 2022.

United Nations (Department of Economic and Social Affairs), Population Division, 2021a. *World Contraceptive Use 2020* (POP/DB/CP/Rev2020).

UN DESA (United Nations Department of Economic and Social Affairs), Population Division, 2020. Estimates and Projections of Women of Reproductive Age Who Are Married or in a Union.

UN DESA (United Nations Department of Economic and Social Affairs), Population Division, 2020a. *World Family Planning 2020 Highlights: Accelerating Action to Ensure Universal Access to Family Planning.* (ST/ESA/SER.A/450).

UN DESA (United Nations Department of Economic and Social Affairs), Population Division, 2019. *World Population Prospects 2019.*

UN DESA (United Nations Department of Economic and Social Affairs), Population Division, 2015. "World Contraceptive Use 2015." Website: un.org/en/development/ desa/population/publications/ dataset/contraception/wcu2015. asp, accessed 26 November 2021.

UN DESA (United Nations Department of Economic and Social Affairs), Population Division, 2013. *Adolescent Fertility since the International Conference on Population and Development (ICPD) in Cairo.*

United Nations Statistics Division, 2020. Global SDG Indicators Database.

UNDP (United Nations Development Programme), 2020. *Human Development Report.* Technical Notes. Website: hdr.undp.org/sites/default/files/hdr2020_technical_notes.pdf, accessed 15 November 2021.

UNDP (United Nations Development Programme), 2005. *Investing in Development. A Practical Plan to Achieve the Millennium Development Goals.*

UN ECOSOC (United Nations Economic and Social Council), 1990. "General Comment No. 3: The Nature of States Parties' Obligations (Art. 2, Para. 1, of the Covenant)." Website: tbinternet.ohchr.org/_layouts/15/treatybodyexternal/Download.aspx?symbolno=INT%2fCESCR%2fGEC%2f4758&Lang=en, accessed 1 December 2021.

UNESCO (United Nations Educational, Scientific and Cultural Organization) and others, 2018. *International Technical Guidance on Sexuality Education: An Evidence-Informed Approach.* Website: unesdoc.unesco.org/images/0026/002607/260770e.pdf, accessed 16 November 2021.

UN ESCWA (United Nations Economic and Social Commission for Western Asia), 2004. "Arab Regional Ten-Year Review and Appraisal of Implementation of the Beijing Platform for Action." Website: un.org/womenwatch/daw/Review/english/documents/ESCWASummaryNationalResponses-English.pdf, accessed 16 December 2021.

UNFPA (United Nations Population Fund), 2022. *Motherhood in Childhood: The Untold Story.*

UNFPA (United Nations Population Fund), 2021. "My Body is My Own. Claiming The Right to Autonomy and Self-Determination." *State of World Population 2021.*

UNFPA (United Nations Population Fund), 2020. Annual report. New York: UNFPA.

UNFPA (United Nations Population Fund), 2020a. *Ensure Universal Access to Sexual and Reproductive Health and Reproductive Rights: Measuring SDG Target 5.6.* Website: unfpa.org/sdg-5-6, accessed 24 November 2021.

UNFPA (United Nations Population Fund), 2020b. "Against My Will. Defying the Practices that Harm Women and Girls and Undermine Equality." *State of World Population 2020.*

UNFPA (United Nations Population Fund), 2020c. *Impact of COVID-19 on Access to Contraceptives in the LAC Region.* Website: lac.unfpa.org/sites/default/files/pub-pdf/technical_report_impact_of_covid_19_in_the_access_to_contraceptives_in_lac_1_2.pdf, accessed 1 December 2021.

UNFPA (United Nations Population Fund) 2020d. *Technical Note on Gender-Transformative Approaches: A Summary for Practitioners.* Website: unfpa.org/resources/technical-note-gender-transformative-approaches-summary-practitioners, accessed 10 February 2022.

UNFPA (United Nations Population Fund), 2019. *Sexual and Reproductive Health and Rights An Essential Element of Universal Health Coverage.*

UNFPA (United Nations Population Fund), 2018. *Women and Young Persons with Disabilities. Guidelines for Providing Rights-Based and Gender-Responsive Services to Address Gender-Based Violence and Sexual and Reproductive Health and Rights for Women and Young Persons with Disabilities.* Website: unfpa.org/featured-publication/women-and-young-persons-disabilities, accessed 7 February 2022.

UNFPA (United Nations Population Fund), 1994. "Programme of Action. Adopted at the International Conference on Population and Development, Cairo, 5–13 September 1994." Website: unfpa.org/sites/default/files/event-pdf/PoA_en.pdf, accessed 26 November 2021.

UNFPA (United Nations Population Fund), n.d. *Adolescents and Youth Dashboard – Sierra Leone.* Website: unfpa.org/data/adolescent-youth/SL, accessed 9 February 2022.

UNFPA (United Nations Population Fund), n.d.a. *World Population Dashboard – Sierra Leone.* Website: unfpa.org/data/world-population/SL, accessed 9 February 2022.

UNFPA (United Nations Population Fund) El Salvador, 2021. *Llegar a cero embarazos en niñas y adolescentes – Mapa El Salvador 2020.* Website: https://elsalvador.unfpa.org/es/publications/llegar-cero-embarazos-en-ni%C3%B1as-y-adolescentes-%E2%80%93-mapa-el-salvador-2020, accessed 1 March, 2022.

United Nations Population Fund, global databases, 2022. Based on official responses to the United Nations 13th and 12th Inquiry among Governments on Population and Development.

UNFPA (United Nations Population Fund) Sierra Leone, n.d. "Gender-Based Violence." Website: sierraleone.unfpa.prg/en/topics/gender-based-violence-11, accessed 9 February 2022.

UN General Assembly, 2007. *Convention on the Rights of Persons with Disabilities*. A/RES/61/106. Website: un.org/development/desa/disabilities/convention-on-the-rights-of-persons-with-disabilities.html, accessed 17 November 2021.

UN General Assembly, 1998. "Rome Statute of the International Criminal Court." Website: icc-cpi.int/resource-library/documents/rs-eng.pdf, accessed 1 December 2021.

UN General Assembly, 1989. *Convention on the Rights of the Child*. A/RES/44/25. Website: ohchr.org/en/professionalinterest/pages/crc.aspx, accessed 17 November 2021.

UN General Assembly, 1979. *Convention on the Elimination of All Forms of Discrimination against Women*. A/RES/34/180. Website: ohchr.org/Documents/ProfessionalInterest/cedaw.pdf, accessed 15 November 2021.

UN General Assembly, 1966. *International Covenant on Economic, Social and Cultural Rights*. Website: ohchr.org/en/professionalinterest/pages/cescr.aspx, accessed 17 November 2021.

UN HRC (United Nations Human Rights Council), 2012. "Report of the Special Rapporteur on Violence Against Women, Its Causes and Consequences, Rashida Manjoo." A/HRC/20/16. Website: ohchr.org/Documents/Issues/Women/A.HRC.20.16_En.pdf, accessed 18 December 2021.

UN Women, 2021. *Beyond COVID-19: A Feminist Plan for Sustainability and Social Justice*. Website: unwomen.org/sites/default/files/Headquarters/Attachments/Sections/Library/Publications/2021/Feminist-plan-for-sustainability-and-social-justice-en.pdf, accessed 1 December 2021.

UN Women, 2012. *Facts & Figures: Rural Women and the Millennium Development Goals*. Website: https://www.un.org/womenwatch/feature/ruralwomen/facts-figures.html, accessed 1 December 2021.

Utomo, Budi and others, 2021. "The Impact of Family Planning on Maternal Mortality in Indonesia: What Future Contribution can be Expected?" *Population Health Metrics* 19: 2.

Vanden Broek, Jana and others, 2016. "Antenatal Care Use in Urban Areas in Two European Countries: Predisposing, Enabling and Pregnancy-Related Determinants in Belgium and The Netherlands." *BMC Health Services Research* 16: 337.

Vlassoff and others, 2018. Economic impact of unsafe abortion-related morbidity and mortality: evidence and estimation challenges. Brighton, Institute of Development Studies (IDS Research Reports 59).

Vu, Alexander and others, 2014. "The Prevalence of Sexual Violence among Female Refugees in Complex Humanitarian Emergencies: A Systematic Review and Meta-Analysis." *PLOS Currents Disasters*. Edition 1, doi: 10.1371/currents.dis.835f10778f-d80ae031aac12d3b533ca7.

Wellings, Kaye and others, 2013. "The Prevalence of Unplanned Pregnancy and Associated Factors in Britain: Findings from the Third National Survey Of Sexual Attitudes and Lifestyles (Natsal-3)." *Lancet* 382(9907): 1807-1816.

Westhoff, Charles F., 2010. *Desired Number of Children: 2000-2008*. DHS Comparative Reports No. 25. Calverton, Maryland: ICF Macro.

White, Kari and others, 2015. "Contraception after Delivery and Short Interpregnancy Intervals Among Women in the United States." *Obstetrics & Gynecology* 125: 1471-1477.

White Ribbon Alliance, 2019. *What Women Want: Demands for Quality Reproductive and Maternal Healthcare from Women and Girls*. Website: whiteribbonalliance.org/wp-content/uploads/2019/06/What-Women-Want_Global-Results.pdf, accessed 24 November 2021.

WHO (World Health Organization), 2021. WHO Guideline on Self-Care Interventions for Health and Well-Being. Website: who.int/publications/i/item/9789240030909, accessed 18 November 2021.

WHO (World Health Organization), 2021a. 'Infant and Young Child Feeding: Key Facts.' Website: who.int/news-room/fact-sheets/detail/infant-and-young-child-feeding, accessed 18 November 2021.

WHO (World Health Organization), 2020. "Preventing Unsafe Abortion: Key Facts." Website: who.int/news-room/fact-sheets/detail/preventing-unsafe-abortion, accessed 15 November 2021.

WHO (World Health Organization), 2020a. "Pulse Survey on Continuity of Essential Health Services during the COVID-19 Pandemic: Interim Report, 27 August 2020." Website: who.int/publications/i/item/WHO-2019-nCoV-EHS_continuity-survey-2020.1, accessed 24 November 2021.

WHO (World Health Organization), 2020b. "Adolescent Pregnancy: Key Facts." Website: who.int/news-room/fact-sheets/detail/adolescent-pregnancy, accessed 18 November 2021.

WHO (World Health Organization), 2020c. "Family Planning/Contraception Methods: Key Facts." Website: who.int/news-room/fact-sheets/detail/family-planning-contraception, accessed 15 November 2021.

WHO (World Health Organization), 2019. "Global Health Estimates: Life Expectancy and Leading Causes of Death and Disability." Website: who.int/data/gho/data/themes/mortality-and-global-health-estimates, accessed 27 November 2021.

WHO (World Health Organization), 2019a. *Breaking Barriers. Towards More Gender-Responsive and Equitable Health Systems.* Website: who.int/healthinfo/universal_health_coverage/report/gender_gmr_2019.pdf, accessed 1 December 2021.

WHO (World Health Organization), 2019b. "High Rates of Unintended Pregnancies Linked to Gaps in Family Planning Services: New WHO Study." Geneva: WHO. Website: who.int/news/item/25-10-2019-high-rates-of-unintended-pregnancies-linked-to-gaps-in-family-planning-services-new-who-study, accessed 1 December 2021.

WHO (World Health Organization), 2019c. *RESPECT Women: Preventing Violence Against Women.* WHO/RHR/18.19. Geneva: WHO. Website: apps.who.int/iris/bitstream/handle/10665/312261/WHO-RHR-18.19-eng.pdf?ua=1

WHO (World Health Organization), 2018. *Family Planning. A Global Handbook for Providers.* Geneva: WHO. Website: apps.who.int/iris/bitstream/handle/10665/260156/9780999203705-eng.pdf, accessed 26 November 2021.

WHO (World Health Organization), 2017. Unpublished report.

WHO (World Health Organization), 2016. "WHO Recommendations on Antenatal Care for a Positive Pregnancy Experience." Geneva: WHO. Website: who.int/publications/i/item/9789241549912, accessed 18 November 2021.

WHO (World Health Organization), 2015. "Safe Abortion: Technical & Policy Guidance for Health Systems." Geneva: WHO. Website: apps.who.int/iris/bitstream/handle/10665/173586/WHO_RHR_15.04_eng.pdf, accessed 18 November 2021.

WHO (World Health Organization), 2014. "Ensuring Human Rights in the Provision of Contraceptive Information and Services: Guidance and Recommendations." Geneva: WHO.

WHO (World Health Organization), 2007. *Report of a WHO Technical Consultation on Birth Spacing. Geneva, Switzerland, 13–15 June 2005.* WHO/RHR/07.1. Geneva: WHO. Website: apps.who.int/iris/bitstream/handle/10665/69855/?sequence=1, accessed 25 November 2021.

WHO (World Health Organization) and others, 2019. "Trends in Maternal Mortality: 2000 to 2017." Geneva: WHO. Website: data.worldbank.org/indicator/SH.STA.MMRT, accessed 15 November 2021.

Wilcox, Allen J. and others, 2001. "Likelihood of Conception with a Single Act of Intercourse: Providing Benchmark Rates for Assessment of Post-Coital Contraceptives." *Contraception* 63(4): 211-215.

Women's Refugee Commission and others, 2012. *Adolescent Sexual and Reproductive Health Programs in Humanitarian Settings: An In-Depth Look at Family Planning Services.* New York: Women's Refugee Commission. Website: unfpa.org/sites/default/files/resource-pdf/AAASRH_good_practice_documentation_English_FINAL.pdf

Wondemagegn, Amsalu Taye and others, 2018. "The Effect of Antenatal Care Follow-Up on Neonatal Health Outcomes: A Systematic Review and Meta-Analysis." *Public Health Reviews* 39: 33.

World Bank, 2021. *Gender Indicator Report: Women Who Believe A Husband Is Justified In Beating His Wife When She Refuses Sex With Him.* Databank: Gender Statistics. Website: data.worldbank.org/indicator/SG.VAW.ARGU.ZS, accessed 20 October 2021.

World Bank, 2021a. *Women, Business and the Law, 2021.* Washington, DC: World Bank. Website: wbl.worldbank.org/content/dam/sites/wbl/documents/2021/02/WBL2021_ENG_v2.pdf, accessed 1 December 2021.

Xu, Fujie and others, 2010. "Women Who Have Sex With Women in the United States: Prevalence, Sexual Behavior and Prevalence of Herpes Simplex Virus Type 2 Infection – Results From National Health and Nutrition Examination Survey 2001-2006." *Sexually Transmitted Diseases* 37(7): 407-413.

Yazdkhasti, Mansureh and others, 2015. "Unintended Pregnancy and Its Adverse Social and Economic Consequences on Health System: A Narrative Review Article." *Iranian Journal of Public Health* 44(1): 12-21.

Zhou, Jacy and others, 2020. "Systematic Review of Early Abortion Services in Low- and Middle-Income Country Primary Care: Potential for Reverse Innovation and Application in the UK Context." *Globalization and Health* 16: 91.

Zuniga, Carmela and others, 2020. "The Impacts of Contraceptive Stock-Outs on Users, Providers, and Facilities: A Systematic Literature Review." *Global Public Health* 2020 doi: 10.1080/17441692.2020.1850829, online ahead of print.